Captured by the Media

Captured by the Media
Prison discourse in popular culture

Edited by Paul Mason

WILLAN
PUBLISHING

Published by

Willan Publishing
Culmcott House
Mill Street, Uffculme
Cullompton, Devon
EX15 3AT, UK
Tel: +44(0)1884 840337
Fax: +44(0)1884 840251
e-mail: info@willanpublishing.co.uk
website: www.willanpublishing.co.uk

Published simultaneously in the USA and Canada by

Willan Publishing
c/o ISBS, 920 NE 58th Ave, Suite 300
Portland, Oregon 97213-3786, USA
Tel: +001(0)503 287 3093
Fax: +001(0)503 280 8832
e-mail: info@isbs.com
website: www.isbs.com

Paperback
ISBN-13: 978-1-84392-144-8
ISBN-10: 1-84392-144-8

Hardback
ISBN-13: 978-1-84392-145-5
ISBN-10: 1-84392-145-6

British Library Cataloguing-in-Publication Data

A catalogue record for this book is available from the British Library

Typeset by GCS, Leighton Buzzard, Beds
Project management by Deer Park Productions, Tavistock, Devon
Printed and bound by T.J. International, Padstow, Cornwall

Contents

Acknowledgements

Thank you to all the contributors who gave the time to produce such high-quality work and to be open to editorial changes and suggestions. My thanks also to Brian Willan who continues to be one of the very few publishers prepared to stick his neck out and support projects based on their intrinsic value and not on how many units he can shift in the textbook market.

Most of all to Helen Caswell, now Mason, for everything.

Notes on contributors

Rob Allen was Director of Rethinking Crime and Punishment, a four-year funding programme set up by the Esmée Fairbairn Foundation to explore public attitudes to prison, from 2001 to 2005. Previously, he was Director of Research and Development at the crime reduction charity Nacro, which he joined in 1989. Between 1992 and 1995, Rob was seconded to the Criminal Policy Department of the Home Office and has been a member of the government's Youth Justice Board since its formation in 1998. In addition, he has undertaken a wide range of consultancy work on criminal and youth justice in the UK and abroad. His publications include *Children and Crime – Taking Responsibility* (IPPR 1996) and he is a regular contributor to journals and periodicals. Rob was appointed Director of the International Centre for Prison Studies at King's College London in March 2005.

Jamie Bennett has been a prison professional since 1996 and is currently Deputy Governor at HMP Whitemoor. He has previously held a number of posts, including Deputy Governor of HMP Gartree and Head of the Dangerous and Severe Personality Disorder Unit at HMP Whitemoor. He has written on a range of criminal justice matters, including prison films, for publications including *The Prison Service Journal*, *Criminal Justice Matters* and *Journal for Crime, Conflict and Media Culture*.

Steve Chibnall is Professor of British Cinema and Co-ordinator of the British Cinema and Television Research Group at De Montfort University, Leicester. Since completing a PhD and writing a book on crime reporting in the British press (*Law-and-Order News*, 1977), he has written extensively on aspects of cultural history and on British cinema. Recent books include studies of British directors J. Lee Thompson (2000) and Peter Walker (1998), and the crime films *Get Carter* (2003) and *Brighton Rock* (2004). He has also co-edited collections on *British Crime Cinema* (1999) and *British Horror Cinema* (2001). His articles on British crime films have appeared in *The British Cinema Book* (edited by Robert Murphy 2002), *Sight and Sound*, *Cineaste* and *Film International*. He is currently researching a history of the British 'B' film.

Chris Greer is Senior Lecturer in Criminology at City University, London. He has published widely in the areas of crime and media. Some recent publications include: 'Crime and media: understanding the connections' (2005), 'Extremes of otherness: media images of social exclusion' (with Y. Jewkes 2005) and (forthcoming) 'Representing victimhood: media constructions of crime and suffering'. Chris is also a founding editor (with Yvonne Jewkes and Jeff Ferrell) of *Crime, Media, Culture*.

Brian Jarvis lectures in American literature, film and popular culture at Loughborough University. He is the author of *Cruel and Unusual: Punishment and US Culture* (Pluto 2004) and *Postmodern Cartographies: The Geographical Imagination in Contemporary American Culture* (Pluto 1998), as well as essays on detective film, dirty realism and 9/11.

Yvonne Jewkes is Reader in Criminology and a member of the International Centre for Comparative Criminological Research at the Open University. She has published widely on both prisons and the media, including *Captive Audience: Media, Masculinity and Power in Prisons* (Willan 2002) and *Media and Crime* (Sage 2004). She is editor of the forthcoming *Handbook on Prisons* (Willan) and a founding editor (with Chris Greer and Jeff Ferrell) of the new Sage journal, *Crime, Media, Culture*.

Helen Johnston is Lecturer in Criminology at the University of Hull, where she teaches a course on the history of crime and punishment. Her doctoral thesis was concerned with transformations of local imprisonment during the nineteenth century. She is currently compiling *Prison Readings* (Willan) with Yvonne Jewkes and publishing articles from her thesis.

Anna King joined Keele University in September 2005. She recently earned her PhD at the University of Cambridge where she was a Gates scholar and co-ordinator of the CUPOP (Cambridge University Public Opinion Project). Some of the preliminary findings from this research have already been published in a chapter (co-authored with Shadd Maruna in A. Bottoms, S. Rex and G. Robinson (eds), *Alternatives to Prison: Options for an Insecure Society* (Willan 2004). Her research interests include identity and narrative, public opinion towards lawbreakers, and crime and the mass media.

Shadd Maruna is a Reader in Law and Criminology at Queen's University Belfast. Previously he has held lecturing positions at the University of Cambridge and the State University of New York. His book *Making Good: How Ex-convicts Reform and Rebuild their Lives* (APA 2001) was named the Outstanding Contribution to Criminology by the American Society of Criminology in 2001. He is also the co-editor of two recent books from Willan Publishing, *After Crime and Punishment* (2004) and *The Effects of Imprisonment* (2005).

Paul Mason lectures in the School of Journalism, Media and Cultural Studies at Cardiff University and is Editor of the *Journal for Crime, Conflict and Media Culture*. His books include *Policing and the Media: Facts, Fictions and Factions* (with Frank Leishman, Willan 2003) and *Criminal Visions: Media Representations of Crime and Justice* (Willan 2003). He is currently writing *From Fugitive to Redemption – Exploring the Prison Film* for Wallflower Press.

Mike Nellis is Professor of Criminal and Community Justice in the Glasgow School of Social Work, University of Strathclyde, and has long been involved in the training of probation officers. He has written extensively on the changing nature of the probation service, the promotion of community penalties, the significance of electronic monitoring and the cultural politics of penal reform (including the use of prison movies and prisoner's autobiographies). His most recent book (edited with Eric Chui) was *Moving Probation Forward* (Longman 2003).

Mick Ryan is Professor of Penal Politics at the University of Greenwich. He has published extensively on criminal justice matters, most recently, *Penal Policy and Political Culture in England and Wales* (Waterside Press 2003).

Enver Solomon is head of policy and research at the Revolving Doors Agency. He worked for two and a half years as the Prison Reform Trust's senior policy officer, co-ordinating the organization's policy and media work. Before joining PRT he was a BBC journalist for nearly ten years, latterly as a home affairs reporter on Radio 4's *The World Tonight* programme. He has also worked for local and national newspapers.

Chapter 1

Turn on, tune in, slop out

Paul Mason

Images of justice and just images

How would you feel if a bloke on early release attacked your daughter? Are you thinking what we're thinking?[1] I'm thinking that with an increasingly politicized law and order built primarily on a foundation of fear and with victims centre stage, Garland is right to draw parallels between the 'repersonalization' (2002: 465) of criminal justice in the USA and the UK. The populist turn in criminal justice has often been cited in discussions of an increased punitiveness in Britain and elsewhere (Garland 2001; Pratt 2002; Roberts and Hough 2002; Roberts *et al.* 2002; Ryan 2003a; Pratt *et al.* 2005) – we live, suggests Mick Ryan, 'in irrational punitive times' (Ryan 2003b). This bottom-up pressure from an angry public, driven onwards by screaming red-top headlines, demands more displays of repressive punishment: longer prison sentences, boot camps, ASBOS and, most recently, proposals for young offenders to wear uniforms whilst carrying out community service (*Guardian* 15 May 2005). Punishment becomes crueller (Simon 2001) as the late-modern 'politics of insecurity' (Crawford 2002) justifies hostility and retribution on the criminal.

Whether one accepts this position – Matthews, for example, argues that punitiveness and populism have been 'poorly theorised... selective and unconvincing' (2005: 195) – none of the criminological writing on penal populism and punitiveness seeks to engage on any meaningful level with how various forms of media construct prison and punishment;[2] how such penal discourse is received and interpreted by the audience; or how it may contribute to a populist and punitive criminological imagination. It is ironic that whilst Garland talks of 'the made for television' quality of social control in late modernity (2001: 133), the television remains switched off for penologists and criminologists alike.

This book turns it on, opens the newspapers, goes to the cinema and assesses how punishment is 'performed' (Cottle 2005: 51) in media culture – what we might alternatively call 'the regimes of penal representation'. *Captured by the Media* can be seen as one response to McLaughlin *et al.*'s call for an examination of:

> how and why conventional criminological understandings are in danger of being overwhelmed by (a) images of crime and control gleaned from novels, magazines, films, music, cyberspace and computer game simulations and (b) tabloid news media representations that can generate sharp swings in the politics of law and order (2003: 8).

And no, let's not ghettoize it as 'cultural criminology' (70s retro chic) but locate media discourse on prisons firmly within the penal policy/public opinion complex. Whilst *Bad Girls, The Shawshank Redemption*, jail cams (Lynch 2004), advertising (Girling 2004) and debates about televising executions[3] continue to ebb and flow in contemporary culture, ignoring such constructions, absences and silences would be foolish. As Valier argues, the 'power to punish is a power of the image' (2004). From Aeschylus' depiction of the torment of Prometheus in 457 BCE and Plato's account of Socrates (Morris and Rothman 1998: 8), it is the persistence of this spectacle of punishment – despite Foucault's contention to the contrary (1979) – that demands investigation. The contested meanings of punishment in media discourse and the politics of representing imprisonment require discussion. To this end, one could well adopt/adapt Jean-Luc Godard's maxim and ask is this not a just image. Is it just an image?

Prisons and the public sphere

The contributors to this volume have been chosen from a variety of backgrounds and disciplines. I wanted to offer interdisciplinary academic accounts but also to move beyond the academy to those working in, with and, sometimes, against the prison system. Thus the prison service, Revolving Doors and Rethinking Crime and

Punishment are all represented, as well as a plethora of academic disciplines including cinema and cultural studies, criminology, journalism and history.

We begin with the fundamental concern of this book – how public opinion, punitivism and the media may mesh together. Anna King and Shadd Maruna's work for the Cambridge University Public Opinion Project adopts research on crime narratives in popular culture, and audience reception, to explore opinions about prison and punishment. It is surprising, given the amount of research undertaken in each of these distinct fields, that few have asked how the three might inter-relate. Indeed, systematic audience research on crime in media culture is surprisingly rare, with only Gillespie and McLaughlin having begun to investigate how public opinion and media discourses of crime relate to one another (2002, 2003). It appears that when it comes to media constructions of crime, audiences are either forgotten, taken for granted or speculated about. It may also be the case that crime and media researchers remain fearful of falling head first into the black hole of the media effects tradition, and consequently tiptoe round the edge of audience research, their backs pressed firmly against content/textual/discourse analysis.

King and Maruna however offer a way forward, suggesting that an exploration of social attitudes and their consumption can be undertaken through audience interpretation of crime stories. Specifically, they look at punitive attitudes as part of personal identity and suggest that 'the types of stories to which members of our punitive sample tend to gravitate may play a useful role in sustaining and maintaining a punitive mindset'. By adopting an interdisciplinary approach as posited by the constitutive criminology of Henry and Milovanovic (1996, 1999) and acknowledging the complexities of identity, King and Maruna found that their highly punitive group of respondents identify with crime narratives offering clarity in right and wrong. In contrast, stories which were less clear about morality, and which challenged the polarizing of good and evil, were enjoyed by the less punitive group.

The question about public opinion and punitive attitudes is explored by Mick Ryan in Chapter 3, who traces the development of this public voice and its intervention in penal politics from what he terms 'old times' to 'new times'. Questioning the pessimistic view of the public voice as merely a crude tool used to beat out the rhythm of vengeance, punishment and cruelty, Ryan suggests a more optimistic and positive use for public opinion. He points out that new information technologies and social movements illustrate

3

the possibility of a 'communicative rationality' in the public sphere of penology.

Ryan maps the shift from the 'old times' of the top-down policy-making of the Whitehall metropolitan elite to the 'new times' of the independent and resonant public voice. He suggests that the decline in public deference – from what Inglehart calls 'elite directed' to 'elite challenging' activity – is a product of mass education and the growth of the information society, e-culture and the Internet blog. Recent events such as the fuel cost protests and Paulsgrove estate disturbances, both in 2000 illustrate, for Ryan, an upgrading of the public voice beyond simply the party political opportunism of the 1979 Conservative law and order manifesto (Butler and Kavanagh 1980) or New Labour's reconstruction and repositioning of 'community' to underpin its legislative programme (McLaughlin 2002).

Ryan's call for a wider and more creative engagement with the public on penal issues is taken up in the subsequent two chapters by Enver Solomon and Rob Allen. As a former journalist and former senior officer at the Prison Reform Trust, Solomon is well placed to offer an informed account of how the media, government and public interact on prison issues. Drawing on the sociology of the media, and echoing Jewkes contention below, he argues that prison stories rarely make the news, suggesting that only two stories in a national newspaper per month would be a good return for a home affairs correspondent. Against the background of celebrity gossip and what Solomon refers to as 'consumer-orientated' stories, the space for penal policy coverage, he argues, is marginal. This ever-decreasing communicative space further hampers the attempts by groups such as the Prison Reform Trust, Rethinking Crime and Punishment and SmartJustice to communicate the utility of community sentences over custodial ones. Director of SmartJustice, Lucie Russell, has noted how the complexity of community penalties compared to the comprehensible notion of prison makes marketing non-custodial sentences to the public through the media problematic (2005). Indeed, Solomon argues that to attempt to promote penal reform via the media is, ultimately, naïve and that it is through reconfiguring the public debate about prison and punishment that progress lies.

This development in penal reform – to sidestep the media or at least to refocus efforts on the public directly, on Ryan's upgraded public voice – has been adopted by both SmartJustice and Rethinking Crime and Punishment (RCP). The latter's work is discussed by its former Director, Rob Allen, in Chapter 5. RCP advocate informing the public more effectively in order to dispel some the myths about criminal transgression and disposal, and to build public support for community penalties. As Ryan suggests earlier, the media's construction of public opinion is one of vengeful punitiveness, yet often this stems from the government's claims to be speaking on behalf of the people, subsequently reported by the media, rather than the people themselves – what has been dubbed 'ventriloquist populism' (Matthews 2005). Allen reports that RCP's research also questions the accuracy of this media construction of public opinion, suggesting it is far less punitive than is often cited. Amongst their findings, Allen demonstrates more public support for preventative measures to reduce crime, alternatives to incarceration and widespread scepticism about the aim and role of prison.

In Chapter 6, Chris Greer widens the discussion beyond prison to punishment and state executions and explores the US press coverage of the death penalty. Specifically, he examines how the botched executions in Florida in the 1990s were 'made to mean' in America and beyond. Echoing Edward Herman's observation that media normalize the unthinkable for the general public (1995), Greer discusses the normalizing of the death penalty in the US print media and argues that the botched execution challenges the state's preferred reading of it. He suggests the news media coverage of these events is not so much a way of seeing state killing, but seeing killing through the state's eyes. The state-driven morality play of executions is performed in the pages of the US media where 'a dangerous guilty offender is seen to pay the ultimate penalty for a free willed evil act' (Garland 2002: 459). Whilst Greer points out a number of counter-discourses in the press at the time calling for abolition, or at least an informed debate about the death penalty, he argues that the reporting of the gruesome deaths of Jesse Tafero, Pedro Medina and Allen Lee Davis in Florida in the 1990s was one of 'political support and cultural reinforcement'.

Sarat (2002) has argued that the cultural reinforcement to which Greer refers also takes place in American cinema. Like Greer, Sarat focused on the 1990s, and at three films depicting the death penalty – *Dead Man Walking* (Tim Robbins 1996), *Last Dance* (Bruce Beresford 1996) and *The Green Mile* (Frank Darabont 1999). Sarat suggests that, despite their ostensibly critical perspective, these films ultimately focus on moral choices and protagonists, which leaves them silent on the fundamental issues concerning state killing whilst essentially reproducing the values on which it is based. In Greer's analysis, this is paralleled in the media's discussion over the proper administration of the death penalty in Florida (electric chair or lethal injection?)

rather than a more elementary dialogue over its very existence. Sarat has argued that state killing obscures the complex questions around crime and social control, instead simply reducing them to notions of revenge. Central here are the use of victim impact statements, 'a vehicle for resurrecting the dead and allowing them to speak as their killers are being judged' (Sarat 2002: 52).

The relationship between the media, public opinion and government penal policy is not new. In Chapter 7, Helen Johnston provides an account of how cultural constructions of the Victorian prison system impacted on public attitudes to punishment. She traces the development of incarceration from the prison hulks in the late eighteenth century to the rise of the separate system at Millbank penitentiary and later at Pentonville which opened in 1842. Through an analysis of the writings of Dickens and reports in *The Times*, Johnston reveals an inconsistent attitude to imprisonment during the mid-nineteenth century. She argue that Dickens' writings at the time illustrate this diversity, fiercely critical of the cruelty of the separate system in *American Notes* and *A Tale of Two Cities* but, later, in *David Copperfield* reflecting public anxiety over the utility of prison and the leniency of the system. Johnston draws contemporary parallels with the concern expressed by Dickens over prison conditions and in particular the inmates' diet. She suggests that the disquiet over prisoners 'rioting in gluttony' persists in late-modern penal discourse where claims of prisons as holiday camps, insufficiently harsh, are expressed in the news media.

Screening imprisonment

The second half of this book shifts its focus to television and film and begins with an account of documentary film-maker, Rex Bloomstein. In an attempt to redress the kinds of concern about prisons discussed by Johnston and to challenge the accepted wisdom about incarceration and the incarcerated, Bloomstein has spent 30 years documenting life in prison for the marginalized and disenfranchised. In doing so, his work has made a significant contribution to criminological debates about social control and imprisonment. In Chapter 8, Jamie Bennett, a former prison deputy governor, charts Bloomstein's criminal justice œvre from *The Sentence* in 1976 to *Lifer: Living with Murder* (2003).

Bloomstein is probably best known for the eight-part series about HMP Manchester, *Strangeways*, first broadcast in 1980. The series resulted from Home Secretary William Whitelaw's new 'open policy' towards prison, and consequently the BBC were invited to make what became 'a frank and uninhibited series about life in prison' (*Guardian* 16 October 1980). The visual impact of the prison iconography, revealed in tracking shots of stairwells, landings and bars – the 'human warehouse' of the first episode – would resonate in future prison films both factual and in fiction (Mason 1996). In 1983, Channel 4's three-part treatise of the British penal system, *Prison*, noted that the 'very success of the *Strangeways* series, especially its visual impact ironically, has helped constrict the meaning of prison to that particular prison's interior. To the public eye, prison means *Strangeways*' (*Prison: The Bankrupt Estate*, tx. 16 March 1983, 2100, Channel 4).

Equally striking about *Strangeways*' communicative design was the use of fly-on-the-wall camera work, or *cinema verité*. Bennett argues that Bloomstein has remained loyal to the technique as it enables his films to capture the essence of inmates in their penal environment: 'these human stories provide the most powerful examples of Bloomstein's art.' He further suggests that such an approach reinfranchises the inmates and their families, providing an opportunity for them to challenge the cultural othering of the prisoner (Garland 2001; Greer and Jewkes 2005).

Bennett's description of Bloomstein's films as 'an important media space for more considered and thoughtful reflection' of prison issues is well founded. The question remains, however, whether such films ultimately have the power to reform or challenge public attitudes about prison. Both King and Maruna earlier, and Yvonne Jewkes in Chapter 9 point out that it is what audiences *do* with crime and punishment narratives in media culture that is important. Jewkes asks how popular televisual constructions of imprisonment such as *Porridge* and *Bad Girls*, and those in the printed press, may contribute to public debates about prison. Supporting the findings of King and Maruna and Solomon, she suggests that the representation of prisons in news and on television will be viewed empathetically by those who share the narrative's perspective. However, she makes two important further points. First, that the identification with prison and its inmates is often driven by a victim-led and punitive attitude which only serves to alienate further the prison population by 'institutions resonant with symbolic moral disapproval, and then further censure by a media industry who strive to achieve public census'. Secondly, she bears out Enver Solomon's contention that coverage of penal issues in the printed press is superficial, and extends this to popular television where she considers prison to be relatively invisible.

Research on the distribution and frequency of prison programmes on British television (Mason 1995, 1996) further underscores Jewkes' argument. Between 1 January 1980 and 31 December 1990, Mason found 186 programmes concerned with prison. Even allowing for 41 repeats in this total, that equates to less than two programmes a month broadcast over a decade. It is interesting to note that over this period, episodes of *Porridge* accounted for nearly a quarter of all prison programmes (22 per cent) and was broadcast in seven of the ten years analyzed. The longevity of the series seems set to continue, and if television schedules are any indication of popularity, its status is increasing. A brief examination of terrestrial television schedules since 1995[4] reveals episodes of *Porridge* have been shown 86 times, over twice that of the Mason sample. This does not include episodes shown on cable channels such as UK Gold and the Paramount Comedy Channel. Mason argues that, in his sample, the dominance of *Porridge* owes more to the cast's excellent performances and the quality of the writing than to the prison setting (1996: 54). This explanation is one of three Jewkes identifies in discussions about the sitcom. Is *Porridge* mere wit, sheer grit or something in between, she posits?

Whilst Jewkes remains agnostic about the significance of *Porridge* and its more contemporary dramatic counterpart, *Bad Girls*, she warns against 'assuming that the meaning of any media text is fixed at the point of production' and cites Wilson and O'Sullivan's (2004) claims that *Bad Girls* has elevated penal reform messages as a case in point. Although the popularity of *Bad Girls* and *Porridge* offers some resistance to the claims of the invisibility of prison in popular culture, Wilson and O'Sullivan, and Brian Jarvis in Chapter 10, suggest otherwise. In their work on prison images in popular culture, Wilson and O'Sullivan contend that despite some notable exceptions (*The Shawshank Redemption* – Frank Darabont 1995; *Birdman of Alcatraz* – John Frankenheimer 1962; *Cool Hand Luke* – Stuart Rosenberg 1967) the prison film remains resolutely unpopular and unprofitable, doomed to cult status as a peripheral sub-genre (Wilson and O'Sullivan 2004). Jarvis too argues that 'popular culture has effectively colluded with "the experiment of mass incarceration" and ensured that inmates remain disappeared'. The HBO series *Oz*, a violent prison drama shot over 56 episodes and six years, Jarvis suggests, goes some way to addressing this.

However, for Jarvis, *Oz*'s claims to authenticity and its opportunity to explore and inform the public about prison are lost in a wave of mutilation and brutality. He suggests that the incessant violence leads not only to a desensitization of its effects, but to reduce 'the reality of violence into spectacle'. Thus for Jarvis, *Oz's* 'realism' is mediatized into the hyper-real, existing only in a cultural space. The special unit in which *Oz* is set is called Emerald City (get it?), its characters sketched from Hollywood prison films and its narratives punctuated by the arrival of film crews and journalists reminiscent of Oliver Stone's *Natural Born Killers* (1994).

The intertextual representation of prison is familiar territory in popular culture. There are several prison films such as *Riot in Cell Block 11* (Don Siegel 1954), which have cast inmates to play themselves. This implosion between the real and the imaginary is well demonstrated by events at Attica prison in 1971, in which inmates rioted in a manner similar to the narrative of *Riot* (Buzz Kulik 1969), released by Paramount two years earlier. Furthermore, Rafter notes how inmates at Santa Fe prison in New Mexico got drunk on home-brewed hooch and killed each other in a riot, again in a manner similar to the calls by the crazed Jack Surefoot (Ben Carruthers) also in *Riot*. In addition to what we may term the meta-cinema of some prison films is the self-reflexivity of others. *The Shawshank Redemption*, for example, offers a knowing and nostalgic nod to the prison film tradition (Chapter 12, this volume), whilst *Weeds* (John D. Hancock 1987) parodies the claims to authenticity of the prison film using the inmate-scripted play of its title.

Jarvis describes *Oz* as 'prison drama for the age of terror' where the masculine body becomes the target of random attacks and violent incursion. He also explores the centrality of masculinity to the series which he argues is equivocal and uncertain, offering alpha male violence, and a division of the male body as subject/object. These 'libidinal alchemies' persuade Jarvis to read *Oz* within the context of a crisis in masculinity. Drawing on the work of Bhabha (1995), Faludi (2000) and Robinson (2000), he posits that the inmates' constant display of masculinity, whilst enduring the pain of others' attempts to prove theirs, is indicative of captivity outside the prison: a 'feminine sphere of domesticity and consumption'.

In this respect, *Oz* bears some resemblance to the recent eight-part British prison drama, *Buried* (tx. February–March 2003, Channel 4): the story of Lee Kingley (Lennie James), a new inmate at the fictional HMP Mandrake Hill. The drama charts Kingley's rise to 'king rat of the shit heap', his decline and eventual murder.[5] *Buried* takes its title from a Jacobean play with the line 'art thou poor and in prison? Then thou art buried before thou art dead'. This takes us back, both metaphorically and historically to Helen Johnston's chapter in which she notes Dickens' use of the buried metaphor in *American Notes* and *A Tale of Two Cities*, but also forward, again in two senses to Mike Nellis's chapter on constructions of dystopian penal futures in popular culture. Here, Nellis notes in *Fortress* (Stuart Gordon 1992) that new inmates are informed on arrival that they are already dead, and in *Judge Dredd* (Danny Boyle 1995), Aspen prison is described as 'a tomb of the living'.

Like *Oz*, *Buried* deals with masculinity as contested and multifarious. The extreme violence constructed as validating the hegemonic masculinity of the prison and central to the inmate hierarchy is, at other times, challenged and muddied:

> Behind your cell door mate, that's where you do your bird. Alone behind your door. That's where your time starts. It's that little boy talking in your head. 'Cos out here on the wing, you keep up a front: we act like men. But alone, behind your door, you're just a boy. And if that boy ever shows his face outside your cell, you're a gonna (Rollie Man, *Buried*, episode 3, tx. 28 January 2003, 22: 30, Channel 4).

This vulnerability of exploring 'multiple masculinities' (Schauer 2004: 28) illustrates, and in contrast to *Oz*, a more compassionate view of the prison inmate. *Buried* script-writer Jimmy Gardner has commented how he wished to move beyond the construction of inmates portrayed in *Oz*, to explore prisoners' humanity: 'When I watched *Oz* I remember thinking I was really glad these people were on the inside – locked up and that I was on the outside: I didn't want people to think like that about *Buried*' (cited in Wilson and O'Sullivan 2004: 146).

However infrequent television prison dramas like *Buried* and *Oz* are, the presence of *Bad Girls*, at Jewkes notes, does at least explore women's incarceration. In cinema, women in prison films have been less prevalent than their male counterparts, with many forming a dubious soft-porn sub-genre (Mayne 2000; Walters 2001; Chapter 12, this volume). Cecil B. DeMille's *The Godless Girl* (1929) was one of the first films to feature women in a reform school whilst, in the early 1930s, *Ladies of the Big House* (Marion Gering 1932), *Ladies they Talk about* (Howard Bretherton and William Keighley 1933) and *Anne Vickers* (John Cromwell 1933) soon followed. In Chapter 11, Steve Chibnall notes how, despite the representation of women in Hollywood prison films, it was not until 1948 that a British prison for women was depicted, in *Good Time Girl* (Arthur la Bern 1948).

For Chibnall however, it was J. Lee Thompson's two films, *The Weak and the Wicked* (1954) and *Yield to the Night* (1957) which offered significant cinematic interventions into the debates around women's prisons in Britain. Chibnall tells the extraordinary story of how British film-maker Thompson, having read Joan Henry's *Who Lie in Gaol* – an account of Henry's time in HMPs Holloway and Askham Grange on conviction for fraud – met her, divorced his wife, married Henry and made *The Weak and the Wicked*, the film of Henry's book. Chibnall notes that although focusing on the cruelty of prison, *The Weak and the Wicked* stresses the loss of role for women whilst they remain behind bars. Thus the gendered politics and sanitized account of prison presented in the film suggest it is 'a means of punishing and re-educating women for their gender transgressions as much for their infringements of the law'.

Chibnall argues that the popularity of *The Weak and the Wicked* paved the way for the radical critique of the death penalty in Thompson and Henry's second prison film collaboration, *Yield to the Night*. The film is best remembered for Diana Dors cast against type as the soon to be executed Mary Hilton, and the contribution of the film to the abolition of the death penalty. Chibnall suggests that although the death penalty lasted into the next decade and *Yield to the Night*'s polemic against it may have been ultimately negligible, the film made a crucial contribution to the future of British film-making. Thompson's film, suggests Chibnall, began a shift from oppressive restriction and moral disapproval to a more progressive discourse: 'Mary Hilton had to swing before the sixties could', he comments, darkly.

By the time *Yield to the Night* was first screened, Hollywood had produced nearly 200 prison films. In a discussion of its output in Chapter 12, I offer a theoretical framework for analysing the prison film and its significance. Drawing upon genre theory, Foucault and Hall, I argue that much of the work pertaining to the prison film has been undertaken in a theoretical vacuum, offering mere description and unjustifiable taxonomies. I suggest that the Hollywood prison film should be read as a discursive practice, a regime of re/ presenting imprisonment in particular ways at particular times. In tracing the development of Hollywood's prison film output, I explore 'the mechanistic discourse of incarceration' suggesting the dominant representation of the penal built environment is one of prison as machine.

Hollywood as a discursive practice which temporally/temporarily fixes the meaning of prison is used in a similar way by Mike Nellis's final chapter in this book. He argues that, as cultural resources, films depicting images of the punishment of the future may contribute to 'understanding our contemporary hopes and fears' about prospective penal practice. Nellis's analysis of such images points to a dim penal future. He suggests that from *Punishment Park* (Peter Watkins 1970) to *Minority Report* (Steven Spielberg 2002) the cinematic representation of future punishment is 'consistently and remorselessly dystopian'. If Hollywood is to believed we can expect a literal, rather than my metaphorical, prison machine: increasingly automated, dehumanized and secret. Nellis posits that such a future is on the way to becoming reality, with monitoring technology already up and running and covert internment centres like Camp X-Ray. Perhaps, wonders Nellis, such dystopian images are preparing us for worse penal times ahead. This book suggests that the manner in which those times are captured by the media will be crucial.

Notes

1 Conservative Party election campaign poster, March–May 2005. See also Indymedia (2005).
2 For a rare exception, see Cavender (2004).
3 A 2004 national telephone poll of more than 1,000 people aged 18 or older in the USA reported that two thirds of Americans supported the idea of televising executions. Some 21 per cent said they would pay to watch Osama Bin Laden put to death and 11 per cent said they would pay to see Saddam Hussein executed (CNN 23 February 2004, at http://msnbc.msn.com/id/4353934/).
4 Television and Radio Index for Teaching and Learning (www.trilt.ac.uk).
5 It is unclear at the end of episode eight whether Kingley is actually dead. The narrative appeared to be left open, probably for the second series that Channel 4 never commissioned. Unfortunately, *Buried*'s title was taken rather too literally by Channel 4's schedulers, and was to be found after 22:30 on weeknights, leading to low viewing figures.

References

Baudrillard, J. (1983) *Simulations*. New York, NY: Semiotext.
Bhabha, H. (1995) 'Are you a man or a mouse?', in M. Berger *et al.* (eds) *Constructing Masculinity*. New York, NY: Routledge.
Butler, D. and Kavanagh, D. (1980) *The British General Election 1979*. Basingstoke: Macmillan.

Cavender, G. (2004) 'Media and crime policy: a reconsideration of David Garland's *The Culture of Control*', *Punishment and Society*, 6: 335–48.

Cottle, S. (2005) 'Mediatized public crisis and civil society renewal: the racist murder of Stephen Lawrence', *Crime, Media, Culture: An International Journal*, 1: 49–76.

Crawford, A. (2002) 'The growth of crime prevention in France as contrasted with the English experience: some thoughts on the politics of insecurity', in G. Hughes *et al.* (eds) *Crime Prevention and Community Safety: New Directions*. London: Sage.

Faludi, S. (2000) *Stiffed: The Betrayal of the American Male*. Pymble, NSW: Perennial.

Foucault, M. (1979) *Discipline and Punish: The Birth of the Prison*. Harmondsworth: Penguin Books.

Garland, D. (2001) *The Culture of Control*. Oxford: Oxford University Press.

Garland, D. (2002) 'The cultural uses of capital punishment', *Punishment and Society*, 4: 459–87.

Gillespie, M. and McLaughlin, E. (2002) 'Media and the making of public attitudes', *Criminal Justice Matters*, 49: 8–9.

Gillespie, M. and McLaughlin, E. (2003) 'Media and the shaping of public knowledge and attitudes towards crime and punishment', in *Rethinking Crime and Punishment* (available at www.rethinking.org.uk).

Girling, E. (2004) '"Looking death in the face": the Benetton death penalty campaign', *Punishment and Society*, 6: 271–87.

Greer, C. and Jewkes, Y. (2005) 'Extremes of otherness: media images of social exclusion', in *Social Justice*, 32.

Henry, S. and Milovanovic, D. (1996) *Constitutive Criminology*. Thousand Oaks, CA: Sage.

Henry, S. and Milovanovic, D. (eds) (1999) *Constitutive Criminology at Work: Applications to Crime and Justice*. Albany, NY: State University of New York Press.

Herman, E. (1995) *Triumph of the Market: Essays on Economics, Politics, and the Media*. Boston, MA: South End Press.

Indymedia (2005) 'Are you thinking what we're thinking? Er ... No' (available at http://www.indymedia.org.uk/en/2005/03/307812.html).

Lynch, M. (2004) 'Punishing images: jail cam and the changing penal enterprise', *Punishment and Society*, 6: 255–70.

Mason, P. (1995) 'Prime time punishment: the British prison and television' in D. Kidd-Hewitt and R. Osborne (eds) *Crime and the Media: the Postmodern spectacle*. London: Pluto Press.

Mason, P. (1996) 'Inside out: the British prison on television 1980–1991.' Unpublished PhD thesis, University of the West of England, Bristol.

Matthews, R. (2005) 'The myth of punitiveness', *Theoretical Criminology*, 9: 175–201.

Mayne, J. (2000) 'Caged and framed: the women-in-prison film', in J. Mayne (ed.) *Framed: Lesbians, Feminists, and Media Culture*, Minneapolis, MN: University of Minnesota Press.

McLaughlin, E. (2002) 'The crisis of the social and the political materialisation of community safety', in G. Hughes *et al.* (eds) *Crime Prevention and Community Safety: New Directions*. Milton Keynes: Open University Press.

McLaughlin, E., Muncie, J. and Hughes, G. (2003) 'Introduction: theorizing crime and criminal justice', in E. McLaughlin *et al.* (eds) *Criminological Perspectives: Essential Readings*. London: Sage.

Morris, N. and Rothman, D. (eds) (1998) *The Oxford History of the Prison: The Practice of Punishment in Western Society*. New York, NY: Oxford University Press.

Pratt, J. (1992) *Punishment in a Perfect Society*. Victoria University Press, Wellington.

Pratt, J. (2002) 'Critical criminology and the punitive society: some new "visions of social control" – western gulags and vigilantes', in R. Hogg and K. Carrington (eds) *Critical Criminology: Issues, Debates, Challenges*. Cullompton: Willan Publishing.

Pratt, J., Brown, D., Hallsworth, S., Brown, M. and Morrison, W. (eds) (2005) *The New Punitiveness: Trends, Theories, Perspectives*. Cullompton: Willan Publishing.

Rafter, N. (2000) *Shots in the Mirror*. Oxford: Oxford University Press.

Roberts, J. and Hough, M. (2002) *Changing Attitudes to Punishment, Public Opinion, Crime and Justice*. Cullompton: Willan Publishing.

Roberts, J., Stalans, L., Indermaur, D. and Hough, M. (2002) *Penal Populism and Public Opinion*. Oxford: Oxford University Press.

Robinson, S. (2000) *Marked Men: White Masculinity in Crisis*. New York, NY: Columbia University Press.

Russell, L. (2005) 'Tabloid tactics: pushing prison reduction', *Criminal Justice Matters*, 59: 32–3.

Ryan, M. (2003) *Penal Policy and Political Culture in England and Wales*. Winchester: Waterside Press.

Ryan, M. (2003b) 'The perception and the reality of crime'. Paper presented at the NACRO conference 'Crime watching: crime, public perception and the media', British Library, London, 19 November.

Sarat, A. (2002) *When the State Kills: Capital Punishment and the American Condition*. Princeton, NJ: Princeton University Press.

Schauer, T. (2004) 'Masculinity incarcerated: insurrectionary speech and masculinities in prison fiction', *Journal for Crime, Conflict and Media Culture*, 1: 28–42 (available at www.jc2m.co.uk/Issue3/Schauer.pdf).

Silverman, J. (2003) 'Crime and the media question time.' Paper presented at the NACRO conference 'Crime watching: crime, public perception and the media', British Library, London, 19 November.

Simon, J. (2001) 'Entitlement to cruelty: neo-liberalism and the punitive mentality in the United States', in K. Stenson and R. Sullivan (eds)

Crime, Risk and Justice: The Politics of Crime Control in Liberal Democracies. Cullompton: Willan Publishing.

Valier, C. (2004) 'Introduction: the power to punish and the power of the image', *Punishment and Society*, 6: 251–4.

Walters, S. (2001) 'Caged heat: the (r)evolution of women-in-prison', in M. McCaughey and N. King (eds) *Reel Knockouts: Violent Women in the Movies.* Austin, TX: University of Texas Press.

Wilson, D. and O'Sullivan, S. (2004) *Images of Incarceration: Representations of Prison in Film and Television Drama.* Winchester: Waterside Press.

Chapter 2

The function of fiction for a punitive public

Anna King and Shadd Maruna

> The experience of art is experience in a real sense and we must master ever anew the task that experience involves: the task of integrating it into the whole of one's own orientation to a world and one's self-understanding (Gadamer 1976: 101–2).

We live our lives surrounded by stories. In the UK today, watching television ranks alongside eating, working and sleeping as one of the things people spend most of their lives doing (Office for National Statistics 2002). Around 85 per cent of adults watch television everyday and half of UK homes now receive digital television (Lovatt 2004). Despite fears of decline, DVD sales more than doubled between 2001 and 2002 (Summerfield and Babb 2004). Yet, all this home media consumption has not stopped British citizens from going out to 'the pictures' to consume yet more stories. The year 2003 marked the second highest number of visits to the cinemas in 30 years (Office for National Statistics 2004). One of the only forms of media consumption that has declined at all over the last few decades is the reading of daily, national newspapers. Yet, in Great Britain, still over half the population takes at least one newspaper a day.[1]

Most of this media involves the sharing of stories, fictional and non-fictional, and an overwhelming proportion of these stories touch upon issues of crime and justice, corruption and revenge, good and evil. From police dramas, to serial killer autobiographies, to murder mysteries, to the national and international news reportage, crime and punishment are enormously popular themes in our cultural stories. It may not be true that 'If it bleeds, it leads' (as the journalist slogan would have it), but criminality and its response are certainly ubiquitous in our cultural stories. Reiner (2002) estimates around 25 per cent of the most popular British television programming is made up of 'crime shows', but even situation comedies, documentaries, soap operas and children's cartoons rely heavily on issues of crime, violence and justice to keep viewers tuned in each week. Could our cultural industries survive without prostitution, rape, prisons, gangsters, cops, violence or swarthy 'bad guys' with dodgy facial hair? Many storytellers even seem to find a vicious murder or two to be essential plot devices. Indeed, it is often claimed that, by the time the average child finishes primary school, he or she will have witnessed over 8,000 televised murders (see, e.g., Shalala 1993).

It is little wonder, in such an environment, that media studies research has become of increasing interest to criminology in recent years (Sparks 2001; Jewkes 2004). Considerable research continues to explore the classic question of whether or not the consumption of various media imagery promotes criminal or especially violent behaviour (e.g. Bandura *et al.* 1963). A smaller, but equally influential body of research traces the effects of media stories on public opinion, namely through the production of 'moral panics' (Hall *et al.* 1978; Cohen 1980; Evans 2003). More recently, a survey-based literature tracing the impact of media consumption on fear of crime and/or attitudes towards punishment has emerged (Hough *et al.* 1988; Sparks 1992; Chiricos *et al.* 2000; Ditton *et al.* 2004).

In some instances, the impact of media stories on public views and behaviour is transparent and even direct. For instance, the role of the tabloid paper, the *News of the World*, in the now infamous vigilantism that took place in Paulsgrove in the year 2000 is impossible to dismiss (see Evans 2003). More often, however, the relationship between media consumption and public attitudes or behaviour is a complex web that is difficult to disentangle outside short-term effects in a laboratory setting. After all, in the real world, not only does media consumption influence attitudes, but attitudes also influence choices of media consumption amongst almost infinite choice.

Recognizing this, contemporary media research is moving away from simple models of passive media influence to a more dynamic understanding of the role of the media in a person's life and self-understanding. According to Yvonne Jewkes (2004: 25), beginning in the 1990s:

> Researchers reconceptualized media influence, seeing it no longer as a force beyond an individual's control, but as a resource that is consciously *used* by people ... Researchers had dismissed concerns about what the media *do* to people, and turned the question around, asking instead, 'what do people do *with* the media?'

This is the approach we have taken in our own research. We are interested in the relationship between social attitudes and the consumption and interpretation of stories from various media. In particular, we are interested in the phenomenon of 'punitivism' which we define as the desire to see greater numbers of people punished (i.e. too many offenders 'get away with it') for greater durations (i.e. longer prison sentences) and with increased severity (i.e. no more 'holiday camp' prisons, more 'boot camps' and harsh conditions). In short, punitivism is the 'get tough' mentality that says the solution to the crime problem is to 'lock 'em up' and 'hang 'em high'. We hypothesize that social attitudes of this sort are supported and sustained through the consumption of particular stories. That is, individuals who hold such highly punitive visions regarding justice may find comfort and meaning in particular sorts of stories, which serve to reinforce and strengthen their views.

This is not a new or radical idea. For instance, in an imaginative essay subtitled 'Make my day', Hallsworth (2004) links the punitiveness apparent in American criminal justice thinking over the last 30 years to the popularity of the Clint Eastwood westerns and their themes of rugged individualism and rough justice. However, such discussions are usually speculative, lacking a systematic grounding in research evidence. Our goal was to explore just what stories do appeal most to a sample of individuals who hold strongly punitive attitudes and then try to speculate as to why.

Stories, media and self-identity

Although it is difficult to discern the precise role of the media on influencing behaviour, it is less problematic to examine the role of media consumption in the process of identity development. To psychologists, identity is the person's answer to the question of 'who am I?' Increasingly, the accepted answer to this question is that 'If you want to know me, you need to know my story'. That is, the construction and reconstruction of one's life story narrative (or 'personal myth'), integrating one's perceived past, present and anticipated future, is itself the process of identity development (the process through which modern adults imbue their lives with unity, purpose and meaning). Overwhelmed with the choices and possibilities of modern society (Fromm 1941), modern individuals internalize this autobiographical narrative in order to provide a sense of coherence and predictability to the chaos of their lives: 'To be a self is not to be a certain kind of being, but to be in possession of a certain kind of theory' (Harre cited in Burr 1995: 48).

Over the last two decades, this idea that identity is an internal narrative has achieved a privileged place in the social sciences and humanities, with adherents like Norman Denzin, Paul Ricoeur, Roger Schank and Charles Taylor. The distinguished psychologist Jerome Bruner (1987: 15) argues:

Eventually the culturally shaped cognitive and linguistic processes that guide the self-telling of life narratives achieve the power to structure perceptual experience, to organize memory, to segment and purpose-build the very 'events' of a life. In the end, we become the autobiographical narratives by which we 'tell about' our lives.

The equally distinguished UK sociologist Anthony Giddens (1991: 54) agrees, arguing that, in modernity, a 'person's identity is not to be found in behavior, nor – important though this is – in the reactions of others, but in the capacity to keep a particular narrative going'.

Theodore Sarbin (1986: vii) has argued that the narrative should be seen as the 'root metaphor' for the entire field of psychology and that 'narrative psychology' represents 'a viable alternative to the positivist paradigm'. The idea, building on traditions such as symbolic interactionism, hermeneutics and phenomenology, is that human life is essentially and fundamentally narrated and that understanding human interaction, therefore, requires some understanding of these stories. Indeed, Bruner (1987: 21) largely accepts Jean-Paul Sartre's famous claim that the human being 'is always a teller of stories, (s)he lives surrounded by his (or her) own stories and those of other people, (s)he sees everything that happens to him(her) in terms of stories and (s)he tries to live his(her) life as if (s)he were recounting it'.

Importantly, this storytelling does not take place in a vacuum; these narratives cannot be understood outside their social, historical and structural context (Bertaux 1981). Indeed, the very concept of 'culture' is sometimes understood as a repository of stories. Each person adopts a self-story based on the limited range of interpretations or narrative archetypes 'proposed, suggested and imposed on him by his culture, his society and his social group' (Foucault 1988: 181). Identity stories can be seen as rational adaptations within existing paradigms of public discourse (Henry and Milovanovic 1996). According to Foote and Frank (1999: 177), the 'social availability of preferred stories, and the assimilation of experience to these narratives, is how power works. The power of the dominant discourse is to include some stories as tellable and to exclude others as marginal and abnormal'.

A significant portion of our identities, therefore, is bound up in the media stories we choose to consume. Again, in some cases, the role of media consumption in identity construction could not be more obvious. Members of groups such as the so-called 'Trekkies' or 'Dead Heads' treat their allegiance to some form of entertainment (in these cases, the *Star Trek* series and the band The Grateful Dead, respectively) as if it were a family or clan, sometimes literally shaping their lives around tours, conventions and consumption of the particular medium. Even in less extreme examples, however, the role of media consumption in answering the question 'who am I?' is increasingly important. As the importance of some identity material (allegiance to neighbourhood, family of origin, ethnic identities, religions) decreases for some individuals (particularly middle-class professionals), the importance of 'what you watch' (or listen to, or wear) has taken on increased in importance in identity development. Science fiction enthusiasts living on opposite sides of the world may find that, in some meaningful ways, they have more in common with each other than they do with their neighbours, for instance.

Basically, as anyone who has ever been on a first date knows instinctively, one can learn a lot about a person from a peek into his or her CD and DVD collections, a scan of his or her bookshelves and magazine rack, or a glance at his or her bookmarked Internet websites. These things can both represent an explicit image the person wants to present to the world (a 'Goth', learned intellectual, romantic), and provide a sense of where the person turns for sources of information and inspiration about the world: the *Guardian* or the *Sun*? Jilly Cooper or Ian Rankin? Dylan or Dido? How individuals use the media and what appeals to them in stories, images and songs transcends the notion or 'taste' or preference to become a central aspect of a person's self-identity and individual subjectivity.

The Cambridge University Public Opinion Project

Beginning in 2002, a group of researchers at the University of Cambridge embarked on a psychosocial study of punitive public attitudes involving both quantitative and in-depth qualitative methodologies (see Maruna and King 2004). The goal of the research is better to understand punitive views as a part of a person's personal identity.

The first phase of this work involved the most traditional approach to public opinion: a brief postal survey sent to 3,600 households seeking their views on a variety of criminal justice-related issues. The survey consisted of a newly constructed scale for measuring punitive attitudes, as well as a variety of possible predictors and correlates of punitiveness ranging from demographic details to measures of social capital, personal anxiety and the like. In total, 939 completed surveys were returned from a variety of areas, ranging from the least affluent to the most affluent areas in the east of England according to the 2000 Indices of Deprivation.

From these initial responses, two subsamples were drawn. The first consisted of 20 respondents whose score on our punitiveness scale was at least one standard deviation above the mean for the sample (hereafter the 'punitive' or 'high punitive' group). The second sample consisted of 20 individuals on the opposite end of that spectrum, one standard deviation below the mean: the 'low punitive' group. Sample members in the two groups were matched on a case-by-case basis on demographics such as age, gender, community of origin and class background.[2]

These 40 respondents were asked to participate in a modified version of McAdams' Life Story Interview, an open-ended, semi-structured protocol that asks participants to describe a variety of key episodes in their lives as if they were constructing an autobiography. Our modified version of the interview contained a variety of questions regarding the experience of crime and punishment (victimization experiences, times the interviewee has been punished for something, etc.), as well as specific questions about the stories the individual has been exposed to (in film, literature, etc.) that they have found particularly meaningful or important.

This research was designed to explore inductively the possible patterns in the identity narratives of individuals who hold particularly punitive views, as well as individuals who hold decidedly less punitive views. In particular, for the purposes of this chapter, we are interested in exploring the media preferences of the two groups – i.e. what types of stories appeal to those with a punitive orientation versus those with less punitive views. Our hunch is that the two groups might differ in interesting ways that can tell us about the nature of punitive attitudes as well as about various forms of media consumption.

Importantly, it is impossible to draw any causal claims from these data. That is, we are not arguing that watching certain films or reading particular books directly leads to a punitive orientation, nor are we simply arguing that media choices are somehow determined by one's pre-existing personality type. The relationship between identity and media is more complicated and more interesting than either of these claims because the influence works in both directions (Henry and Milovanovic 1996: 126).

Identity is a fluid and dynamic concept, and identity development does not end when a person reaches any certain age (McAdams 1985). In fact, our stories have to be 'routinely created and sustained in the reflexive activities of the individual' (Giddens 1991: 52). Thus, life experiences – including watching a particularly meaningful film or reading a personally influential book – can alter one's overarching view of the world and one's own self-identity in crucial ways (Miller and C'deBaca 1994). At the same time, these sorts of transformations can be exhausting and even traumatic, so most experiences tend to be worked into pre-existing worldviews (Epstein and Erskine 1983).

This partially explains why most of us, whilst occasionally seeking to challenge ourselves with a new type of media experience, decide fairly quickly on what types of media we like (e.g. 'cop shows', folk rock or liberal opinion magazines) then stick with these same choices that subsequently reinforce our own worldviews. Our argument, therefore, is that the types of stories to which members of our punitive sample tend to gravitate may play a useful role in sustaining and maintaining a punitive mindset. Likewise, the stories selected as important by the low punitive sample may support the maintenance of beliefs that are distinctly less punitive than those of 'average citizens' (as constructed by our survey measures). Importantly, by matching the two groups on important characteristics such as income level and residence in high-crime area, it is unlikely that emergent themes in the data are attributable to these other, obvious differences.

Stories sustaining punitive worldviews

For the punitive sample members, the types of fictional media described as having made the most of an impression on the way they saw themselves were stories that provided clear examples of right and wrong, where justice prevailed, where authority was fair or struggled to be so and where underdogs successfully traversed obstacles. In sum, the stories they described allowed them to experience an idealized world with just resolutions. Often, this sense of orderliness appeared to contrast with the events in their own life stories, which seemed to be less neatly resolved.

Barry's[3] interview illustrates this nicely. A 48-year-old resident of the working-class seaside resort town, Great Yarmouth, Barry had recently experienced the dissolution of his marriage and separation from his only child. In addition, he lost two jobs that had kept him socially active (bar work and driving a bus). He found himself in a state of both isolation and emotional pain. Barry's home, however, reflected a different world, almost literally, with numerous bookshelves lined with fiction rich in moral tales such as Stephen King's work and classic science fiction. He described the appeal of one of his favourite series of books, *The Dark Towers*, by Stephen King: 'There's a very strong sense of right and wrong in that, and justice and fair play…The central character is what we'd call a cowboy basically, but it's in a warped world. And it's, again, it's a very strong sense of right and wrong…' These works might have functioned to present him with a prepackaged, coherent and moral universe on the cheap. Additionally, the fiction offers an idealized version of reality for Barry. For instance, in his own life history, a recurring theme was the idea of sudden and involuntary life change. He would just be hitting stride with a situation and then the rug would be pulled up and his life would change dramatically. This was first described when he was forced to move homes with his family as an adolescent. From this point on, he said, he had to learn to adapt to changes in his own life although this was not something that seemed to come easy to him. On the other hand, in *The Dark Towers* stories, Barry says: 'three characters are brought from our world into the new world. And you see them gradually become used to it, to their new environment and the new people'.

Stories that focus in particular on the personal struggles of authority figures also seemed to make lasting impressions for Barry. For instance, he spoke at length about *Killer: A Journal of Murder* (Tim

Metcalf 1996), a film that – despite its title – is actually more about the experiences of two prison guards with an inmate in Leavenworth prison (USA) than it is about the offender. Its central concern, Barry says, is the meaning of punishment, not crime. What made the film so memorable to him were the choices the prison officers had to make in the film:

> It was the brutality of the guards. If there was – I'm not saying that they should be like that now, but – if there was more respect for the guards and the warders in prison, I think it would be more of a deterrent because people wouldn't be so ready to take a chance to end up in there if there was more authority.

Another interviewee, Sandra, 63, living in a high-crime area in east London described her interest in stories about 'authority' and the justice process: 'Well I love crime and punishment to be honest. I love documentaries on all that. I've read a lot of books...I like authority all that sort of thing. I watch that. I like true crime what they have on Channel 4.' Like Barry, Sandra had worked in an area in which she was frequently in a position to manage other people's behaviour. Barry had talked about his experiences with trying to control rowdy school children on his bus routes, and Sandra had worked as a civil servant in a welfare department in London for years. She talked at length in her interview about her experiences and impressions of managing clients who often had chaotic lifestyles. Also, like Barry, this retired civil servant appeared to be less than satisfied with her current emotional existence. Sandra described the passing of her much loved, chronically ill husband five years prior to the interview as being the most important turning point in her life, and said that most of her familial ties were now 'dying out'. Both Sandra and Barry described themselves as outgoing and social people, but both were living alone. For both these sample members, stories of justice seemed to provide something that was missing in their own lives. Sparks (1992: 28) insightfully notes that the heroes of television crime shows and the like 'not only solve crime but also symbolically reconstitute the integrity of the social body'.

Another recurrent theme amongst punitive sample members involved personal triumphs over adversity. Interviewees spoke enthusiastically about stories that showcased individuals persisting in the face of terrible hardships to emerge triumphant, such as in *The Shawshank Redemption* (Frank Darabont 1994):

Just how it turns round at the end really. How they've wandered, the two of them...one of the best moments is where...He's got his parole and kept getting knocked back all the time. No, he hadn't got it; no he hadn't got it. And how the other one like, he was in a bad situation but he turned it round for himself didn't he – by doing all the bookwork and things he did...I think was just quite, you know, he's in a bad situation but he turned it round to sort of help himself really. You know, he could have got quite bitter in there couldn't he?

Examples of protagonists who are able to break out of cycles of family abuse by personal strength and integrity were exemplified in another story mentioned by the same interviewee, Alice:

The Child Called It, about that little boy who was abused...I felt he was let down by like Social Services and things. He'd been abused by his mum...He's turned his life around and he's been kicked in the teeth by a lot of people, even by his own parents, but he's still gone on to be a stronger person. And I think you have to have admiration for people like that. Because he could have just gone on the same way, you know, had children and beat them up and, you know, because that's all he knew really...That's just one of these things that gets on my nerves with people. You know, 'Why have you abused your children?' 'Oh, because I was abused.' Now to me, I don't know, but you have to stop that cycle. You know, if I was thrashed as a child, you know, loads and loads of times, I know if I'd got a child that I was meant to have loved and, I would not want them to go through the same hurt that I was done like that.

Another punitive sample member, Richard (51 years old and living alone in Great Yarmouth), talked about the stories that had made a lasting impression on how he saw himself in these same terms:

John Steinbeck, Of Mice and Men and Grapes of Wrath...a family having it rough...Everywhere was dried up and they couldn't make a living. They were all driving into towns or into big cities to look for work. It's when the Depression was on...I just like a film where the underdog comes out on top like, you know.

The 'good guys' do not always win in real life, of course, but stories of justice of this sort seem to attract the interest of many of the participants in our punitive sample group.

Stories for the less punitive public

For the participants in the 'low punitive' group (scoring below the mean in punitive views), very different themes emerged in their discussions of the stories that have had a lasting impact on their lives. Their stories were characterized by themes of subversion, where corrupt governments, corporations or authority figures are overthrown or exposed in some way.

Ella, from East London, said she resonated with stories that subverted the established order of things, exposing what is 'underneath' the more comforting portrayal of 'justice' in television programmes like CSI (*Crime Scene Investigators*):

> It is more corruption and the twisted-ness of corruption. So that's the side that would interest me...the different factions within that, and the government...So, actually, although I like CSI – more than that, the ones that do interest me would be are the one's about what's underneath it.

Similarly, Carol, a charity worker from London, said she gravitated to stories of rebellion. In particular, she said that she saw herself in a scene from *The Sound of Music* (Robert Wise 1965):

> There's a particular scene where the nuns in the convent, I think the Nazis have a jeep and they're going to chase the family and the nuns are standing there looking angelic and they kind of, they reveal that they've taken bits out of the engine. And I just really like that because they say – I think the line was, 'Father we have sinned', and they showed that, you know, it's been good...it's like the thing, you know, the good girl with things hidden up my sleeve.

In this wonderful example, like others selected by members of the non-punitive group, 'doing bad' is sometimes necessary to do what is right, and rules are sometimes meant to be broken or inverted. Certainly, those who make and impose the rules are not always to be trusted.

Additionally, stories from the low punitive group highlighted darker aspects of experience (e.g. serial killing) than those described by the punitive sample. Whilst the punitive group seemed more attracted to things that let them experience ideals of justice vicariously, the low punitive interviewees seemed drawn to stories that allowed them to experience 'bad' things vicariously. For example, Louise, 34, a recovering heroin addict living in central King's Lynn, discussed why *The Red Dragon* (Brett Ratner 2002), a film about a serial killer, had left an important impression on her: 'I suppose it's macabre that somebody can actually do that, it's ugh...It's something that's unnatural, that you couldn't see yourself doing, but in a way sort of I wonder what that would be like to do.' Her favourite fiction to read also contained elements of fascination with destructive forces: 'Normally it's got like some kind of mutant thing in there and you know, it's tearing people apart here, there and everything.'

Discussion

The modern age has been referred to as an age of unparalleled uncertainty (Bottoms 1995) where unprecedented proportions of the population are said to be suffering clinical anxiety (Twenge 2000). Apparently, increased freedom from personal constraints and universal values may come with a price: a diminished capacity of culture to guard us against uncertainty. As such, the transition to this late-modern world may be experienced as unpleasant for humans who seem naturally to seek to make meaning out of the chaos of our lives (Frankl 1984 [1959]; Bordwell 1989). In response, many of us turn to stories to create a sense of deeper meaning or order in our lives.

Members of both the punitive and low punitive samples in our study are adapting to the same, late-modern anxieties and fears, but they do so in different ways. Punitive attitudes exist alongside an interest in stories that present an alternative reality that reflects longings for a more just and meaningful world through likeable and triumphant heroes. Sparks writes, it 'may be that the audience turns to crime fiction precisely in consolation for the messy inconclusiveness of the process of justice in the world and its obdurate failure to conform to morally or aesthetically satisfying patterns' (1992: 24). Contrarily, less punitive attitudes coincide with an attraction to tales that showcase worlds in which the structures and constraints of society are less determined. In this way, they may function similarly

27

as outlets for expressing a desire for a different type of world; only the world that is 'just' and 'meaningful' in these stories manifests in different ways. For instance, heroes may not be instantly likeable or may even be anti-heroes (e.g. serial killers) and their triumphs are of a much different nature. Still, the common themes in the content of the stories that each group tells differentiate constellations of symbolic referents that can inform our thinking about what constitutes punitive and non-punitive worldviews.

Notes

1 Of those who do, 5 per cent take the *Daily Telegraph* and a 4 per cent take *The Times*, but the *Sun* (with its infamous 'Page Three' girls) continues to be the most popular, with 20 per cent of UK newspaper readers choosing it each day. The more politically progressive papers, the *Guardian* and the *Independent*, have readerships of 2 per cent and 1 per cent, respectively (Church *et al.* 2000).
2 In some ways, we have modelled the research design on Adorno and colleagues' (1956) highly elaborate, if flawed (see Martin 2001), methodology, as well as the triangulated design of Gaubatz (1995).
3 All names have been changed.

References

Adorno, T.W., Frenkel-Brunswick, E., Levinson, D. and Nevitt Sanford, J. (1956) *The Authoritarian Personality*. New York, NY: Harper.
Bandura, A., Ross, D. and Ross, S.A. (1963) 'Imitation of film-mediated aggressive models', *Journal of Abnormal and Social Psychology*, 66: 3–11.
Bertaux, D. (1981) *Biography and Society: The Life-history Approach in the Social Sciences*. Beverly Hills, CA: Sage.
Bordwell, D. (1989) *Making Meaning: Inference and Rhetoric in the Interpretation of Cinema*. Cambridge, MA: Harvard University Press.
Bottoms, A. (1995) 'The politics of sentencing reform', in R. Morgan (ed.) *The Philosophy and Politics of Punishment and Sentencing*. Oxford: Oxford University Press.
Bruner, J. (1987) 'Life as narrative', *Social Research*, 54: 11–32.
Burr, V. (1995) *An Introduction to Social Constructionism*. London: Routledge.
Chiricos, T., Padgett, K. and Gertz, M. (2000) 'Fear, TV news and the reality of crime', *Criminology*, 38: 755–85.
Church, J., Jackson, J., Jackson, V., Kershaw, A., Lillistone, C., Manners, A., Mill, N. Sharp, D., Shipsey, C. and Short, M. (2000) in J. Matheson and C. Summerfield (eds) *Social Trends: No. 31: 2001 Edition*. London: HMSO.

Cohen, S. (1980) *Folk Devils and Moral Panics: The Creation of the Mods and Rockers*. New York, NY: St. Martins Press.

Ditton, J., Chadee, D., Farrall, S. Gilchrist, E. and Bannister, J. (2004) 'From imitation to intimidation – a note on the curious and changing relationship between the media, crime and fear of crime', *British Journal of Criminology*, 44: 595–610.

Epstein, S. and Erskine, N. (1983) 'The development of personal theories of reality from an interactional perspective', in D. Magnusson and V.L. Allen (eds) *Human Development: An Interactional Perspective*. New York, NY: Academic Press.

Evans, J. (2003) 'Vigilance and vigilantes: thinking psychoanalytically about anti-paedophile action', *Theoretical Criminology*, 7: 163–89.

Foote, C.E. and Frank, A. (1999) 'Foucault and therapy: the disciplining of grief', in A.S. Chambon *et al.* (eds) *Reading Foucault for Social Work*. New York, NY: Columbia University Press.

Foucault, M. (1988) 'Technologies of the self', in L.H. Martin *et al.* (eds) *Technologies of the Self*. Amherst, MA: University of Massachusetts Press.

Frankl, V. (1984/1959) *Man's Search for Meaning: An Introduction to Logotherapy*. New York, NY: Simon & Schuster.

Fromm, E. (1941) *Escape from Freedom* (ed. Farrar and Rinehart). New York: Rinehart and Company.

Gadamer, H. (1976) *Philosophical Hermeneutics*. Berkeley, CA: University of California Press.

Gaubatz, K. (1995) *Crime in the Public Mind*. Ann Arbor, MI: University of Michigan Press.

Giddens, A. (1991) *Modernity and Self-identity: Self and Society in the Late Modern Age*. Stanford, CA: Stanford University Press.

Hall, S., Critcher, C., Jefferson, T., Clarke, J. and Roberts, B. (1978) *Policing the Crisis: Mugging, the State, and Law and Order*. London: Macmillan Education.

Hallsworth, S. (2004) 'Make my day: images of masculinity and the psychodynamics of mass incarceration', in R. Lippens (ed.) *Imaginary Boundaries of Justice*. Oxford: Hart Publishing.

Henry, S. and Milovanovic, D. (1996) *Constitutive Criminology*. Thousand Oaks, CA: Sage.

Hough, M., Lewis, H. and Walker, N. (1988) 'Factors associated with punitiveness in England and Wales', in N. Walker and M. Hough (eds) *Public Attitudes to Sentencing: surveys from five countries. Cambridge Studies in Criminology*. Cambridge: Cambridge University Press.

Jewkes, Y. (2004) *Media and Crime*. London: Sage.

Lovatt, F. (2004) 'Half of UK homes now receive digital TV' (available at http://digital-lifestyles.info/display_page.asp?section=distribution&id=10 43).

Martin, J.L. (2001) 'The authoritarian personality, 50 years later: what lessons are there for political psychology?', *Political Psychology*, 22: 1–26.

Maruna, S. and King, A. (2004) 'Public opinion and community sanctions', in G. Robeinson (ed.) *Alternatives to Prison*. Cullompton: Willan Publishing.

McAdams, D. (1985) *Power, Intimacy and the Life Story: Personological Inquiries into Identity*. New York, NY: Guilford Press.

Miller, W. and C'deBaca, J. (1994) 'Quantum change: toward a psychology of transformation', in T. Heatherton and J. Weinberger (eds) *Can Personality Change?* Washington, DC: American Psychological Association.

Office for National Statistics (2002) '2000 time use survey' (available at http://www.statistics.gov.uk/cci/nugget.asp?id=7).

Office for National Statistics (2004) 'TV and cinema.' UK Film Council; Cinema Advertising Association/Cinema and Video Industry Audience Research; Office for National Statistics (available at http://www.statistics. gov.uk/cci/nugget.asp?id=572).

Reiner, R. (2002) 'Media made criminality: the representation of crime in the mass media', in M. Maguire *et al.* (eds) *Oxford Handbook of Criminology*. Oxford: Oxford University Press.

Sarbin, T. (1986) 'The narrative as a root metaphor for psychology', in T. Sarbin (ed.) *Narrative Psychology: The Storied Nature of Human Conduct*. New York, NY: Praeger.

Shalala, D. (1993) 'Addressing the crisis of violence', *Health Affairs*, 12: 30–3.

Sparks, R. (1992) *Television and the Drama of Crime: Moral Tales and the Place of Crime in Public Life*. Milton Keynes: Open University Press.

Sparks, R. (2001) '"Bringin' it all back home": populism, media coverage and the dynamics of locality and globality in the politics of crime control', in K. Stenson and R. Sullivan (eds) *Crime Risk and Justice*. Cullompton: Willan Publishing.

Summerfield, C. and Babb, P. (2004) *Social Trends No. 34: 2004 Edition*. London: HMSO.

Twenge, J. (2000) 'The age of anxiety? Birth cohort change in anxiety and neuroticism, 1952–1993', *Journal of Personality and Social Psychology*, 79: 1007–21.

Chapter 3

Red tops, populists and the irresistible rise of the public voice(s)

Mick Ryan

The punitive paradox

It has become commonplace to argue that crime rates in many urban societies, including our own ('Longest period of falling crime for 106 years', the *Guardian* 22 July 2004), have been on a downward curve in recent years, yet paradoxically this has not registered with the general public (Roberts *et al.* 2003). Indeed, if anything, fear of crime amongst the public(s) seems to be on the increase. This fear is blamed for ushering in more *punitive times* (Pratt *et al.* 2005). Prisons in Britain, Australasia and America are overflowing, and the conditions attached to traditional alternatives to custody like probation, to include devices like electronic tags and curfew orders, are more restrictive than ever. All this penal repression at a time when we should be feeling less worried about being victims of crime.

Explaining this punitive paradox is no easy business, though it is a tempting to 'round up the usual suspects'. In simple terms, the explanation runs something like this. Most of us are fortunately not routinely the victims of crime, especially serious crimes. And so a lot of what we know about such crimes comes from the media, which as Cohen (1972) and Hall *et al.* (1978) demonstrated long ago, can over-represent the scale of the problem. Or under-represent it for that matter. At the time of the mugging panic in the 1970s, for example, there was not much serious media debate about domestic violence against women or the physical abuse of very young children.

But whatever crimes we are considering, what we normally refer to as public(s) opinion about crime, its extent, what we might do about it, is a problematic social construct which has been put together by a complex set of interactions between the media, the agencies of law and order, pressure groups and, not least, those very politicians who simply claim to be *responding* to it as good democrats (Leishman and Mason 2003). So we have a scholarly duty to interrogate public opinion about crime; we should never be content simply to measure it and then uncritically report what it registers.

First-year sociology and media students will be familiar with this critical approach. They will also have come across claims that British red tops and politicians have been responsible for deliberately and/ or unnecessarily heightening public fears about crime when it was seen to be in their circulation or political interests, so ratcheting up the punitive index even when crime rates are holding steady or in decline (Jewkes 2004).

For example, during the paedophile scare on the Paulsgrove housing estate during 2000 it was difficult for anyone reading the *News of the World* not to have come to the wholly erroneous conclusion that every paedophile was a homicidal maniac who could easily be neutralized by publishing his name and place of residence on a register (Silverman and Wilson 2002; Aldridge 2003). This had devastating consequences for quite innocent people, and some politicians, believing that the *News of the World* had caught the popular mood, were less forthcoming than they might have been in attacking the outbursts of vigilantism it provoked (Ryan 2003).

We trust this demonstrates that we are far from uncritical about how public opinion about crime is *constructed* and used, and in particular, that it is right to be highly suspicious of how red tops and politicians have fuelled what Giles Playfair once described as Britain's *Punitive Obsession* (1971), even when the objective evidence suggests they should be doing quite the opposite.

However, having made this point, the central argument of this chapter is that politicians have far less room to manoeuvre in responding to public opinion and crime and punishment, *however it is constructed*, than in the past; that changes in our political culture and the arrival of new media technologies make the public voice(s) a far more powerful player in the policy-making process than was once the case. Simply deconstructing individual moral panics and chastizing opportunistic politicians and red top editors like Rebekah Wade of the *Sun* no longer has sufficient explanatory potential.

Other forces are at work. This has important strategic consequences, but let me first outline the changes I wish to stress by drawing a contrast between old times and new times.

Old times

After 1945 there were some attempts at liberalizing criminal justice policy. Labour Party supporters acknowledged that many of those at the sharp end of the criminal justice system had been touched by one or more of what were identified as the five great evils: want, squalor, idleness, disease and ignorance. Some offenders were therefore entitled to a measure of welfare and support as well as punishment. However, whilst the impact of deprivation on ordinary people's lives was well understood, many rank-and-file Labour voters supporters, like many of their Conservative Party counterparts, were none the less suspicious of the influence of liberal 'do-gooders' in Parliament who supported measures like the aboliton of corporal punishment in 1948. So the concessions that were secured, including the partial abolition of the death penalty under the Conservative Party in 1957, were hard fought compromises where the opinions of ordinary party members and, indeed, the public at large, were often shunted aside (Ryan 1983).

That such controversial reforms – it took many years of parliamentary and extra-parliamentary agitation to roll back the scaffold – were secured at all is partly explained by the *deferential* nature of the policy-making process in Britain. We draw attention here to Almond and Verba's (1963) widely supported observation that Britain's political culture at this time was highly *deferential*, not least when compared with that of the USA. It was accepted in Britain, albeit sometimes reluctantly, that 'Whitehall' was likely to know best. This allowed senior politicians, civil servants, insider pressure groups like the Howard League and 'experts' serving on government advisory bodies to dominate what was a highly 'closed' policy-making apparatus.

This secretive, 'top down' policy-making apparatus, supported by party loyalty, and reinforced by the ever-present threat of the Official Secrets Act 1911, was nowhere more evident than in the Home Office where leading politicians, civil servants like Sir Frank Newsom, academic experts like Sir Leon Radzinowicz and senior members of the judiciary made criminal justice policy very much as they thought appropriate. Of course, as with corporal and capital punishment, this metropolitan elite ensemble could not *entirely* ignore the public voice(s). But this was monitored, not in order that it might be accommodated, but more in order to out-manoeuvre it. Much the same attitude was taken about the opinions of those operatives, who actually ran the criminal justice system, be they policemen, local

33

magistrates, prison warders, even prison governors; their wishes were almost wholly ignored (Lewis 1997).

How this policy-making process can be squared with our ideas about democracy is a central issue which I shall return to. In the mean time, however, I want to outline how this top-down process was partially opened up, first by the arrival of the counter-culture, and then later, by the rise of the New Right.

New times

The arrival of the counter-culture in the mid-1960s and early 1970s had a very real impact on the way people, particularly young people, looked at how policy decisions were being made, and who was to be included in what had hitherto been a closed process. Activists were far less willing to accept *statist* solutions to complex social problems that were handed down by others – clever, middle-class, Oxbridge-educated chaps, mostly – and instead became far more interested in working outside established processes that simply reproduced prevailing ideologies.

This led to the setting up of alternative or parallel political structures based around local, community-grounded initiatives where those on the receiving end of social provision, be they patients, welfare claimants or drug addicts, were encouraged to speak to each other. They knew where the shoe pinched, it was their turn to define their own needs, to come up with their own solutions rather than having them imposed by bureaucrats from above.

In the case of criminal justice, this movement encompassed groups like the Prisoners' Union, PROP, Up Against the Law and Radical Alternatives to Prison (Ryan 1983). Contact with the academic National Deviancy Conference at various intersections provided some theoretical insights. Although these groups never spoke with a single voice, and were no more representative of the public than the male, metropolitan policy-making elite they challenged, they nevertheless together combined to mount a sufficiently coherent critique of the existing criminal justice system throughout the 1970s.

However, whilst the prison system and the probation service were partly destabilized by these groups the elite, metropolitan policy-making ensemble which I have described carried on operating much as before. Indeed, it was only later disturbed by the rise of the New Right which partly overlaid and then superseded the counter-culture towards the end of the 1970s. Under Margaret Thatcher, the Tories aggressively confronted the Labour government on law and order right from the start.

The Conservative Party election manifesto in 1979 carried a special section on 'The rule of law', immediately followed by one on 'The fight against crime'. This first depicted Labour as having undermined the authority of Parliament, the Conservatives offered to restore this and, *within the same sentence*, to give 'the right priority to the fight against crime' (Conservative Party 1979). Tougher sentences were called for, violent criminals and the young were special targets, and there was even a promise to reopen the debate on capital punishment. In the subsequent election, 87 per cent of Conservative candidates declared themselves in support of tougher measures on law and order.

This populist approach was vigorously challenged by the liberal, metropolitan ensemble that had dictated the shape of criminal justice policy in *old times*. Its members worried that such populist rhetoric would all too easily incite a more punitive attitude towards offenders which had its roots stretching back to the eighteenth century. Mrs Thatcher's response was simply to reply that she was just reflecting the wishes of 'the people of Britain' in these matters (Conservative Party conference address 1977). Put in another way, she represented public opinion in its broadest and most representative sense, and that under her leadership she would not allow this 'grass roots' opinion to be shunted aside as it had been in the past.

So it was 'the people of Britain' the Conservatives were listening to, not to liberal pressure groups like the Howard League, not to sheltered Oxbridge-educated civil servants, not to the far from convincing university experts on criminal behaviour like Sir Leon Radzonowicz, and still less to those radical criminologists whose 'alternative realities' derived from the counter-culture, that handmaiden of the 'permissive society,' that had so offended middle England.

In its essentials, though never quite in its classic form as British society was still too deferential to entertain pure populism, Conservative rhetoric on crime and punishment in the 1970s displayed most of the basic characteristics of populism everywhere. There was a distrust of metropolitan elites, of the academy, of 'backstage' policy-making which favours complicated trade-offs instead of simple uncomplicated solutions – life sentences should mean life – and a strong charismatic leader to convey these essential truths directly to the people (Canovan 1999). As Le Penn was to encourage ordinary French men and women to ignore Parisian metropolitan elites and speak from their hearts, so Mrs Thatcher invited 'the people of Britain' to have their say on law and order. This had great popular appeal. In the run-up to the 1979 General Election law and order was the only major issue on which the Conservative Party was far ahead of Labour.

Political opportunism?

What persuaded the Conservative Party to 'respond' in such an unashamedly populist way in the mid-1970s or, perhaps more accurately, what persuaded it *actively to become part of the cycle that both manufactured and helped to sustain such a hard-line approach*? Part of the answer, clearly, was political opportunism. For a number of reasons, some areas of Britain were under enormous pressure as the postwar consensus between capital and labour was renegotiated (Hall *et al.* 1978). This produced real feelings of insecurity amongst all social classes which the Conservative Party consciously tapped into for electoral reasons (Taylor 1981). It is doubtful that its leading spokespersons really believed that more repressive policies would contain crime, but it was confidently assumed that they would be enthusiastically supported by the public (Windlesham 1993).

Following three successive electoral defeats New Labour's thinking on law and order also became more populist in tone. The party consciously distanced itself from old times, arguing that criminal justice policy had now to take account of a wider, popular constituency. For example, introducing one of New Labour's first major pieces of legislation – branded as social authoritarianism by its liberal critics – the Crime and Disorder Bill 1998, Jack Straw wrote (*The Times* 8 April 1998) that what pleased him most about the bill was not just its contents but the fact that it was 'rooted' in the experiences of 'local communities across the country' rather than reflecting the views of 'metropolitan elites' who lived at a 'comfortable distance' from the 'worst excesses' of crime and other forms of anti-social behaviour. He therefore presented the bill as a 'triumph of democratic politics', a quintessential New Labour measure that had been shaped, not by the interests of well connected, liberally minded, London-based pressure groups, but one which had grown out of 'speaking to people, hearing their worries', of responding to the public voice(s):

So, public opinion broadly defined, diligently gathered through plain-speaking constituency surgeries, and no doubt augmented by opinion polls and the findings from focus groups, became New Labour's primary constituency, not the special publics made up of what Straw was later to refer to as the BMW-owning Hampstead liberals who had disproportionately influenced the policy making process in old times. Eager to demonstrate this commitment, Straw went beyond the hallowed column of *The Times* and *The Guardian*, talking regularly to the red tops, especially *The Daily Mirror.* Also writing in support of the Crime and Disorder Bill (1998) Tony Blair chose another red top, *The News of the World,* to stress his commitment to govern in the interest of 'ALL the country' (*News of the World,* 10 May 1998).

The available evidence therefore appears to confirm that both Labour and Conservative politicians, no doubt willed on by populist red tops, bypassed the metropolitan elite of old times which had seen itself as the bulwark against a vengeful, not to say ignorant, public, and that they consciously did this to secure votes, to win electoral advantage. This electoral competition continues to fuel the public's fear of crime in very recent times, even when crime rates have declined. For example, a recent British Crime Survey has suggested that risk of becoming a victim of crime has fallen from 40 per cent in 1995 to 26 per cent in the 12 months to March 2004, its lowest level since the crime surveys in their modern form began in 1981 (*Guardian* 22 July 2004). In spite of this improvement, the prison population has spiralled upwards and the Conservative opposition has only recently, in August 2004, promised to build even more prisons.

As I mentioned earlier, when faced with these statistics it is certainly tempting to 'round up the usual suspects', to blame our punitive paradox on manipulative politicians and editors like Rebekah Wade. Furthermore, the evidence we have produced in this chapter *does* suggest that both should take some share of the blame. It is therefore easy to agree with Thomas Mathiesen's observation that, nowadays:

> communicative rationality lives its life in the secluded corners of the professional journals and meetings, while the public debate, flooded as it is by dire warnings by the police and sensational crime stories, and significantly, by opportunistic political initiatives in the context of burlesque television shows called 'debates' is predominately characterised by the rationality of the market place (1995: 8).

However, my argument is that there are other forces at work in our political culture which suggest that placing *all* the blame on the usual suspects in this way is simply wrong; that *other* forces have

37

contributed to the growing resonance of the public voice(s); and that its *enhanced presence* in the policy-making process cannot just be explained by the manipulative actions of red-top editors and/or politicians. It is this possibility that we now seek to interrogate.

The irresistible rise of the public voice(s)

We are not much interested here in contesting whether or not the desire of the old metropolitan elite to influence the direction of penal policy behind closed doors represented little more than a snobbish, educated, liberal disdain for the views of ordinary people in these matters. We are, however, interested to emphasize that the power of that elite became circumscribed. The hierarchical society that underpinned it the 1940s and 1950s, battered by the radicalism of the 1960s and 1970s and then further undermined by the consumerism of the 1980s and 1990s which transformed criminal justice system into a service to be measured and consumed, has irrevocably changed.

People are less and less prepared to leave questions, including difficult penal questions, to their 'masters'. Nor are they, in less ideologically inclined times where less than a third of the electorate can see much differences between the parties, willing to leave such questions to 'their' party which they are increasingly less inclined slavishly to vote for, that is even if they bother to vote at all. In short, to argue for what John Stuart Mill described as the value of the 'superior wisdom' of elites, be it of politicians, pressure groups, university professors like Leon Radzinowicz, nowadays cuts far less ice in a political culture which is moving *away from deference*, trusting instead to exerting more direct pressure through mechanisms outside of the formal political process and its network of consultative committees and processes.

This growing public 'independence' is evident in a number of modern democracies; it is a postmodern phenomenon that has been extensively researched. Robert Inglehart, for example, writes:

> Mass publics have played a role in national politics for long time of course, through the ballot and in other ways. Current changes enable them to play an increasingly active role in formulating policy, and to engage in what might be called 'elite-challenging', as opposed to 'elite-directed' activities. Elite-directed participation is largely a matter of elites mobilising mass support through established organisations such as political

parties, labor unions...and so on. The newer elite-challenging style of politics gives the public an increasingly important role in making specific *decisions*, not just a [mere] choice between two or more sets of decision makers (1997: 3).

Two things are driving this long-term change. The first is mass education, the second is the growth of the information and communication society. These enable the masses to participate more in politics, they help ordinary people to acquire the skills (and information) previously enjoyed only by elites within the formal political and administrative networks. One result of this shift is that:

Western publics are developing an increasing potential for political participation. This...does not imply that mass publics will simply show higher rates of participation in traditional activities such as voting, but that they may intervene in the political process on a qualitatively different level. Increasingly they are likely to demand participation in making major decisions, not just a voice in selecting the decision makers...These changes have important implications for political parties, labor unions and professional organisations; for mass politics are increasingly likely to be elite-challenging rather than elite-directed (Inglehart 1997: 294).

Whilst Britain still remains a less deferential society than Ronald Inglehart's America, the shift that has already taken place here is clearly apparent. British parties have become far more responsive to changing public sentiment on specific issues as opposed to offering broad, ideologically distinctive programmes to the electorate once every four or five years. In its turn, the electorate has shown less and less inclination to turn out to vote, believing that it does not matter that much which party is in power. The force of these changes in our political culture was brought home to Britain in the summer of 2000. During August of that year a few lorries began picketing an oil refinery just outside Manchester. This was in protest against fuel costs that had steadily risen, partly because of price rises on the international market, and partly through the application of the 'fuel tax escalator' first introduced by a previous Conservative government. Within a week the picketing lorry drivers were joined by other disaffected groups, including small dairy farmers with their tractors, and quickly Britain's fuel supplies were almost curtailed and the government lurched into a full scale political crisis with opinion polls showing overwhelming support for the protesters who, through their skilful use of digital mobile telephone and fax networks, seemed to have the country at their mercy. It is no exaggeration to say that the government came close to being toppled (Rawnsley 2001).

When this loose alliance eventually broke up after the government signalled that it would make some concessions in the forthcoming budget, particularly to the road haulage industry, the long-term damage to the New Labour government was not serious; the protest was not an ideologically based protest in the traditional sense of being an old-fashioned party struggle between capital and labour, rather it was a 'consumers' protest'. Within a year, New Labour was returned with another huge majority, but significantly it was the lowest turn out at any general election since 1918.

It is, of course, easy to berate the simplicity of the arguments of many of those who took part in this protest. Like the people of Paulsgrove we referred to earlier, they wanted simple populist solutions to what are, in truth, complex policy problems. However, the crucial point is that the protest reveals how easily the public voice(s) can be translated into effective political action quite outside the parties or, indeed, any of the other traditional institutions that channel communication between people and government in modern democratic societies. Furthermore, although New Labour mishandled this protest, as it arguably mishandled the Paulsgrove protest, both are testimony to the claim that there is: 'An upgrading of the public voice in political communication. Instead of being positioned only to attend to and overhear the views and arguments of others (politicians, journalists, pressure group spokesmen) the experience and opinions of quite ordinary people are being aired more often' (Blumler and Gurevitch 1996: 129). This upgrading of the public voice(s) is partly a consequence of the growth in commercial media outlets from the late 1950s onwards and new media technologies. The days have long since gone when the only voice governments had to listen to on controversial issues like capital punishment was Lord Reith's respectful BBC. The introduction of commercial television began upgrading the public voice, and with the recent arrival of digital networks, there are so many outlets that just about anyone is invited on air to give his or her views on such subjects; indeed, some even do some agenda setting of their own. Or if you cannot get air space to talk about what concerns you, why not email the Prime Minister's Office, or log on to the Downing Street web page? In early 2003, the government launched yet another electronic initiative, inviting the public to participate in the Prime Minister's 'Big Conversation' with the British people.

Commenting on the growing influence (and potential) of the new information and communication technologies in promoting new and, arguably, more democratic forms of political action in Britain, Will Hutton recently observed that:

> [the] number of bottom-up campaigns into which people are throwing themselves with enthusiasm on left and right alike is growing by the year…
>
> All are networks that depend on the new information and communication technologies (ICT) to create the multiple linkages and co-ordination for large-scale mobilisation of people; without the mobile and the internet they would be impossible.
>
> Such networks can be very local…Groups form via, and remain in contact through, the internet and the mobile, and bring formidable pressure on local councillors, and harried councillors give way under their force…They are…a tribute to the newly emerging local and partially formed public realm…
>
> All this is in its infancy, but the direction is clear; ICT is facilitating forms of interaction which both deepen local social relationships and offer a platform on which to co-ordinate any political action they might want to take. It is not so much that politics is dead; it's that the structures in which politics is taking pace are mutating…in the past established political parties, indeed the state itself, could compete to run society only because they controlled the information necessary to do so.
>
> That era is passing; political parties are not the agency of the citizen, but rather try to coerce the citizen into supporting what the party leadership has already decided – an inversion of the democratic process and of which the Iraq war recently has been the quintessential expression (*Observer* 1 August 2004).

Whilst it is important (and necessary) to point out that analysts like Hutton seriously underestimate the part still played by traditional branches of the media in mobilizing some of the campaigns we have referred to (for example, the campaign generated around Paulsgrove relied heavily on key, national red tops), there is surely no doubt that the new information and communication technologies are steadily increasing the public's reach and influence. Governments now have to listen much more attentively to what the public thinks about this or that policy initiative. Ordinary people are no longer prepared to be 'air brushed' out of the penal equation. Instead, they transmit their views on these sensitive matters to home secretaries, and they expect to be listened to.

This indicates a significant, long-term shift in our political culture, about the nature of modern governance, and the new communication technologies that are driving that change. Understanding this change requires that we look beyond the discourse of moral panic theorists who all too frequently take the easy option of apportioning *all* the blame for Britain's continuing punitive paradox on to irresponsible red tops and opportunistic politicians.

The active citizen

These changes to our political culture which have upgraded the public voice have also been reinforced by significant changes in the operation of the criminal justice system itself. That is to say, the repositioning of the public voice is a partly a reflection of the simple fact that governments now need to engage with the public in a way that was not envisaged in the decades immediately after 1945. At that time the machinery of law and order, as we have seen, was firmly in the hands of a highly centralized state and its operatives. This slowly began to change in the 1980s when it became apparent that the central state could no longer deliver on law and order from the centre and the result has been has been the restructuring of the delivery of these services, including penal services, to engage the public. Sometimes it engages them in a voluntary rather than a paid capacity, sometimes they participate at local rather than national level (Garland 1996).

The consequence is that as individuals and as groups, often in partnership with professionals from both the private and public sectors, citizens in these new times are being invited back into the criminal justice network. This increasing public stake has enhanced the public voice(s). Governments cannot mobilize active citizens and then ignore them. A dialogue is now increasingly demanded; it is now firmly embedded in the architecture of the policy-making process.

This development is *also* best understood by using an analytic framework that distances itself from the formal sociology of moral panics which is inclined to interpret (and project) the public voice(s) as being simply a 'construct' in the service of self-seeking, opportunistic politicians and red-top editors.

Again, we do not doubt that there been countless occasions when political parties and red-top editors *have* deliberately helped to construct or, at the very least, sustain moral panics for their own wider political or circulation purposes, tapping into public fears about crime and punishment and producing a punitive backlash. We have made it clear the Conservatives did this without the slightest compunction in the 1970s and New Labour, though to a far lesser extent, did so around the murder of James Bulger in the 1990s. However, the changes traced in this chapter suggest there are *other forces* at work.

Democracy and the public voice(s)

I now want to raise the difficult question of whether or not this upsurge in the public voice(s), and the necessity for politicians to pay more heed to it, is a good or a bad thing for democracy, and then conclude by considering what strategic lessons it poses for those lobby groups who see their role as unravelling – and contesting – Britain's punitive paradox.

On the first question we have to acknowledge the perhaps uncomfortable truth that democracy is less about government by the people, but more a set of complicated institutional arrangements whereby the various publics in any society, including what we have referred as public opinion more broadly defined, work out compromises which are, by and large, accepted by all the parties, including the broader public. This is sometimes a lengthy, messy and infuriating business, but it is none the less the way business mostly gets done in modern pluralist democracies. To illustrate this process at work, just consider the issue of capital punishment that we raised earlier in this chapter.

The House of Commons was overwhelmingly in favour of its abolition, as were important insider pressure groups like the Howard League. On the other hand, the House of Lords vehemently opposed abolition, as did a clear majority of the public. The messy compromise in this case was the Homicide Bill 1957 that drew what eventually turned out to be an unworkable distinction between capital and non-capital murders.

This sort of compromise continues to be struck even in new times. For example, the campaign for a paedophile register in the form of Sarah Law's was not accepted by New Labour. The public, if we are to believe polls conducted in behalf of Sky Television, were massively in favour of it, as were the people of Paulsgrove. Parliament, the NSPCC and the Association of Chief Police Officers, on the other hand, were far more cautious, and this opinion eventually prevailed. However, the tense compromise finally negotiated has entailed the release of more information on and surveillance of individual paedophiles than any government has ever contemplated in the past.

Given this choice of examples you might ask, what then is the difference between old times and new times? The answer is that in the messy business of thrashing out such compromises – the process we identify as democracy – the public voice(s) now carries more clout than in the past. The broader public now demands the right to have its views known and represented – very often in the past this has *not* been case. Too often difficult issues were quietly settled, not least in matters of crime and punishment, between government and the cognoscenti with consumers of such services, battered women for example, being left out in the cold. The rise of the public voice is therefore about putting the consumers' views in the frame, of acknowledging that in today's society the public voice(s) can no longer be ignored.

Of course, this chapter is testimony to the obvious truth that we should be critically attentive to how the broader public voice(s) we (and others) claim to is now being listened to is *socially constructed*. To ignore this would be sociologically naïve. Furthermore, we should be careful to avoid the tendency of slipping into the habit of speaking as if the broader public voice(s) is far more homogeneous than it really is, as if translating this voice is sufficient to secure accountability and legitimacy (Hancock 2004). None the less, the argument that governments increasingly have to attend to the public voice(s), and that this may be no bad thing for democracy, surely has some validity, even if it threatens to make the difficult business of governance even more fraught than it was in the 1940s and 1950s.

Democracy should never *just* be articulated as a complicated way of reaching decisions, its promise is that the manner in which decisions are settled confers some power and authority on those who participate, including the broader public(s), *that is what underpins its legitimacy* (Canovan 1999). There is not much mileage in trying to mobilize the people around the idea that democracy is *just* a series of checks and balances, that democratic politics is little more than a series of messy compromises arrived at behind closed doors amongst the cognoscenti. Of course, selling this more 'engaged' version of democracy by suggesting at heady moments that 'The people are the masters now' runs the risk of stoking up populist expectations, but as Canovan argues, it is not unreasonable to view populism as the necessary 'shadow of democracy' (1999).

Some strategic consequences

The changes in the policy-making process that we have outlined have some obvious strategic consequences for those progressive lobby groups seeking to unravel Britain's punitive paradox.

First, these groups need to understand that they no longer have governments all to themselves, that the growing clamour of the public voice(s) cannot be turned off, let alone quietly sidelined. This suggests a requirement that works *outwards* and not just *inwards*. Progressive forces need to engage more directly with the wider public rather than concentrate their efforts on the corridors of power in Parliament and Whitehall. That they have currently failed to make this adjustment accounts for the harsh judgement that they have had 'little impact in terms of restraining the development of penal populism' (Roberts *et al.* 2002). Secondly, progressive forces need to engage *differently*, to improve and vary their styles of communication and, above all, to think more strategically about the sites on which populist sentiment is best confronted (Roberts *et al.* 2002).

Making these adjustments is no easy business. Who would rather not look *inwards* than confront marauding parents using children who can barely walk in their ill-informed crusade against paedophiles named and shamed by the *News of the World*? Who does not despair when another cynical red-top editor wheels out, nearly 40 years after the event, the still-grieving mother of Lesley Anne Downey whose daughter was so brutally murdered by Myra Hindley and Ian Brady? The difficulties of engaging in a rational dialogue with the public on the subject of law and order are daily obvious.

However, commentators like Golding (1995) and Hutton (2004) have done well to remind us that there are other more optimistic views about the possibility of a 'communicative rationality' around the emergence of the new information and communication technologies and new social movements which suggest a more vibrant, progressive, less purely nationally focused, homogeneous 'public voice(s)' than we sometimes suppose. So there is some hope for Thomas Mathiesen's 'alternative' public forum (1995). If people, often young and poorly resourced people, can organize across-national boundaries and mobilize against world trade negotiators using the new technologies

I fail to see why others cannot do the same on narrower terrain. Indeed, there are already a number of quite sophisticated 'alternative' websites on penal questions, including capital punishment (Roberts *et al.* 2002).

So, the liberal penal lobby needs to engage more. Without reaching out, say through the Howard League's commendable, but limited, initiative on citizenship and crime, or making more of Mike Hough's research which shows that if properly informed the *public voice(s)* is not as crude as the red tops represent it, the lobby will be left simply reacting to punitive populist responses (Hough and Roberts 1998). Of course, conventional lobbying will continue to be needed, and defensive initiatives will also be required from time to time. Some credit should therefore be given to NACRO, the chief police officers involved through ACPO and the chief officers of probation (ACOP) who took on the *News of the World* over its crude campaign to 'unmask' paedophiles (6 August 2000). However, in new times where the power of the public voice(s) is growing, a far more proactive approach is needed and a successful strategy needs to involve more than just making sure that Hampstead liberals have access to Whitehall.

References

Aldridge M. (2003) 'The ties that divide: regional press campaigns, community and populism', *Media, Culture and Society*, 25: 491–509.

Almond, G. and Verba, A. (1963) *The Civic Culture*. Princeton, NJ: Princeton University Press.

Blumler, J. and Gurevitch, M. (1966) 'Mass media and society', in J. Curran and M. Gurevitch (eds) *Media Change and Social Change.* London: Arnold.

Canovan, M. (1999) 'Trust the people! Populism and the two faces of democracy', *Political Studies*, XLV: 2–16.

Cohen, S. (1972) *Folk Devils and Moral Panics*. London: Palladin.

Conservative Party (1979) *Conservative Party Manifesto*. London: Conservative Party.

Garland, D. (1996) 'The limits of the sovereign state; strategies of crime control in contemporary society', *British Journal of Criminology*, 30: 449–74.

Golding, P. (1995) 'The mass media and the public sphere; the crisis of information in the "Information Society"', in S. Edgell *et al.* (eds) *Debating the Future of the Public Sphere*. Aldershot: Avebury.

Hall, S., Critcher, C., Jefferson, T., Clarke, J. and Roberts, B. (1978) *Policing the Crisis: Mugging, the State and Law and Order*. London: Macmillan.

Hancock, L. (2004) 'Criminal justice, public opinion, fear and popular politics', in J. Muncie and D. Wilson (eds) *Criminal Justice and Criminology*. London: Cavendish.

Hough, M. and Roberts, J. (1998) *Attitudes to Punishment: Findings from the British Crime Survey. Home Office Research Study* 179. London: Home Office.

Hutton, W. (2004) 'Why politics must connect', *The Observer*, 1 August 2004.

Inglehart, R. (1997) *The Silent Revolution*. Princeton, NJ: Princeton University Press.

Jewkes, Y. (2004*) Media and Crime*. London: Sage.

Leishman, F. and Mason, P. (2003) *Policing and the Media: Facts, Fictions and Factions*. Cullompton: Willan Publishing.

Lewis, D. (1997) *Hidden Agendas*. London: Hamish Hamilton.

Mathiesen, T. (1995) 'Driving forces behind prison growth: the mass media.' Paper presented at the conference 'International conference on prison growth', April, Oslo (available at http://www.fecl.org/circular/4110.htm).

Playfair, G. (1971) *Punitive Obsession*. London: Gollancz.

Pratt, J. *et al.* (2005) *The New Punitiveness*. Cullompton: Willan Publishing.

Rawnsley, A. (2001) *Servants of the People*. London: Hamish Hamilton.

Roberts, J., Stalans, L., Indermaur, D. and Hough, M. (2002) *Penal Populism and Public Opinion*. Oxford: Oxford University Press.

Ryan, M. (1983) *The Politics of Penal Reform*. London: Longman.

Ryan, M. (2003) *Penal Policy and Political Culture in England and Wales*. Winchester: Waterside Press.

Silverman, J. and Wilson, D. (2002) *Innocence Betrayed; Paedophilia, the Media and Society*. Cambridge: Polity Press.

Taylor, I. (1981) *Law and Order Arguments for Socialism*. London: Macmillan.

Windlesham, Lord (1993) *Responses to Crime*. Oxford: Clarendon Press.

Chapter 4

Crime sound bites: a view from both sides of the microphone

Enver Solomon

Along with estate agents, journalists tend to come out at the top of surveys of professions which the public dislike and distrust. I was well aware of this when I worked as a reporter, so when meeting people for the first time I would always try to be economical with the truth about what I did. It was particularly tricky whilst working on local papers which are considered by many to be populist rags not worth the paper they are printed on. However, nothing had quite prepared me for the disdain, and sometimes pure venom, reserved for the media that I came across when I left journalism and joined the Prison Reform Trust.

On numerous occasions people throughout the criminal justice sector lambast the media for creating a punitive climate which is blamed for the relentless rise in prison numbers.[1] The media is seen as the irresponsible bogeyman that fails to report the facts and is hell bent on whipping up fear with sensationalist reporting. It is blamed for playing on people's emotions and then demanding tough action from government and long sentences from the courts. This is a common view held with great passion by many academics and professionals, including prison governors, probation officers and voluntary sector leaders. Professor Richard Sparks articulates a sense of deep-rooted frustration and anger towards the media: '[w]hy the endless concentration on the bad news about crime? Is there some malign intent to inflame public passions and play upon our fears? ... Must every progressive initiative be undermined – or every challenging research finding reduced to sound bites? (Sparks 2001: 6).

The list of complaints levelled at the media is comprehensive. It is blamed not only for being sensationalist but also for misrepresenting the facts on crime, for misinforming the public, for oversimplifying complex issues and ignoring important developments or ground-breaking projects. But there are reasons why the media conduct themselves in this manner. Journalists operate on the basis of unwritten newsroom rules and values. They have specific ways of working unique to their profession. These need to be understood and placed in a broader social and political context in order to move towards a more sophisticated and constructive analysis that is not simply about blaming the media.

The intention in this chapter is neither to defend my previous occupation nor to justify the way journalists work. Instead it is to provide a reflective commentary based on my experiences working as a journalist and in the non-governmental sector. I intend to question assumptions about what role the media should play in raising the level of public debate about penal policy and crime in general. If those who campaign for penal reform and those who work in the criminal justice sector want to use the media to convey their messages more effectively they must begin to understand why it is prone to distort the facts and exaggerate. It is also vital to recognize the social and political environment that the media operate in. Only then will we be able to realize the limitations of using the media and develop more effective strategies for communicating our messages.

Sensationalism

Life on local newspapers often provides memorable moments. There were many during my early career in journalism working on the weekly *Middleton and North Manchester Guardian*. Being told to provide some additions to the letters page was always great fun, especially when given free reign to make up any old letter as long as it was from a 'Mr Angry'. There were also the appalling headlines that were written in great haste by the editor. 'Parrot Dies' was my favourite. But despite the boredom of local politics and the lack of earth-shattering events unfolding on my doorstep, it was a vital education in the basics of journalism that even today provides an important understanding of how the media function.

The gruff editor who was slightly batty and always had a cigarette hanging out his mouth gave me instructive lessons about news values on a regular basis. In my first week he came up to me and barked:

'What do you think makes news, young lad? I'll tell you. People. It is as simple as that. And the nastier the things that happen to them the better the news story.' It is difficult to argue with this interpretation. And a glance at any newspaper or watching any TV news bulletin confirms it. Inevitably when people are robbed, attacked, beaten, abused or murdered, journalists regard it as a good story, or as I have heard many times in newsrooms, 'it's a great tale'. Not surprisingly, therefore, crime stories will always be picked up by the media and the more sensational the better. As Mike Hough has noted, 'news values favour the extraordinary' (Hough 1996).

A study of changing media representations of crime since the Second World War (Reiner *et al.* 2000) which looked at a sample of stories from the *Daily Mirror* and *The Times* found that homicide was by far the most common type of crime featuring in news stories in both papers throughout the period, accounting for about one third of all crime stories. Other violent crimes were the next most common in both papers, for most of the years studied. For reporters, particularly in the local press, such crimes provide a steady flow of copy ensuring they maintain a high profile in the newspaper. It might seem sensationalist always to splash murders on the front pages but, for journalists, it simply provides a good story.

Apart from homicides and violent crimes, the study by Reiner *et al.* found that there were significant shifts concerning other types of offences. In particular there was a marked decline in the proportion of stories featuring volume property crimes such as burglary in which no violence occurred. In the 1940s and 1950s a substantial proportion of crime stories were about routine property offences but this declined after 1965. This demonstrates the fact that news values are not politically neutral. Newspapers reflect the public mood, society's hopes and fears, aspirations and anxieties. These are often determined by the government and politician's agendas. The recent furore over anti-social behaviour which has had a impact on the numbers being remanded into custody, particularly amongst children, demonstrates this very clearly (Morgan 2003). I vividly remember sitting in a BBC editorial meeting shortly after Labour had been elected in 1997 when a programme editor suggested a story about the level of litter, dog fouling and nuisance caused by youths on his local high street. He was, in effect, talking about low-level anti-social behaviour. But this was long before the government had launched its blitz on anti-social behaviour and the story never made it to air. Since then hundreds of column inches, a lot of it sensationalist in tone and content, have been devoted to the subject. It is doubtful this would have happened had it not been such a hot political issue. Indeed, those crimes which are not given great political prominence are overlooked. Corporate crime has remained marginalized for a long time and so the media rarely give it much prominence. If ministers were to talk it up and provide the same number of sound bites that have been delivered on anti-social behaviour it would certainly rise up the news agenda.

Another significant change in media reporting over the past 50 years has been the polarization in the portrayal of victims and offenders (Reiner 2001). In the postwar years there was more of an attempt to make the perpetrators of crime comprehensible. This fitted well with the rehabilitative social agenda that was dominant at the time (Feeley 2003). Since the 1970s stories have become increasingly victim centred. Reiner notes that offenders 'became demonised as dangerous predators whose vicious actions called for harsh but justified retribution on behalf of the vulnerable innocents they savaged' (2001).

What happens to high-profile offenders such as Maxine Carr and Ian Huntley in prison attracts far greater media attention than almost any other prison-related story. Even those who commit less serious offences are singled out and demonized. Many young children are often portrayed by the media as 'evil yobs'. Sensationalist reporting, particularly in the tabloid press, labels prisons as being too 'soft' for them and refers to young offender institutions as 'holiday camps' (Shape 2003). But this development is not simply driven by sensationalist news values. Once again journalists and editors are acting out a political discourse which reflects the prevailing law and order consensus. An over-reliance on punishment as deterrence reproduces an ideology of 'them and us', a criminology of 'the other', as David Garland has called it (2001). Those who commit crimes are constructed as 'the threatening outcast, the fearsome stranger, the excluded and embittered' against whom the rest of us – the law-abiding moral majority – must be protected. Their menacing mug shots appear in the media to instil fear in us all and victims are portrayed as figures that are disadvantaged and neglected by the authorities. Ministers take the lead demanding that the criminal justice system is rebalanced in favour of the victim (Home Office 2004).

It is important to acknowledge that the media are not operating in a political vacuum. Editorial decisions are also affected by the prevailing punitive law and order discourse which infects all sections of the media. The balance of power ultimately rests with politicians, who have the levers of state power in their control, and not with the media. If politicians start talking up a particular issue journalists in the national media who work in the Westminster village will soon become infected by this and it will not be long before it is headline news across the country. This then has an impact on people's perceptions about law and order. At the same time the prevailing fear of crime is affected by macro shifts in the economic and political landscape. The problems on many council estates where fear of crime is particularly high are a consequence of long-term structural change in the labour market and, more broadly, the rise of free market ideology (Young 1999).

An equally important factor which determines why the media are sensationalist is the simple fact that the press needs to sell newspapers to survive. It is easy to forget that the media is big business. From the smallest local newspaper to the *Sun*, they all rise or fall on the state of their profit margins. Executives keenly keep up with circulation figures. In a world where newspaper sales are in long-term decline, both locally and nationally, the press is constantly fighting for survival (Peak and Fisher 2004). Fewer people are buying newspapers than ever before and, as the media become more diverse with more people getting news and information from the Internet, even broadcast news organizations are losing audiences. Executives at Channel 5 or ITV are desperate to maintain high ratings and ensure healthy advertising revenues. In such a climate editorial values are skewed towards making the product, and it should not be forgotten that like any other consumer goods, newspapers and television bulletins are products, more attractive. Commercial pressures will mean editors are minded to be more sensationalist in order to sell their papers. And the pressures also determine the kind of stories that get into the paper. Today, the *Sun*, the *Daily Mirror* and the *Daily Star* regularly splash stories of celebrity misdemeanours across their front pages. When the *Independent* was first launched in the early 1980s it decided not to cover gossip stories about the royal family. But that is no longer the case. Even today the BBC has an entertainment reporter whose main brief is to do celebrity stories. Media executives believe that in today's market they cannot afford to ignore these matters. Issues of social or penal policy are of secondary importance and struggle to make it into the media.

Overall, the general trend in the media has been towards consumer-orientated issues. It is common today for the press to advertize itself not on the back of its journalism but with endless promotions for flights, cinema tickets or meals out. Editors therefore become more consumer orientated, and the complexities of criminological research findings are overlooked. A home affairs correspondent on a leading national newspaper that has recently changed its format has been told by his editors that policy developments are to be given a lower priority. He knows that stories about debates over the reorganization of the probation and prison services and the creation of a new National Offender Management Service will not generate any interest with his news desk. The gradual shift away from reporting policy issues in detail has even affected the BBC. When the government published its long-awaited review of correctional services led by Patrick Carter in January 2004 I was told in advance by a BBC correspondent that it would be hard to get the story on air as editors were not interested in structural reorganization or proposals to rebuild the use of fines. This change in the news agenda is not to be underestimated. Despite the huge expansion in the number of media outlets with the creation of the Internet and 24-hour news channels, there is probably less space in newspapers and on news bulletins for serious debate and political critique. Over the past 20 years it has therefore become much harder for issues relating to penal policy to get media coverage. And when they do it is not as common as it once was for the issues to be presented in a straight, intelligent format.

Distortion, misrepresentation and misinformation

One of the first lessons in journalism is how to identify the top line of a story, or for those in the broadcast media, the key sound bite. Journalists are taught to read through long and complex reports and come up with a single sentence that sums up the most newsworthy aspect. This often results in oversimplification into what might appear to be misleading messages. The journalist will have chosen what he or she believes is the sexiest line that will find favour with the news desk and so have a fighting chance of making it into the newspaper or on to the television or radio news bulletin. The process of selection means that many often important findings in a study will be ignored and omitted in the final news report. To the authors it can easily appear to be a clear-cut case of distortion and misrepresentation. But it is important to understand what decision-making process the journalist goes through in determining the line to take on a story.

Beyond the factors already outlined in explaining why journalism is by its nature sensationalist and less inclined today to focus on penal policy there are other important factors that must not be overlooked.

Journalists will always look for the most critical or controversial line in a report. Even if it is only a minor aspect of the report or a line which is not developed in any detail, in the journalist's mind it is controversy which makes news. A good example is the publication in November 2004 of the Coulsfield inquiry into alternatives to custody (Coulsfield 2004). The report produced by a team led by the eminent Scottish judge, Lord Coulsfield, was the centrepiece of the three-year Rethinking Crime and Punishment initiative of the Esmée Fairbairn Foundation which was intended to raise the level of public debate about prison and community alternatives. The message which the report's authors were keen to get across was that the public should be given a greater say about the kind of community punishment undertaken by offenders. However, buried in the report is a brief paragraph which expresses concerns about how the early release of prisoners under the Home Detention Curfew (HDC) scheme could undermine public confidence. This line was leapt on by the media. HDC has been controversial with the Conservatives consistently criticizing Labour and pledging to scrap the scheme if they are elected. When an independent judge also voiced concern, for journalists, it was clearly a good story – for both the national news agency, the Press Association, and the BBC which were given exclusive advance briefings on it. The BBC stated 'Tagging criminals "damages trust"' (BBC News Online, 15 November 2004), and this was the message that reached the public. The key theme of the report, that the public's trust in alternatives to custody needs to be rebuilt with a number of new initiatives such as allowing the public to have a greater say in deciding how to use the millions of hours of community work that criminals are ordered to do each year, was unfortunately overlooked.

Whilst journalists will always pick up on controversy, newspaper reporters are also influenced by the partisan position of their owners. The *Daily Mail*, the *Sun*, the *Daily Express* and the *Daily Telegraph* all have right-wing proprietors which produce editorials that favour locking up more offenders and building more prisons.[2] They call for tougher sentencing and tend to ridicule alternatives to custody as the soft option. The facts are regularly distorted; the public are told that the courts are more lenient when in fact the government's own review of correctional services has shown that, over the last decade, proportionally more people have been sent to prison and for longer (Prime Minister's Strategy Unit 2004). As long as the press is used by its owners to wield political power and influence it is inevitable that the public will be misinformed about penal policy. Newspapers are organs of political power and always have been. Distorting the facts or putting a particular spin on information is a consequence of advancing their own political agendas. And the newspapers often define themselves on the basis of their political beliefs. The *Guardian* prides itself on promoting progressive liberal values and attempting to imbue the wider public with these values.

We are, of course, living in an age of political spin. The sections of the media which are impartial and non-partisan have to work even harder so they do not misrepresent the facts. This is particularly the case for BBC journalists. Public relation companies will push journalists to take a particular line on a story and the New Labour government has a notorious reputation for using its spin doctors to influence them. It is not uncommon for BBC correspondents to be called by minister's senior media advisers after appearing on the BBC Radio Four *Today* programme to be questioned about why they have interpreted the latest government initiative in a particular way. The government has worked harder than most at getting the messages it wants in the media and the tactics have been particularly aggressive. Ministers will happily distort the facts if it serves their own political ends and journalists can be complicit in this if by doing so they are getting an exclusive story and thus gaining credibility with their own editors.

Misrepresentation and oversimplification are also a function of the changing nature of news production. Today, news programmes are on air 24 hours a day with dedicated news channels on radio and television. These channels have to churn out stories without having the time or space to sit back and make considered editorial judgements. They will often take the lead from what is in the morning's newspapers or what the news wires are reporting on a particularly story and so repeat the distortions that have been produced elsewhere. Reporters and producers working on 24-hour news channels struggle to read the relevant government report or research study. Increasingly it is only the specialist home affairs correspondents who will actually read the report and even then only some of them will have read it from start to finish. Time pressures mean that subtle arguments will be overlooked and for broadcasters the aim will be to get a clear, pithy sound bite. News editors, particularly in broadcasting, increasingly believe that viewers' attention spans are limited so the emphasis is always on keeping a story uncluttered, telling it in an A, B, C fashion. Oversimplification can easily lead to misrepresentation.

Communicating the message

Journalists receive endless press releases; many go straight in the bin. So when I left journalism to join the Prison Reform Trust (PRT) I found myself thinking 'will anybody ever read this?' as I sent out my first press release. I also pondered the merit of sending out press release after press release. Whilst at the BBC I had received several from NACRO, the Howard League and PRT and only a couple had resulted in a story making it on air. Often the press releases were pretty straight bland statements about prison overcrowding, young girls in custody or the dramatic rise in the women's prison population. My own interest in the subject and my editor's interest in prisons helped to get some of them on air. But the brutal reality is that, for a BBC news programme like *Today* or *Newsnight*, there is a limit to how many prison stories will be covered. A home affairs correspondent on a national newspaper told me he thinks he has done well if he gets one or two prison stories in his newspaper each month. So it is an uphill struggle for the penal reform charities. Yet despite this there has been some limited success.

It is now firmly embedded in the public consciousness that prisons are overcrowded institutions that are struggling to provide decent regimes. Most people acknowledge that overcrowded prisons are not effective places of rehabilitation. Overall there remains a certain amount of cynicism about how effective prison can be in turning criminals away from a life of crime (Roberts and Hough 2002). Research has found that people think prevention programmes and better parenting are more effective (Rethinking Crime and Punishment 2004). The message has also got through to policy-makers that prison numbers have increased not due to a rise in crime or because more criminals are being convicted but because the courts have become much more punitive in their sentencing. And ministers accept that short sentences can do more harm than good. However, the government is still reluctant to talk up alternatives to custody. Sentence lengths are becoming longer and longer (Hough *et al.* 2003). Prison remains society's default setting and is seen as the most acceptable form of punishment. Alternatives to custody lack credibility and both political and public support. There is little doubt that the penal reform sector has not been very successful in shifting the terms of the debate on crime and punishment and needs to rethink its media strategies. There is a need to develop a more sophisticated understanding about why journalism is by its nature sensationalist and why journalists distort information. But before attempting to examine how the sector should be working more effectively with the media, it is instructive to look at one example.

'The decision to imprison'

In 2002 the Esmee Fairbairn Foundation's Rethinking Crime and Punishment project commissioned Professor Mike Hough and colleagues to carry out a study examining the causes of rising custody rates in England and Wales. It was agreed that the study would be managed, published and disseminated by the Prison Reform Trust. The final report, *The Decision to Imprison: Sentencing and the Prison Population* (Hough *et al.* 2003), was based on an analysis of sentencing trends over the previous decade and interviews with more than one hundred magistrates and judges to determine what factors influence sentencing. It found that the prison population had risen because the courts have become much tougher sending far more people to jail and for much longer. But the reasons behind this toughening up were complex and not clear cut. The research found that a number of factors were important. A more punitive legislative and legal framework had certainly had an inflationary effect on jail terms. The study also found that the climate of political and media debate about crime and sentencing had become more punitive and this had affected magistrates and judges. However sentencers, particularly magistrates, strongly believed that changing patterns of offending were extremely important, despite the fact that there was no statistical evidence to suggest this. They consistently said that offending, linked to drug addiction, had become more violent, resulting in an increased use of custody. The report states: '[the] senior judges argued that violent offences had become more violent; and that crimes related to dependent drug use have become more serious' (Hough *et al.* 2003). One district judge simply said 'I think we are seeing more nastier work more often'.

The report could easily have led to two different set of headlines. Either that judges and magistrates are toughening up in response to a punitive political climate or that judges and magistrates believe more violent crime is behind the dramatic rise in the prison population. The latter was a story which would find favour in the right wing press and the media in general which often claim that drug and alcohol-fuelled violence is out of control on our streets. This therefore meant the publication of the report had to be carefully handled. It was felt that if the report was to have an impact it had to challenge the perception held by the public and often emphasized by the media that the courts have become too lenient.

Under a headline 'Judges and magistrates toughen up in response to a punitive political climate', the press release that accompanied the report said it 'explodes the myth that magistrates and judges in England and Wales are soft on crime and calls for decisive political leadership in reducing the prison population'. A few weeks ahead of publication part of the report had been given in advance to the *Independent* which had taken a very similar line. This had ensured that the message we wanted to get across would be clearly set out in advance as well as on the day of publication. The intention was to make sure our message was clear so that journalists could be steered in the direction that we wanted them to take and away from focusing on sentencers believing crime had become more violent. If our strategy failed it would also mean that the wrong message was received by policy-makers.

In the end the media reports focused on sentencing becoming harsher. The BBC said 'tough sentencing by judges, rather than a rise in crime, has led to the record prison population' (BBC News Online, 1 July 2003). Even the *Daily Mail*'s story had a similar headline.[3] The message also got through clearly to policy-makers and government advisers. The government's review of correctional services concluded that tougher sentencing had been the key factor driving up prison numbers (Prime Minister's Strategy Unit 2004). So why was this report not distorted by the media? What had ensured that the message the authors wanted to convey was successfully communicated? One critical factor had been making sure that there was a strong headline which would provide a good story for the media. The press release was also quite detailed and carefully laid out the complexities of the story. And importantly it included supporting quotations from the Lord Chief Justice and the Magistrates Association. This meant that the message was not just being delivered by the authors and the Prison Reform Trust but that key figures in the judiciary were backing it up. We had also chosen actively to engage with the media ahead of publication by trailing ahead the report in a national newspaper in order to generate early interest from journalists in the message that we wanted to convey. But critically, the report fitted in with a view that was being pushed within government at the time by the Treasury that something had to be done about the relentless rise in prison numbers. Officials also accepted that the courts were at fault for toughening up and so the message the report was conveying was, in a sense, politically acceptable.

Towards a future strategy: how to work more effectively with the media

In my experience there tends to be a begrudging reluctance within the criminal justice sector about having to deal with the press. Professionals and campaigning groups are well aware of the power of the media to shape public opinion and understand that it is important to attempt to get messages across via the media. But at the same time deep-held suspicions of journalists and how they operate mean that organizations are often wary and uneasy about getting too close to the media. It is understandable that criminal justice organizations might be defensive when contacted by journalists who they suspect are attempting to dig the dirt or undermine their organization. And there are, of course, important issues of confidentiality and the sensitive nature of many cases. But this is no excuse for hunkering down and automatically taking a defensive position. The former *Observer* correspondent and investigative journalist David Rose is highly critical of the criminal justice sector for the way it relates to the media: 'the criminal justice agencies often seem barely to have considered an appropriate way to inter-act with the media in a modern, democratic state' (2001). Rose goes as far as suggesting that the sector has itself to blame for the media's reporting: 'some of the media's failings originate with the very bodies which attack them. If the papers are full of sensational and inaccurate reports, to some extent this is because it can be so difficult to acquire information about anything else.'

In the same way that it is naïve simply to blame the media for creating today's climate of penal populism, the criminal justice sector is not solely to blame for the sensationalism and distortions that are a common characteristic of many crime stories. But there are a number of ways in which the sector could improve how it deals with the media.

Engage with enthusiasm

The media should not been seen as the enemy. As is the case in any profession there are some journalists who have low standards but the majority are decent people simply doing their job. The criminal justice sector would be much better off if it engaged with greater enthusiasm and opened up more information channels so that journalists are better informed.[4] For a reporter who is up against a tight deadline and is not a specialist in criminal justice matters somebody on the other end of the phone who is prepared to help him or her navigate round a complex story and provide him or her with a solid background briefing is invaluable. Apart from some of the home affairs correspondents on national newspapers and in the BBC, journalists know very little, if anything, about criminal justice. They need somebody metaphorically to hold their hand and help them out. They will not know where to find relevant statistics or who are the most knowledgeable and accessible commentators on a particular subject. This is particularly the case for journalists from local and regional media and also the 24-hour news channels. They need to be guided and informed of the basic facts. It is therefore vital to be prepared to give them time and engage instead of being suspicious and trying to get them off the phone as soon as possible. Ultimately, choosing not to co-operate or assist the media can be counterproductive especially if it leads to inaccuracies and gross distortions that could have been corrected in advance.

Spin

In a world of political spin it is important to be clear what your message is and then to be realistic about whether it is the kind of story that will make it into the news. I have found that sometimes those campaigning for penal reform are not very strategic about putting out their press releases. There is almost an expectation that the story should make it into the news and if it doesn't the media are blamed for being biased or irresponsible. But given the way the media work and the changing nature of journalism it will always be a struggle to get issue-based prison stories into the press. This requires thinking carefully about what the message should be, how it should be spun. It might even mean headlining a controversial aspect of research so that it gets into the news and then provides the opportunity to air any other issues raised. Doing this will, of course, be a risky strategy, but it is worth considering.

The messenger

The messenger is just as important as the message. It is too often the case that the head or policy director of a criminal justice organization will speak to the press or appear on television. This is particularly the case for the campaigning non-governmental organizations. Yet research has found that messages resonate more strongly with the media if they come from ex-offenders themselves and also victims of crime (Rethinking Crime and Punishment 2004). If a victim of a serious crime is arguing passionately on the radio or television for the perpetrator not to be imprisoned it will certainly cause more people to sit up and listen than hearing well rehearsed arguments from the director of the Prison Reform Trust. However, there are not many opportunities for the media to hear from ex-offenders or victims.[5] There is also a need to hear more from professionals working at the coal face. Unfortunately it is rare that prison governors appear on the radio talking about the futility of short prison sentences or of locking up severely mentally disordered offenders.

The wider context

Given that the media are not immune from the wider political, economic and social context shaping society it is vital that if any campaigning organization is going to have an impact on penal issues and crime debates it has to engage with these issues. Having something meaningful to say about the rise in the prison population and about crime and the fear of crime therefore requires developing arguments and ideas that feed into wider debates on social policy. This, in effect, means developing strategies that enable campaigning organizations to influence the big policy ideas. A theme that has been emerging amongst some organizations campaigning for penal reform is that there needs to be a new narrative on punishment which emphasizes the limits of imprisonment in tackling the causes of crime.[6] Prison should be a place of genuine last resort and not a cheap social service. More broadly there needs to be a reconfiguration of the debate on crime so that solutions are found outside the criminal justice agencies. Communicating these ideas must be central to any penal reform strategy.

Conclusion

In this chapter I have attempted to set out why the media concentrate on bad news about crime, why they are sensationalist and why they misrepresent and misinform the public. It is hoped that this will provide a greater understanding of the media and how they operate. This in turn should allow those who work in the criminal justice sector to have more realistic expectations of journalists. It should also lead to the sector rethinking how it engages with the media and encourage the development of new strategies.

The biggest failing of campaigners for penal reform has been to have the wrong expectations of the media. It is näive to expect newspapers and broadcast news organizations to be responsible conduits of information. That is the job of government and its agencies. It is therefore critically important to be honest about the limitations of any media strategy. If the public is to be better informed about penal issues, and to have a greater understanding and confidence in alternatives to custody, this cannot be achieved through the media. The solution lies elsewhere. The conclusion of the Rethinking Crime and Punishment initiative was that there needs to be a government co-ordinated public education campaign that is supported by a government-led marketing campaign to promote alternatives to custody (Rethinking Crime and Punishment 2004). This could have an impact provided it is backed up by genuine political leadership that emphasizes the goal of reducing the use of prison and talking up alternatives to custody. But such leadership is unlikely to emerge unless there is an ideological shift away from the current punitive consensus on law and order. Therefore, the critical long-term challenge facing penal reform groups is to reconfigure the debate on crime and punishment by feeding into policy discussions that exist beyond the media and that will determine future thinking. This requires an engagement with the wider political, social and economic trends that shape society and the development of a new narrative on punishment so that imprisonment does not continue to be society's default setting.

Notes

1   This chapter is mainly focused on the news media, newspapers, television and radio news, rather than media in the broader sense.
2   It is important to note that changes in newspaper ownership will lead to shifts in allegiances. Before Richard Desmond bought the *Daily Express* it took a more liberal stance and under the editorship of Rosie Boycott in the 1990s it campaigned for the reclassification of cannabis.
3   Only the *Times* chose to highlight the fact that the report found that 'criminals have become nastier, more prolific and more dependent on drugs in the last decade, according to judges and magistrates' (1 July 2003). This was because the home affairs correspondent read the report in detail and picked out a line that fitted his newspapers partisan position and recognized that this was a strong story. This demonstrates that there will always be limitations even to a carefully thought-out communications strategy and to the extent that the media can be 'spun' to deliver campaigning messages.

4 The 'crimeinfo' website set up by the Centre for Crime and Justice Studies is an attempt to address this (see www.crimeinfo.org.uk and also the Prison Reform Trust fact file available at www.prisonreformtrust.org. uk).

5 The Voicing Success Case Study Project run by Staffordshire probation service is attempting to address this by providing the media with a range of ex-offenders' life experiences (see www.staffordshireprobation. org.uk/probation/stories.htm).

6 See the Crime and Society Foundation (www.crimeandsociety.org.uk).

References

Ashford, B. and Morgan R. (2004) 'Criminalising looked after children', *Criminal Justice Matters*, 57: 8–9.

Coulsfield Inquiry (2004) *Crime, Courts and Confidence: Report of an Independent Inquiry into Alternatives to Prison*. London: Esmee Fairbairn Foundation.

Feeley, S. (2003) 'Crime, social order and the rise of neo-Conservative politics', *Theoretical Criminology*, 7: 111–130.

Garland, D. (2001) *The Culture of Control*. Oxford: Oxford University Press.

Home Office (2004) *Cutting Crime, Delivering Justice, A Strategic Plan for Criminal Justice*. London: HMSO.

Hough, M. (1996) 'People talking about punishment', *Howard Journal Criminal Justice*, 35: 286–306.

Hough, M., Jacobson, J. and Millie, A. (2003) *The Decision to Imprison: Sentencing and the Prison Population*. London: Prison Reform Trust.

Morgan, R. (2003) 'Rebalancing penal policy: using the probation and prison services more cost-effectively.' Annual lecture, King's College Centre for Crime and Justice Studies, December (available at http://www.kcl.ac.uk/depsta/rel/ccjs/home.htm).

Peak, S. and Fisher, P. (2004) *The Media Guide*. London: Guardian Books.

Prime Minister's Strategy Unit (2004) *Managing Offenders, Reducing Crime*. London: Cabinet Office.

Reiner, R. (2001) 'The rise of virtual vigilantism: crime reporting since World War II', *Criminal Justice Matters*, 43: 4–5.

Reiner, R., Livingstone, S. and Allen, J. (2000) 'No more happy endings? The media and popular concern about crime since the Second World War', in T. Hope and R. Sparks (eds) *Crime, Risk and Insecurity*. London: Routledge.

Rethinking Crime and Punishment (2004) *Rethinking Crime and Punishment: The Report*. London: Esmee Fairbairn Foundation.

Roberts, J. and Hough, M. (2002) *Changing Attitudes to Punishment, Public Opinion, Crime and Justice*. Cullompton: Willan Publishing.

Rose, D. (2001) 'What's in it for us?', *Criminal Justice Matters*, 43: 8–9.

Shape (2003) 'Ignoring the facts is the biggest crime' (available at http://www.shapethedebate.org.uk/mediareport.pdf).

Sparks, R. (2001) 'The media, populism, public opinion and crime', *Criminal Justice Matters*, 43: 6–7.

Young, J. (1999) *The Exclusive Society*. London: Sage.

Chapter 5

What works in changing public attitudes to prison: lessons from Rethinking Crime and Punishment

Rob Allen

> Everybody thinks our system is becoming soft and wimpish. In point of fact it's one of the most punitive systems in the world (Lord Bingham, cited in Rethinking Crime and Punishment 2003).

Rethinking Crime and Punishment (RCP) has been a four-year, £3 million programme set up by the Esmee Fairbairn Foundation to raise the level of debate about the use of prison and alternatives. RCP funded more than 60 projects including research, public education campaigns, events and public involvement activities (Rethinking Crime and Punishment 2004). Amongst these has been a major independent inquiry into alternatives to prison chaired by Lord Coulsfield, whose findings were published in November 2004 in the report, *Crime Courts and Confidence* (Coulsfield *et al.* 2004). RCP has had an overarching focus on public attitudes to prison and alternatives, and much has been learnt both about what people really do think about the best way to deal with offenders and how attitudes can be changed.

The research RCP commissioned and the projects it funded include three opinion polls, conducted by Mori; four substantial research studies; and a number of projects whose primary focus was to impact on public attitudes through the provision of information or influencing in other ways. These include the Local Crime Community Sentence project (LCCS) in which presentations are made by magistrates and probation staff to community groups; the Case Study project which trains ex-offenders to appear on the media; and the crimeinfo.org which has created a website designed to provide good, accessible, accurate and objective information to the public on crime and criminal justice issues. The Common Purpose 'Broadening the debate' project has aimed to deepen the understanding and quality of debate about crime and punishment amongst leaders in the UK, and other projects have sought to raise issues with particular groups: churchgoers, trade unions, professional groups and parliamentarians. The Prison Film project organized weekend prison film festivals in three cities to stimulate debate and discussion. RCP also produced its own guide to *What you Really Need to Know about Criminal Justice* (Rethinking Crime and Punishment 2003). In addition, the Coulsfield Inquiry commissioned a body of research into alternatives to prison (Bottoms *et al.* 2004) which included a review of existing literature on public attitudes and a significant piece of research on attitudes in two high-crime areas (Bottoms and Wilson 2004).

The RCP's work has identified important lessons in four main areas: what the public actually think, what lies behind the variability of attitudes of individuals, the role of the media, and how attitudes can change. Before looking at the findings, it is worth discussing the context of penal policy and practice and why public attitudes have become so important.

Why are attitudes important?

Over the last 12 years or so, there has been a growing sense amongst opinion formers and the public that in many respects the British penal system was not working as it should. The prison population has been rising steadily since 1980 but particularly sharply since 1992 (Figure 5.1), and is amongst the highest per capita in Western Europe. Home Office projections have since suggested it might rise to more than 87,000 by 2010 (Home Office 2005). But there is little evidence that society feels increasingly protected from violence and crime as a result of this. A high proportion of prisoners, particularly young people, are known to reoffend within a short period, with three quarters of young prisoners and over half of adult prisoners reconvicted within two years of release. Most of those leaving prison do not seem equipped for constructive employment in society.

As a result, it seemed to the trustees of the Esmée Fairbairn Foundation that there was a strong case for giving thought to alternative forms of punishment for some categories of offender. In 1997 the House of Commons Home Affairs Select Committee had

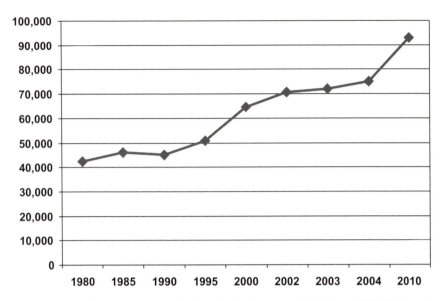

Figure 5.1 The prison population in England and Wales, 1980–2004 and projection to 2010

undertaken a thoroughgoing inquiry into alternatives to prison, considering evidence from a wide variety of sources. They had reached the view that:

> The rapidly escalating prison population makes it of paramount importance to investigate credible alternatives to custody and to use them wherever appropriate. Prison will always be necessary for the most dangerous and/or persistent criminals, but it must be closely targeted on them, with other offenders being given non-custodial sentences which are effective *and in which sentencers and the public have confidence* (Select Committee on Home Affairs 1998: para. 17, emphasis added).

Research and experience have shown the many disadvantages of over using imprisonment. Imprisonment can harm the chances people have to make amends and fulfil their potential as citizens. By definition prison limits the opportunities people have to contribute to civil society and democratic life. Prison is a very expensive and largely ineffective measure, which can harm the prospects not only of offenders but also of their families. In theory, prison could provide its captive audience with decent education, training and employment opportunities. With notable exceptions in the form of resettlement prisons, such opportunities are not provided on anything like the scale required. Most prisoners therefore leave prison no better equipped to fit into society than when they entered it. Some leave a good deal worse off.

At its worst, prison simply provides a reinforcement of delinquent attitudes and skills and contact with delinquent accomplices. It almost certainly involves disruption and severance from family, friends and employment. A third of prisoners lose their homes as a result of going to prison. Almost nine out of ten prisoners face unemployment on release. None the less, despite these disadvantages, imprisonment has been enjoying growing appeal as a political response to crime not just in Britain but also around the world. The UK's use of prison does not yet approach that of the USA who on any one day lock up a quarter of the world's prisoners and more than one in 150 of their own citizens (International Centre for Prison Studies n.d.). Yet some of the ingredients for a US-style expansion have been put in place here, such as mandatory sentencing and increasingly punitive enforcement of probation violations. A consensus has emerged too amongst Labour and Conservative politicians that it may be necessary to have more people in prison in order to deal with law and order problems. The compelling arguments for a sparing use of prison are often heard but seldom listened to even when made by such senior and experienced figures as successive lord chief justices and chief inspectors of prisons.

The main reason for this has been the increasingly important role in policy-making and in practice played by 'public opinion' – or more accurately the pressure to introduce the harsher measures, which the public is perceived to demand. The Court of Appeal has ruled that sentencing must reflect public opinion and when it decides to frame or revise a sentencing guideline, must have regard to the need to promote confidence in the criminal justice system. Politicians are ever more sensitive to the perceived electoral consequences of their policies. Decisions about the release of prisoners on parole have had since 1993 to take into account acceptability to the public. In this area all seem to agree that what the public demand is a tougher and tougher response. In the words of Lord Bingham:

> So we have the extraordinary paradox that judges and magistrates have been roundly criticized for over-lenient sentencing during a period when they have been sending more defendants to prison for longer periods than at any time in the last 40 years.

The increase in the prison population is not explained by any increase in sentencing powers, and I have no doubt that it is related to the pressure of public opinion (Bingham 1997: para. 17).

In an era of increasingly direct accountability, if politicians and courts are to rely less heavily on prison, they will need to be confident they will not be punished at the polls or in the media. Changing public attitudes and the perception of those attitudes have become an important issue of public policy. Helping to ensure that those attitudes are based on a better understanding of the facts about crime, the effectiveness of prison and of non-custodial alternatives seems to be an urgent task. Factual information, however, about prison and the alternatives to it is fragmented and the quality of public debate, particularly in the popular media, leaves much to be desired. The Esmee Fairbairn Foundation decided that this important subject should be seriously studied and debated through a specific and directed programme of work. The foundation also agreed it was important for there to be understanding of the attitudes held by the public towards prison and alternative punishments, and how these are formed and changed. The Rethinking Crime and Punishment initiative was therefore set up to achieve this.

What the public actually think

Perhaps the most important finding from the work of the RCP is that although public attitudes are complex, sometimes contradictory, and often highly dependent on the wording of poll questions, they are in general much less punitive than is often thought to be the case. The analysis undertaken by the University of Strathclyde in 2002 (Rethinking Crime and Punishment 2002b) suggested that the general public have lost confidence in criminal justice and are looking instinctively for a simple and robust solutions. They want safety and fear produces punitiveness. They need simple fables in which wrong-doers get punished, not cared for. Yet public attitudes are full of contradictions, supporting effective prevention and more lenient towards cases where an offender's decision-making may have been affected by drugs or mental illness or where effective preventive action could be taken. RCP's work has tended to confirm this initial analysis with four particularly significant sets of findings.

First, it is clear from Figure 5.2 that there is a good deal of support for prevention. Asked what would do most to reduce crime in Britain, six out of ten people say better parenting (Mori 2003), 55 per cent more police, 45 per cent better school discipline and 41 per cent more constructive activities for young people. When we asked in 2001 how the public would spend a notional £10 million on dealing with crime, the most popular option was to set up teams in 30 cities to work with children at risk (RCP 2002a), as illustrated in Figure 5.3.

Nearly three quarters of people think schools and colleges have an important role in preventing young people from offending and reoffending, with teachers seen as more important in this regard than police, courts or custody (Ecotec 2005). These findings confirm the findings of an European Union-wide survey in 2002 which found more support for targeted prevention programmes than tougher sentencing (European Opinion Research Group 2002).

Secondly, as Figure 5.4 shows, there is a great deal of scepticism about prison. About half of the public think that offenders come out of prison worse than they go in and a third don't know (Mori 2003). Only 2 per cent choose to spend the notional £10 million on prison places (Rethinking Crime and Punishment 2002a) and when asked how to deal with prison overcrowding, building more prisons is the least popular option with the support of only a quarter of people

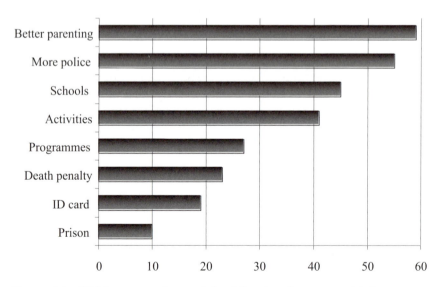

Figure 5.2 Which two or three of the following factors would do most to reduce crime?

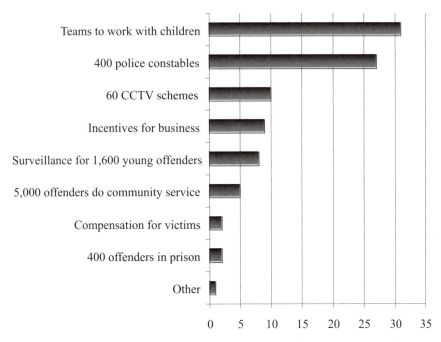

Figure 5.3 How respondents would spend £10 million on crime reduction (per cent)

(Mori 2003). This reflects the finding that only one in ten people think more offenders in prison would do most to reduce crime in Britain (Mori 2003).

Thirdly, there is a desire for better alternatives. To deal with prison overcrowding more than half the public would prefer tougher community punishments to be developed (Mori 2003). Nine out of ten agree that there should be more use of intensive community punishments to keep track of young offenders (RCP 2002a). Focus group research by Strathclyde University found that people want non-custodial sentences that get offenders to pay back and learn their lesson (RCP 2002b). Research on the reputation of alternatives to prison found a need to benefit victims, communities and offenders in what has been called a triple bottom line (Macmillan *et al.* 2004).

Fourthly, Figure 5.5 shows that there is a lot of support for treating rather than punishing underlying problems. More than half the public think that the best way of dealing with prison overcrowding is to build more residential centres so that drug-addicted offenders can receive treatment (Mori 2003). In focus group research, 'almost all respondents, including tabloid readers adopted liberal positions

71

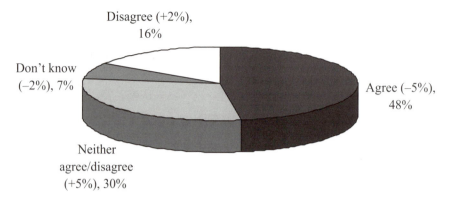

Figure 5.4 To what extent did respondents agree or disagree with the statement 'Most people come out of prison worse than they go in'?
Notes
(Per cent change since 2001 shown in brackets)
Base: all respondents (2,154) November 2003

on the issue of drug crime and felt strongly that drug users should be treated rather than punished' (RCP 2002b: 4).

For young offenders, education is seen as playing an important role. Two thirds of people agree (a third strongly) that under 18s who have offended and cannot read and write should receive compulsory education rather than custody (Ecotec 2005). People think preventing offending, rehabilitation and education are more important than punishment in dealing with young offenders.

These four findings might seem to be somewhat at odds with the prevailing wisdom about public attitudes. Evidence from opinion polls is usually taken to suggest that people in Britain have harsher attitudes towards offenders than the RCP's work suggests. It is true that when asked if they want stiffer sentences, seven out of ten people will say 'yes', and between a quarter and a third will 'strongly agree' that the courts are 'too lenient'. Moreover, three quarters of people think that the police and the courts are 'too lenient' when dealing with young offenders (Mattinson and Mirrlees-Black 2000). However it is well established that people simply do not know how severe the system actually is in terms of the use of, and the length of, custodial sentences. Over half of people make large underestimates of the proportion of adults convicted of rape, burglary and mugging who go to prison, for example, and research conducted for the Sentencing Advisory Panel in 2001 (Home Office 2001) confirmed this picture. Nearly three quarters of people believed that sentences for domestic

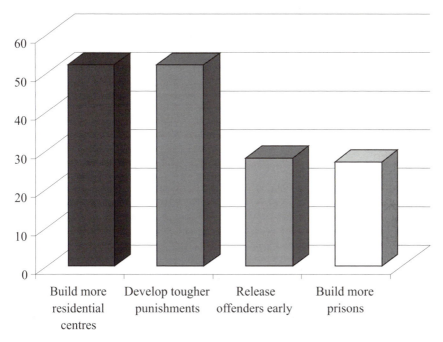

Figure 5.5 How would respondents deal with prison overcrowding? (per cent)

burglary were 'too lenient', and nearly half that they were 'much too lenient'. However, people consistently underestimated the degree to which courts actually imposed prison sentences. Close analysis would suggest that there is something of a 'comedy of errors' in which policy and practice are not based on a proper understanding of public opinion, and that the same opinion is not based on a proper understanding of policy and practice. As the Home office Review of the Sentencing Framework put it in 2001, 'tough talk does not necessarily mean a more punitive attitude to sentencing' (Home Office 2001: 118).

The International Crime Victims survey also suggests that in comparison with other countries, the British tend to want to use prison more readily. Using a burglary case study the survey found UK countries consistently near the top of the table in terms of preference for prison (Van Kesteren *et al.* 2000). On average 34 per cent of respondents from 16 countries preferred prison, with a range of 56 per cent in the USA to 7 per cent in Catalonia. Just over half the British sample opted for prison. Interestingly, most of the countries with above-average support for prison have cultural origins in Britain,

America, Canada and Australia. The exceptions are Japan and the Netherlands, both of which have seen sharp increases in popular support for prison in recent years. On the whole, the countries in the least punitive half of the table share a mainland European or Scandinavian heritage. In all these countries community service is more popular than prison. Quite why this is so is not clear.

One explanation may be that people in the UK are unaware of what community sentences are available or what they involve. Social psychology shows that, to change minds and inform opinions, people need to know that there are viable alternatives. It has been suggested that fewer people are concerned about global warming than five years ago because they do not think anything can be done about it. Lack of awareness of alternatives to prison is suggested by the belief, reported in the British Crime Survey (Home Office 2004), that the youth courts do not have adequate powers. Three quarters of people think this. However, when invited to propose additional powers, many of the respondents tend to suggest provisions that are already available to the court. This is mirrored by research carried out for the Review of the Sentencing Framework that found that less than a third of people could recall three or more disposals unprompted. Somewhat implausibly only 67 per cent remembered prison, a half community service and 49 per cent fines (Home Office 2001).

RCP's work has confirmed the low visibility of community sentences. *The Decision to Imprison* (Hough *et al.* 2003) found that some sentencers, let alone members of the public, were poorly informed about the full range of community penalties and about their benefits. Most sentencers recognized that the general public were ill informed about most community penalties (Hough *et al.* 2003). Research on the role of the media in shaping attitudes found that most viewers had very little understanding or knowledge of alternatives to prison. Where it did exist, knowledge of retributive and rehabilitative elements of justice was much more evident than of restorative justice. Henley Management College's survey found that many people know little or nothing about prison alternatives (Macmillan *et al.* 2004). There is a particular lack of knowledge amongst the public about where community sentences have been successful. This causes many people to be unsupportive of community sentences, even though they know that prisons do not work. Ecotec (2005) found that, to the general public, community sentences lack a clear brand image in contrast to imprisonment and are often seen as having ineffective coercive elements, with insufficient overtones of both punishment and restitution. The potential for widespread support of community options is further limited by sensationalist media coverage of high-profile cases of young people who offend and the pervasive twin beliefs that crime by young people is rampant and that their sentences are increasingly lenient. Furthermore, the causes of crime tend to be seen to lie in young people's individual choices and actions rather than structural or system issues. This means that for the public and many professionals the potentially powerful preventive role of being included and attaining in mainstream education is considerably underestimated.

The Lord Chief Justice has said that neither the public nor sentencers have sufficient confidence in the community alternative (Woolf 2002) and when the Home Affairs Select Committee published their report on alternatives to prison in 1998 (Select Committee on Home Affairs 1998), they concluded that confidence was key: 'Unless the public has confidence, far from reducing the prison population there will be calls for increasing it' (Select Committee on Home Affairs 1998: para. 4). This has to a large extent come to pass.

The communications challenge is to demonstrate that prison alternatives are capable of rehabilitating offenders whilst involving some element of punishment. Their ability to take account of victims' views and contribute to community safety is also important to members of the community.

Variations in attitudes

The second main conclusion is that these aggregate findings, of course, mask wide variations in attitudes. The Centre for Social Marketing at the University of Strathclyde (Rethinking Crime and Punishment 2002b) identified three groups which they referred to as 'hangers and floggers', 'the moderate majority' and the 'liberals'. A review of psychological research for the RCP looked at what might lie beneath the variety of attitudes to crime and punishment (Wood and Viki 2001). It found, for example, that in times of prosperity and optimism, attitudes to offenders are more sympathetic, and in times of economic crisis less so. Most studies have shown that older people are more punitive than younger, and manual occupations more punitive than non-manual. The Rethinking Crime and Punishment survey found that, whilst more people are likely to see reducing prison numbers as a 'bad' rather than a 'good idea' in overall terms, the reverse is true amongst those in social classes A and B and those who read broadsheet newspapers (Mori 2003). People who fear crime are more likely to think that courts are lenient, and advocate heavier sentences. But, surprisingly, victimization does not seem to affect punitive attitudes.

There are some more predictable links between ideological beliefs and attitudes to crime. Studies, mainly North American, have shown that highly religious people and those with a strong belief in a just world – the belief that good things will happen to good people and bad things will happen to bad people – held the most punitive attitudes to offenders (Wood and Viki 2001). Other studies have found that Christian fundamentalism strongly predicted support for the use of punitive criminal justice policies (Wood and Viki 2001).

Not surprisingly, conservative beliefs – measured by agreement with statements endorsing traditional social values – are linked with punitiveness and liberal political views with more lenient attitudes. This is confirmed by detailed analysis of survey data in Britain. The British Social Attitudes survey in 1999 (National Centre for Social Research 1999) found that support for stiffer sentences ranged from 59 per cent amongst salaried Liberal Democrat voters to 90 per cent amongst working-class conservatives (and, surprisingly, working-class Liberal Democrat supporters.) Amongst Labour voters, 70 per cent of salaried, 77 per cent of self-employed and 85 per cent of working-class respondents supported a tougher approach.

A similar pattern was found in Mori's poll on attitudes to burglars. Conservative voters favoured imprisoning a first-time burglar by 50 per cent to 41 per cent, Liberal Democrat voters favoured community service by 54 per cent to 38 per cent whilst Labour supporters were equally divided. When, in work undertaken for the RCP, Mori asked if it was a good or a bad idea to reduce the prison population, they found that respondents intending to vote Conservative were more likely to think it a bad idea (53 per cent) than Labour voters (45 per cent) or those supporting other parties (37 per cent).

Psychological research suggests that, at the individual level, attitudes to punishment are mediated by psychosocial factors: emotional orientation, prejudice and fear of crime may be particularly important in this respect (Wood and Viki 2001). We also know something about the factors that seem to concern people most about offending. Not surprisingly, the vulnerability of the victim and the persistence of the offending seem particularly significant. Research is consistent in finding that repeat offenders elicit little sympathy (Wood and Viki 2001). Interestingly, people prefer tougher measures for 'persistent' young offenders than for adult offenders 'with previous convictions', suggesting that the term 'persistent' (although defined by the researchers as having three convictions) may trigger an association with the highly prolific young offenders allegedly responsible for very many more crimes, and about whom there was so much concern in the early 1990s.

Research carried out for the Coulsfield Inquiry found sharply contrasting attitudes to punishment between the residents of two high-crime areas. More punitive attitudes were prevalent in an area where residents felt a strong sense of rootedness but experienced increasing disorder in public space and a lack of optimism about the future; less punitive attitudes were present in an area with more of a sense of social control and safety (even where crime rates were equally high). In both areas most residents were positive about the idea of offenders moving out of crime and going on to lead useful lives. The researchers found reasonable public support for the idea that offenders should be allowed to redeem themselves and this is the case in areas with high punitiveness as much as in other areas (Bottoms and Wilson 2004).

The role of the media

The third main finding relates to the role of the media. In modern culture, the media have taken over the role of primary storytellers, providing many of the signs by which people navigate the complexities of the social world. In general, the media systematically misrepresent the level of, and nature of, criminal acts. There are links between media consumption and fear of crime. People who watch TV most tend to be most fearful, and watching crime programmes increases the desire to see offenders punished (Wood and Viki 2001).

Research carried out for the RCP at the Open University looked at the role the media play in shaping attitudes (Gillespie and McLaughlin 2003). It found that viewers often blur the boundaries between information and entertainment programmes. Crime stories, in different forms, are common and a pervasive part of most people's media experiences. A great deal of knowledge about criminal acts, policing and detection is gained from television. In contrast, the sample viewers recall very little knowledge about punishment. The public has high levels of ignorance about sentencing and negative attitudes towards sentencers who are seen as inconsistent and out of touch.

Whilst TV plays some part in forming opinions and attitudes, tabloid newspapers are more directly and noticeably influential in conditioning and reinforcing punitive attitudes, and in shaping punitive rhetoric, than television. Saturation coverage of *specific* (often extreme and unrepresentative) cases may be particularly important in shaping attitudes to crime in *general*. Viewers are just as likely to gain and recall useful information about criminal justice from dramas, especially soap operas, as from news, current affairs and documentaries.

Changing attitudes

The final area in which the RCP has identified lessons relates to how public attitudes can be changed. Mike Hough and Alison Park's analysis of a deliberative poll (2002), in which a random sample of the public were exposed to a weekend of facts and argument about crime and punishment, found that information and discussion could trigger significant shifts in attitudes about the best ways of controlling crime. For example, 35 per cent of participants initially thought that 'sending more offenders to prison' would be a very effective way of reducing crime. After the weekend, only one in five took this view. Whilst 50 per cent initially thought that 'stiffer sentences generally' would be a very effective way of reducing crime, ten months later only 36 per cent thought the same. Support for community penalties was originally quite high and remained largely unchanged. By no means all people adopted more liberal views after the event; many adopted tougher views. In general, people adopted less extreme views after the event, with a *net* shift in a liberal direction. Ecotec (2005) found that information about the educational deficits of young offenders reduces popular support for custody. Focus group work conducted by Strathclyde University (Rethinking Crime and Punishment 2002b) suggested that key message strategies to engage public support for non-custodial sentences include:

- instillation of responsibility and discipline;
- having to work hard, emotionally and physically;
- putting something back;
- paying back to victims;
- restriction of liberty and requirement to change behaviour; and
- treatment of causes of offending.

Messages that focus on the *costs of custodial sentences, the rising prison population or humanitarian arguments* are less persuasive.

Gillespie and McLaughlin found deeply entrenched views are hard to dislodge but more reasoned responses to the complexities and purposes of sentencing arise when people are confronted with different perspectives and become aware of the gaps in their own knowledge. Focus group discussions suggest the ways in which viewers discuss their media experiences in everyday life. In every focus group, discussion participants, even the most vociferously punitive, worked through some of the contradictions in their views and opinions. Macmillan *et al.* (2004) concluded that building support for alternatives to prison requires getting across positive stories about performance with offenders from the perspective of victims and communities. This is not simply a question of public relations. The actual work undertaken with offenders out of prison must afford a higher priority to the interests of victims and local communities.

This finding was mirrored in a small-scale study conducted for the RCP by the Scottish Council Foundation, which identified the values which people consider important if criminal justice is to meet the public interest (Scottish Council Foundation 2004). Considered alongside Bottom's finding of 'a high degree of potential support for community penalties even in high punitiveness areas', there seem substantial opportunities for shifting attitudes in a positive direction. The Local Crime Community Sentence project found that case study presentations by probation officers and magistrates to community groups is one way of putting this into practice (King and Grimshaw 2003).

Implications for policy

If many members of the public are inclined to exaggerate the extent and gravity of crime, on the one hand, whilst underestimating the nature of sentences on the other, then something should surely be done to correct such misunderstandings. Moreover, if the very same misunderstandings then go on to influence criminal justice policy formation, then the need to inform public opinion arguably becomes more pressing still. Suggested below is a strategy aimed at impacting both on the attitudes which people may hold for *instrumental reasons* ('more prison keeps me safe') and those which are held for *expressive reasons* ('more prison gives offenders what they deserve'). The strategy comprises three prongs: to *inform*, to *influence* and to *involve* the public.

79

To inform

The evidence above suggests that communicating accurate and accessible information about crime; the options available to the courts; and their effectiveness and costs must be the cornerstone of a strategy to raise the level of debate. The Home Office Sentencing Review (Home Office 2001) found that it was possible to raise levels of knowledge through printed information, a video and attendance at a seminar. Interestingly, the 'informed public' who had been given key facts were less punitive in their sentencing preferences than the general public. The review recommends that the Home Office should be required to disseminate information about the effectiveness of sentencing as part of its duties under s. 95 of the Criminal Justice Act 1991, and should consider ways of increasing public knowledge about how sentencing is intended to work and how it is working in practice (Home Office 2001). One of the respondents to the consultation on the sentencing review suggested that schools should be required to promote understanding of crime and the justice system.

To influence

As well as informing what people *know* about youth crime and young offenders, there is a need to influence how people *feel* about the subject. Indeed, attitudes are formed on the basis of what people think *and* what they feel. There is good reason to suppose that, however compelling the content and logic of information, attitudes to crime contain a strong emotional element. This may be based on personal experience. On the whole victims of crime do not appear to be more punitive than non-victims, although victims of burglary were more likely than others to say in the 1998 *British Crime Survey* that immediate imprisonment in a young offender institution was the best way to deal with a male juvenile burglar. Attitudes may also be based on local experience. Those who believe that juvenile courts are doing a 'poor' or 'very poor' job were most likely to say that teenagers hanging around the streets locally present a very big problem. Fear of crime is likely to be an important mediating variable. Helping people to feel safer seems a prerequisite for developing more constructive attitudes. People high in anxiety (or in certainty) are low in persuadability. Influence is also needed to counteract the effects of the media.

Simple information may be sufficient to dispel common myths but a good deal more work needs to be undertaken to identify the impact which different messages have on the public. Reformers have often produced information about the costs of incarceration; assuming that people will be sufficiently shocked to find out that it costs £35,000 a year to keep someone in prison that they will change their views about the desirability of doing so. However, American evidence suggests that for the general public cost may be a marginal issue if they think you are in a 'war on crime'. For some, the lesson may be that prisoners should be kept in more Spartan and inexpensive conditions whilst, for others, 'jail is cheap at the price; just think of how much more it would cost repeatedly arresting and processing and trying and monitoring him on probation or on community service, which won't work anyway' (Marrin 2002).

In similar vein, evidence from the Office of National Statistics that most young offenders in prison have mental health problems might be thought likely to influence people towards alternative approaches, but what attitude are they likely to adopt? Some might think better health care in prisons is the answer; others might want new secure psychiatric institutions. Others might think that longer or even indeterminate sentences are needed to protect them from offenders who are not only 'bad' but also 'mad'.

It is therefore crucially important to promote viable alternatives to criminal prosecution and penal custody. Restorative and reparative disposals, for which surveys suggest there is a sizeable baseline of support, seem particularly ripe for promotion. The British Crime Survey found that restorative or reparative disposals were a popular sentencing preference in respect of juveniles committing first offences. Research for the Halliday Review found a majority supported the idea that, if offenders were made more aware of the impact of their crime on the victim, they would be less likely to reoffend (Home Office 2001). Intensive community supervision programmes such as the Youth Justice Board-funded Intensive Supervision and Surveillance projects are also capable of active promotion, although this needs to be done in a way that avoids less eligibility arguments – that young offenders are getting better education, health care or recreation than law-abiding young people.

To involve

The third strand of the strategy to promote a positive change in attitudes is to encourage greater public and community involvement in the criminal justice system. There are a number of reasons for supposing that the 'seeing is believing' inherent in involvement will not only help to inform and influence attitudes, but might bring about a more fundamental reorientation towards offending. It has been estimated, for example, that only one in five of the population has been into a prison in one capacity or another. For the vast majority opinions on prisons are second hand.

Two insights from social psychology suggest that increasing involvement can impact forcefully on attitudes and might therefore be a way of producing more positive opinions towards offenders. First, the so-called 'contact hypothesis' argues that prejudice can be reduced through contact between groups, but only under certain circumstances: when the contact is intensive and frequent; has support from the leadership of the groups involved; and where groups are of equal status. These are obviously problematic but not impossible criteria to meet when one of the groups consists of offenders. Secondly, there is evidence that people who express emotional attitudes to an abstract issue (crime) may develop different attitudes when given responsibility for solving a practical problem in the real world (an individual offender). It is a psychological commonplace that attitudes and behaviour are often not closely related. This suggests that the more people involved in direct work with offenders in one way or another the better. Encouraging such involvement has been the aim of a further strand of work conducted by the RCP but is beyond the scope of this chapter.

References

Bingham, LCJ (1997) *Evidence in Select Committee on Home Affairs (1998) Third Report: Alternatives to Prison Sentences* (Cm 486). London: HMSO.

Bottoms, A., Rex, S. and Robinson, G. (eds) (2004) *Alternatives to Prison.* Cullompton: Willan Publishing.

Bottoms, A. and Wilson, A. (2004) 'Attitudes to punishment in two high crime areas', in A. Bottoms *et al.* (eds) *Alternatives to Prison.* Cullompton: Willan Publishing.

Coulsfield, Lord *et al.* (2004) *Crime, Courts and Confidence.* London: Police Foundation.

Ecotec Research and Consulting (2005) *Unlocking Learning.* London: Rethink Briefing, Esmee Fairbairn Foundation.

European Opinion Research Group (2002) *Eurobarometer 58.0: The Attitude of Europeans towards the Environment.* http://europa.eu.int/comm/public_opinion/archives/ebs_181_sum_en.pdf

Gillespie, M. and McLaughlin, E. (2003) *Media and the Shaping of Public Knowledge and Attitudes towards Crime and Punishment.* London: RCP.

Home Office (2001) *Making Punishments Work: Report of a Review of the Sentencing Framework* (Halliday Report). London: HMSO.

Home Office (2004) *Crime in England and Wales 2003/4*. London: HMSO.

Home Office Statistical Bulletin (January 2005) *Prison Population Projections 2005–2011*. London: HMSO.

Hough, M., Jacobson, J. and Millie, A. (2003) *The Decision to Imprison: Sentencing and the Prison Population*. London: RCP/Prison Reform Trust/South Bank University.

Hough, M. and Park, A. (2002) *Attitudes to Crime and Punishment: The Results of a Deliberative Poll of Public Opinion*. London: RCP.

International Centre for Prison Studies (n.d.) *World Prison Brief* (avilable at www.prisonstudies.org).

King, J. and Grimshaw, R. (2003) *Evaluation of LCCS*. London: Centre for Crime and Justice Studies.

Marrin, M. (2002) 'The ugly truth is that Britain must build a lot more jails', *The Sunday Times*, 10 March.

Macmillan, K., Money, K. and Hillenbrand, C. (2004) *The Reputation of Prison Alternatives*. London: RCP.

Mattinson, J. and Mirrlees-Black, C. (2000) *Attitudes to Crime and Criminal Justice: Findings from the 1998 British Crime Survey. Home Office Research Study* 200. London: Home Office.

Mori (2003) *Crime and Prisons Omnibus Survey*. London: Mori.

National Centre for Social Research (1999) *1999 British Social Attitudes Survey*. London: National Centre for Social Research.

Rethinking Crime and Punishment (2002a) *Briefing 1: What Does the Public Think about Prison?* London: RCP.

Rethinking Crime and Punishment (2002b) *Briefing 3: What Do the Public Really Feel about Non-Custodial Penalties?* London: RCP.

Rethinking Crime and Punishment (2003) *What You Really Need to Know about Criminal Justice*. London: RCP.

Rethinking Crime and Punishment (2004) *The Report*. London: RCP.

Scottish Council Foundation (2004) *Criminal Justice and the Public Interest*. Edinburgh: Scottish Council Foundation.

Select Committee on Home Affairs (1998) *Third Report: Alternatives to Prison Sentences* (Cm 486). London: HMSO.

Van Kesteren, J., Mayhew, P. and Nieuwbeerta, P. (2000) *Criminal Victimisation in Seventeen Industrialised Countries*. The Hague: Dutch Ministry of Justice.

Wood, J. and Viki, G.T. (2001) 'Attitudes to punishment.' Unpublished research for Rethinking Crime and Punishment.

Woolf, LCJ (2002) 'Making the punishment fit the needs of society.' Speech to the Prison Service annual conference, 5 February.

Chapter 6

Delivering death: capital punishment, botched executions and the American news media[1]

Chris Greer

Introduction

Since the nineteenth century, executions have been transformed from public events to 'behind-the-scenes' bureaucratic procedures, increasingly hidden from the public gaze. Today, for the vast majority of American citizens, capital punishment is rendered visible *only* through its representation in various forms of media. Media representations, then, are closely interconnected with how the death penalty is 'made to mean' throughout the USA and the rest of the world. This chapter explores the construction of juridical killing in the American press by considering the representation of three 'botched executions' (executions in which the apparatus of death, in this case the electric chair, malfunctions) which took place in Florida during the 1990s. Botched executions are of particular interest for at least two obvious reasons. First, they represent a direct challenge to the state's desired presentation of capital punishment as quick, clean and painless. Secondly, by making the violence inherent in capital punishment clearly visible, and raising questions about the suffering of the condemned, they present abolitionists with an important opportunity to mobilize support against the continued use of the death penalty. How the press construct botched executions offers useful insights into the contemporary meaning of capital punishment in America, and demonstrates how attempts to challenge the cultural hegemony of state killing in the media may ultimately serve to reinforce it.

Crime as news

Most crime news stories, largely irrespective of market or medium, bear certain key elements in common (for useful reviews, see Reiner 2002; Jewkes 2004; Greer 2005). They focus disproportionately on the most serious and violent crimes, and generally seek to establish narrative closure, culminating in a reaffirmation of moral and social order. One of the most important journalistic devices through which crime stories derive their potency is the establishment of oppositional binaries – good and evil, innocent and guilty, pure and depraved and, frequently, black and white (Chibnall 1977; Hall *et al.* 1978; Schlesinger and Tumber 1994). The resonance of these binaries has been amplified with the emergence of the 'victim culture' in recent decades (Maguire and Pointing 1988; Garland 2001). Whereas the position of victims in news stories used to be at best shadowy, they now provide the central focus around which crime narratives are increasingly structured. The plight of the victim is often portrayed in sympathetic, emotive terms which encourage empathy and identification from the news consumer (Reiner *et al.* 2000; Greer 2004). One consequence of this growing victim-centricity has been a shift towards stories which promote vengeance and retribution against the offender – in the name of the victim, whose suffering must be acknowledged, validated and avenged – over restitution and rehabilitation.

The most dramatic and compelling crime stories, then, are frequently those that feature the straightforward and uncontested binary of 'idealized victim' and 'absolute other' (Greer and Jewkes 2005). This requires stories to be individualized. Aetiology tends to be addressed in terms of free will and rational choice – reflecting classical conceptions of the hedonistic, calculating transgressor – and there is seldom any consideration of the wider socioeconomic and cultural conditions which may have contributed to precipitating the criminal event: responsibility and blame can be attributed more easily and dramatically to individuals than structures. By highlighting deviance and attributing blame, crime narratives often function as 'moral fables' (Sparks 1992). They promote social cohesion throughout respectable society by marginalizing and demonizing those 'not like us'. They invite consumers to engage collectively in the affirmation of virtuous identities through pointing to and denunciating the criminal 'other'.

Executions as news

Executions carried out by the state, in this case in the USA, embody many of the key determinants of newsworthiness. They represent the most forceful expression of sovereign power (state killing) and the ultimate form of closure (the death of the convicted offender), in response to the most violent of crimes (nearly always murder), by individuals legally judged to be unfit for membership of the human community (supposedly the most unequivocal examples of 'absolute other'). Furthermore, whilst the binaries established in most crime news stories serve to distinguish between those who are good and those who are evil, those who are guilty and those who are innocent, execution narratives make an additional crucial distinction – between those who deserve to live and those who deserve to die.

It is curious, then, that most executions fail to attract much attention in the news media, and many pass virtually unnoticed outside the states in which they are carried out. At the prosecution and sentencing stages of capital trials, race appears to be a central determining factor. Cases featuring black offenders and white victims – the binary of black and white – generally attract higher levels of media attention than those involving black victims, mirroring wider racial tensions throughout American society (Sarat 2002). But the apparent lack of media interest in the vast majority of executions indicates just how 'normal' the practice of capital punishment in the USA has become. Clearly, only certain examples of state killing fulfil the criteria required to come within the horizons of newsworthiness, and attract media attention on a national scale.

Media interest in executions may be determined primarily by the nature of the crime(s) for which the death sentence was originally passed. More dramatic crimes – involving serial and mass murderers and spree killers – will naturally attract more media attention at the time of their commission, and throughout the investigation, trial and sentencing stages of the penal response than bungling, panic-stricken murderers of store attendants during a robbery-gone-wrong (see Caputi 1987; Jenkins 1994).[2] Phenomenal in terms of their media presence, those rare cases involving the multiple murders of unsuspecting innocents by unrepentant offenders exemplify the binaries of good and evil, human and inhuman, 'idealized victim' and 'absolute other'. In both the scale of violence and the incontestability of guilt, they also support the most compelling emotional-moral arguments in favour of capital punishment. If people like Timothy McVeigh and people like John Gacy do not deserve to die, who does (see Sarat 2002: ch. 1)? In important ways, then, the high-profile coverage of executions in the American press is oriented towards reporting those cases that tend – whether intentionally or otherwise – to support the institution of state killing, rather than challenge it. This has implications for wider perceptions of the legitimacy of capital punishment throughout American society.

Sometimes, however, it is not the nature of the crime or the criminal, but the nature of the execution itself that provides the main focus for media attention. When the technologies of execution malfunction, the physical effects on the body of the condemned can be horrific, presenting a visual spectacle too dramatic for the media to ignore. Botched executions raise serious questions regarding the pain and suffering of the condemned on the path to death. They carry the potential to shift attention away from the lethal violence for which the offender was sentenced and on to the lethal violence the state uses to sanction its 'worst' offenders. Whilst press representations of the (straightforward and smooth-running) execution of America's most prolific murderers tends to legitimate the practice of capital punishment, stories of botched executions – by exposing state inefficiency and incompetence, and potentially generating sympathy for the condemned – might be expected to have the opposite effect.

The civilized killing of the savage

Capital punishment in America is intended only for the most serious offenders who have committed the most heinous crimes, though the extent to which this legal mandate is upheld in practice remains a major source of global concern (Bedau 1997; Hood 2002; Zimring 2003). In the courtroom prosecutors merge verbal and visual grammars of violence, depravity and senselessness – through detailed descriptions and dramatic reconstructions, crime scene photographs and victim impact statements – to depict capital defendants as monsters unfit to live. Lynch (2005) has noted the paradox in a legal process where those facing the death penalty are characterized as rational, calculating and free-willed, yet also as 'alien' and 'other'. This image of the rational, calculating 'other' is not only echoed in media narratives, it has become one of the mainstays of late-modern crime reportage. Yet despite the construction of the condemned in legal and mediatized discourses as inhuman monsters, the state seeks to deliver death in a humane way. Sarat (2002) queries why the state, which actively and openly uses the death penalty as a means of deterring offenders and of satisfying victims' demands for justice, goes to so much trouble to minimize the suffering inflicted on the condemned. Garland (2002: 466) takes up this question:

> The answer would seem to be that the modern state seeks to disguise the violence that it uses to sanction the violence of others. It seeks to escape the contradiction of taking life in order to condemn the taking of life. The killing state *kills*, of course, but it strives to legitimate these killings by representing them as something other than they are – for example, as painless, sterile medical procedures. In the modern welfare state, executions can no longer be public displays of awe-inspiring force and sovereign power like those of the *ancient regimes* of early-modern Europe...Instead, executions have become behind-the-scenes, bureaucratic procedures in which the offender's life is terminated with a minimum of pain and physical suffering.

Paradoxically, through the very act of killing the state seeks to demonstrate its higher moral standing. The death penalty is mobilized as a means of affirming the state's humanity, even mercy, expressed through the delivery of death using less painful, less barbaric, more civilized means than those used by the condemned in committing his or her capital crime(s). Both the punisher and the punished use lethal violence, but where the condemned inflicts physical pain and suffering, the state strives to administer a death which is sterile and painless. Where the condemned disregards victims and their loved ones, the state places them, both symbolically and literally, at the heart of the criminal justice response. Where capital murders so often represent an enraged loss of control, the state aims always to be impartial, dispassionate and measured.

This is what separates the state, which kills lawfully and 'in the name of the people', from the murderers it puts to death. If death can be delivered in a quick, clean and painless manner, it can be rendered humane and, therefore, civilized. The delivery of a painless death thus establishes a further crucial binary, between 'the civilized and the savage' (Sarat 2002: 82). Since executions are made visible to the vast majority only through their media representation, the positioning of the audience in news stories is vital. Foucault (1979) describes how, in early-modern Europe, people attending public executions were compelled not only through fear, but also through complicity. By seeing the spectacle with their own eyes, they became 'voyeur accomplices' (Thompson 2000), guarantors of the punishment who, to an extent, took part in it. Then, as now, for its legitimacy to prevail, the consciousness of those who regard state killing must be aligned with the consciousness of the authority that sanctions and administers it, not with those condemned to die. One of the reasons that public executions died out was the fear of the crowd, horrified by the torture being inflicted, mobilizing behind the condemned. Contemporary news media may render executions visible on a far greater scale than anything imaginable two centuries ago. At the same time, however, the violence inherent in state killing is increasingly disguised and hidden from public view. Precisely because the act of killing is presented as sanitized and bureaucratic, if the state's use of lethal violence is shown to be anything else – if death is not delivered quickly and cleanly, if the condemned, no matter how heinous his or her crime, is seen to suffer physically – then the crucial gap between lawful and unlawful killing, between civilized and savage, between 'virtuous identity' and 'absolute other', closes in.

Botched executions are the most vivid manifestation of the state's failure to deliver death in this idealized way. Their representation presents the opportunity for a more penetrating, challenging and involved way of 'seeing' – a way of 'witnessing' (Girling 2004), of *seeing through* the state's preferred reading of juridical killing as efficient, painless and sterile. In such cases, the consciousness of those regarding capital punishment may not be aligned so readily with the state, whose exhibition of fallibility and incompetence – should it be communicated to a mass audience – is surely more likely to create 'doubters than converts' (Zimring 2003: 196). Media representations of botched executions thus constitute sites on which the conceptual foundations and perceived legitimacy of capital punishment may, in theory, be fiercely contested and forcefully undermined.

When state killing goes wrong

Throughout the 1990s, the state of Florida executed 23 death-row inmates by electrocution (www.deathpenaltyinfo.org). Three of these were botched, giving Florida one of the worst records in the USA for botched executions that decade.

Jesse Tafero was sentenced to death in 1976 for the murder of two police officers. He was executed on the 4 May 1990. When the first surge of current was applied, flames arced from beneath the leather death hood, inflicting third-degree burns to Tafero's face and head. Though the burning filled the execution chamber with smoke, witnesses observed that even after a second surge of current the condemned's head and chest continued to move. Over a four-minute period, the current was applied a total of three times, with each surge producing more flames and smoke. It was not until seven minutes after the execution had begun that Jesse Tafero was pronounced dead.

The 25 March 1997 execution of Pedro Medina, condemned to die for the murder of a neighbour in 1982, was striking in its similarity to Jesse Tafero's. The first application of current caused flames to erupt from the headpiece, filling the execution chamber with smoke and, according to some witnesses, the stench of burning flesh. One witness recalled that it was like 'watching someone being burnt alive' (*Daily News of Los Angeles* 26 March 1997). Again, three surges of current were needed before death was finally pronounced.

On 8 July 1999, Allen Lee Davis was executed for the 1982 murders of a pregnant woman and her two young daughters. During the execution, those present watched as blood seeped from Davis's facial area and dripped on to his torso, where it created a stain that continued to spread across his white shirt. The condemned tried to cry out, but his screams were muffled beneath the thick leather straps bound tightly across his face. By the pronouncement of death, 11 minutes after the execution had begun, the bloodstain on Davis's shirt was the size of a dinner plate.[3]

In each case, the visual manifestation of pain and suffering depicted the literal inscription of sovereign power on the body of the condemned. The scenes recalled the prolonged and tortuous sanctions of a bygone age, and echoed an era in state punishment that was believed to belong firmly in the past. The gruesome nature of the spectacles, and the controversy of Florida's preferred method of execution malfunctioning to such an extent and with such horrific consequences, ensured that the Tafero, Media and Davis stories were reported nationwide. These executions presented a clear opportunity for death penalty opponents to challenge the legitimacy of capital punishment in the USA, not through scarcely visited websites or specialist 'alternative' media, but through mainstream outlets with audiences that are, by comparison, massive and highly diverse.

The savage killing as civilized

In light of the gruesome nature of Tafero's execution, it seems remarkable that most newspaper headlines failed entirely to mention

that it had been botched. Instead, they stressed the reasons why
Tafero had been condemned to die in the first place, with some
alluding disapprovingly to the fact that he had spent more than a
decade on death row – 'Convicted cop-killer executed' (*United Press
International* 4 May 1990); 'Killer of two police officers executed in
Florida' (*New York Times* 5 May 1990); 'Tafero executed for killing two
officers 12 years ago' (*Associated Press* 4 May 1990). Of course, the
nature of Tafero's death was too sensational not to be described in
the main body of stories. But even when descriptions were detailed,
any sympathy the reader might feel for the condemned was pre-
emptively challenged in stark headlines that reinforced the binaries of
good and evil, innocent and guilty, foregrounding images of Tafero's
murderous criminality and consolidating his status as 'absolute
other'. Further reminders came as the narratives unfolded, lest it be
forgotten that 'Tafero coldly took the lives of two officers 12 years
ago' (*Associated Press* 4 May 1990). That there were serious questions
regarding Tafero's guilt was scarcely mentioned.

News reports tended also to downplay any notion that Tafero
had experienced physical pain when he caught fire. Some stories
noted that witnesses had observed Tafero's chest heaving and head
bobbing after two surges of electric current had been administered.
But such observations were invariably printed alongside official
statements by prison representatives, insisting unequivocally that
Tafero had not suffered. The prison spokesman was widely quoted
reiterating the physician's view: 'Tafero was dead within seconds of
the first jolt…there was no indication he felt pain' (*Associated Press* 4
May 1990). In other reports the prison physician was quoted directly,
confirming his belief that Tafero 'was unconscious the minute the
current hit him' (*Associated Press* 4 May 1990).

Thus, whilst there was considerable scope to develop a dramatic
and critical account of the state's failure to deliver death cleanly
and quickly, the vast majority of reportage downplayed the botch,
or glossed over it altogether. The *New York Times* (5 May 1990) was
the most economical in this respect. Beneath the headline 'Killer of
two police officers executed in Florida', it simply stated 'Because of
a malfunction it was necessary to administer three jolts of electricity
to carry out the execution'. Rallying cries and abolitionist calls from
anti-death penalty organizations – either because these calls had
failed to make final copy, or because they hadn't been advanced
in the first place[4] – were noticeable by their absence. What little
attention the efforts of anti-death penalty activists received was
couched in dismissive terms. Descriptions of the candlelight vigil

held in silent protest against Tafero's execution diminished the event by stressing that 'fewer than a dozen death penalty opponents' took part (*Associated Press* 4 May 1990).

Of all the sources quoted, condemnation came from Tafero's defence attorney alone. 'Death warrants in this state tend to come out of the governor's office like junk mail', he protested, 'If they cannot execute correctly, they can't execute at all' (*United Press International* 4 May 1990). Creating a marginal space of resistance, the lawyer appealed to the Governor to 'suspend all executions' (*United Press International* 4 May 1990). But the most thoughtful reflection on the case came in an editorial in the *St Petersburg Times* (8 May 1990), headlined 'There is no clean way to kill'. It read: 'The United States, lacking the collective will and national leadership to fight crime in more effective ways, keeps company with South Africa and the Soviet Union as the only developed nations that routinely look to executions for deterrence and catharsis.' This article stood amidst a remarkably consistent body of reportage which defended the humanity of state killing by downplaying the botch and the pain and suffering it may have caused, whilst stressing the inhumanity of the condemned by focusing on the crimes for which he had been sentenced. Press coverage not only supported the continued use of the death penalty, it also advocated the continued used of the electric chair. The clear message imparted in the majority of news stories was that the situation may have been ugly, but the condemned would not be missed and, in the end, justice, however unsightly, had been served.

Whilst headlines after the Tafero execution focused on the nature of his crimes, those following the execution of Pedro Medina seven years later were explicit in foregrounding the gruesome nature of his death: 'Condemned man catches fire in electric chair' (*Daily News*, New York)[5]; 'Flames erupt at man's execution in Florida (*Daily News of Los Angeles*); 'Electrocution triggers fire – prisoner's mask burns' (*Chicago Sun-Times*); 'Gruesome execution in Florida' (*Atlanta Journal-Constitution*). Some hard-line conservatives expressed approval, suggesting that the spectacle may serve well to deter others. Florida's Attorney General warned: 'People who wish to commit murder, they better not do it in the state of Florida because we may have a problem with our electric chair' (*Daily News of Los Angeles*). And one state Republican reasoned: 'It all comes out the same way. I just don't have a problem with it any way it goes' (*Ledger*, Lakeland, Florida). The majority of commentators, however, were appalled and, whilst Tafero's execution had attracted remarkably little criticism beyond the condemned's defence attorney, this time both pro- and anti-death penalty supporters were vociferous in their calls for an end to the electric chair.

Medina's counsel recalled 'it was brutal, terrible, it was a burning alive, literally' (*Commercial Appeal*, Memphis; *Chicago Sun-Times*). Beneath the headline 'Get rid of the chair, foes urge', the American Civil Liberties Union of Florida insisted that 'It's time to retire "Old Sparky". It's time for Florida to shut this machinery of death down' (*Miami Herald*). And a number of newspapers debated the possibility of switching to lethal injection as the default method of execution in Florida. For Sarat (2002), however, these criticisms and calls to retire the electric chair fell short of challenging the legitimacy of capital punishment on anything more than a technical level. Most press reports, he argues, 'treated the Medina story as a mere technological glitch rather than an occasion to rethink the practice of state killing' (Sarat 2002: 62). The Fort-Lauderdale *Sun-Sentinel* claimed that Florida 'is justified in imposing the death penalty…but it has no justification for retaining a method…that is so gruesome and violent and sometimes flawed'. Furthermore, as with the Tafero execution, prison officials sought to downplay any suggestion that Medina experienced physical pain. The medical examiner stated that, despite the flames and the smoke, he saw no evidence that Medina suffered, nor found any burns on his head (*Chicago Sun-Times*). She even went so far as to say: 'In my opinion, he died a very quick, humane death' (*Daily News*, New York).

On closer inspection, however, the press construction of the Medina execution was less one-sided than Sarat suggests. Many news stories expressed deeper concerns about the validity, not just of the electric chair, but of the wider institution of capital punishment, and there were impassioned and widely reported calls for its outright abolition. Some of these calls emanated from powerful sources. Condemnation came from as far afield as the Vatican, which was resolute in its demand for an end to all executions in the USA. It was widely reported that the Pope had personally entered a plea for executive clemency (*Chicago Sun-Times*; *Associated Press*; *San Hose Mercury News*). 'That this incredible, tragic event might cause justice officials to reflect and abolish capital punishment', one Vatican representative exhorted, 'is the least one can hope for' (*Associated Press*). Abolitionist arguments came from journalists too. The *St Petersburg Times* insisted: 'The horrific scene in the death chamber Tuesday should outrage even supporters of the death penalty and force all Floridians to reassess whether their state should continue to kill people.' Further challenging the legitimacy of state killing, many stories disclosed that Medina had maintained his innocence until the end, that much of the evidence in the case was circumstantial and that there were questions regarding his sanity (*Palm Beach Post*; *St Paul Pioneer Press*, Minnesota; *San Antonio Express*; *Washington Post*). The *Gainesville Sun* revealed that 'Medina was executed despite a life-long history of mental illness, and the Florida Supreme Court split 4–3 on whether to grant an evidentiary hearing because of serious questions about his guilt'. The condemned man's last words, 'I am still innocent', featured prominently (*Miami Herald*; *New York Times*; *San Hose Mercury News*).

Most notable, though, were the widely cited views of the murder victim's daughter. Lindi James openly opposed the execution and maintained that she 'had never believed that Medina had committed the murder', insisting that her mother would not have wanted him put to death (*Palm Beach Post*; *USA Today*; *Associated Press*). In a 'victim culture' where the views and interests of the aggrieved are made paramount, and increasingly provide the focus for criminal justice policy and crime news stories, the dissemination of such responses clearly matters. Certainly, press coverage of the Medina execution can be read as much more critical than Sarat's (2002) analysis indicates. The condemned's status as rational, calculating 'absolute other' was problematized and the normally clear-cut distinctions between good and evil, innocent and guilty, were blurred by those who placed the state at the scene of a public burning. Though the botch was dismissed by some, it provided a platform from which anti-death penalty commentators – with the support of the Catholic Church, the victim's family and certain newspapers – could launch a vocal attack on the death penalty in America.

Like the headlines describing Medina's death, those appearing in the wake of Allen Lee Davis's execution focused on its gruesome nature: 'Execution of 344-pound inmate turns bloody' (*Charleston Gazette*); 'An execution causes bleeding' (*New York Times*); 'Execution turns bloody' (*Sarasota Herald-Tribune*, Florida). Aside from the obvious contrast between burning and bleeding, there was another key aspect of Davis's execution that set it apart from Tafero and Medina: there was no question over his guilt. Rather than using his last words to maintain innocence, 'Tiny' Davis remained silent in the execution chamber. In the absence of last words, a suggestion of Davis's final thoughts came from the victims' family. This time, the family's message positioned the reader firmly with the victim. Making eye contact as the leather hood was placed over

Davis's head, the surviving husband and father recalled, 'He didn't show an ounce of remorse. He knew who I was and he didn't care. Not a bit'.

Condemnation came almost exclusively from anti-death penalty groups. The American Civil Liberties Union repeated the plea it had made following Medina's death, and called for all Florida executions to be suspended 'until the state can ensure that they can be conducted humanely' (*Charleston Gazette*, West Virginia; *Associated Press Online*; see also *New York Times* 8 July 1999). The National Coalition to Abolish the Death Penalty claimed that 'No civilized society should be using this apparatus, and I hope what happened today moves Florida toward a speedy end to the electric chair' (*USA Today* 9 July 1999). It was widely reported that Davis's ordeal had constituted sufficient grounds for Florida's Supreme Court to delay the execution of the next inmate in line for the electric chair (*Miami Herald*; *Florida Times-Union*). But only one organization, Amnesty International USA, called for an outright ban on capital punishment, insisting that Davis's bloody execution demonstrated that Florida 'cannot remove the cruelty inherent in state killing' (*St Louis Post-Dispatch*, Missouri, 9 July 1999).

Thus, whilst most expressed horror at the barbarity of the spectacle, and many called for a suspension of all further executions by electric chair, the vast majority of responses were reported in a manner which criticized the technological administration of state killing, but remained silent about its wider practice. Sarat's (2002) observations regarding the limits of mediatized protest following the Medina execution can be applied with much greater accuracy here. Even the *St Petersburg Times*, which had been so damning of capital punishment after Medina, was muted by comparison: 'The image of condemned killer Allen Lee Davis bleeding from behind his death hood in the electric chair Thursday is renewing a wrenching political debate: Should Florida retire the chair and switch to lethal injection?' (9 January 1999).

The demise of Ol' Sparky and Florida's switch to lethal injection

In the wake of the botched executions of Jesse Tafero, Pedro Medina and Allen Lee Davis, pressure mounted on the state of Florida to reconsider its use of the electric chair. The legislature remained committed. A temporary suspension was put in place following

Tafero, and executions were stayed during legal challenges following Medina and Davis, but in 1999 – having considered all three botches, with particular attention to Davis – Florida's Supreme Court came to the 4–3 majority ruling that execution by electric chair is painless and, therefore, not unconstitutional (*Provenzano* v. *Moore*, 95, 973). In an unprecedented move, one of the dissenting justices appended to his opinion post-execution colour photographs of Davis, depicting his contorted face and bloodstained body immediately after death and before he had been removed from the electric chair. These photographs were made available via the website of the Supreme Court of Florida and, at the time of writing (March 2005), could be accessed and viewed online via a hose of anti-death penalty websites.

Then, in January 2000, faced with an impending US Supreme Court hearing on the constitutionality of the electric chair, Florida's legislature voted overwhelmingly to switch to lethal injection as the default method of execution in that state (Hood 2002). By adopting lethal injection, the legislature ensured the continued retention of capital punishment in the state of Florida, even in the event that the Supreme Court might rule the electric chair a violation of the Eight Amendment, which prohibits 'cruel and unusual' punishment. Since the switch meant that electrocution was no longer Florida's sole method of delivering death, the challenge to its constitutionality, by death-row inmate Anthony Bryan, was dismissed by the US Supreme Court as moot and the case was never heard. In the five years since the Florida vote, all but one of the remaining states that offered the electric chair as their sole method of execution have adopted lethal injection, leaving Nebraska with the dubious distinction of being the only US state that currently requires electrocution (Death Penalty Information Centre). The electric chair is still available in the state of Florida. But only on written request from the condemned (Hood 2002).

Many abolitionists would rightly regard the widespread adoption of lethal injection, in Florida and elsewhere, as a significant step forward. Lethal injection is by no means problem free, and has accounted for 23 of the 36 bungled executions since 1976, most often due to difficulties in finding a suitable vein for insertion of the IV needles (Death Penalty Information Centre). Most would accept, however, that this method of execution is a less barbaric and almost certainly less painful alternative to the electric chair (Hillman 1993). And nationwide press coverage of the three Florida botches, which in the cases of Medina and Allen presented forceful and cohesive condemnations of electrocution, may well have played its part. In terms of promoting a more reflexive *public* debate on the legitimacy and continued used of capital punishment in the USA, however, the role of press representations bears further consideration.

Only in the Medina case was the death penalty represented as more than merely an issue of technological proficiency. Condemnation of the death penalty, in all its forms, and calls for its outright abolition were widespread and emanated from influential sources. In stark contrast, representations of the botched executions of Tafero and Davis – ironically through exposing the state's failure to deliver a clean, quick and painless death – may actually have reinforced the legitimacy of capital punishment. The prevailing message following these cases was that, whilst botched executions are unacceptable and to be avoided, there is nothing wrong with state killing provided the chosen method works on the day. It was the administration of the system rather than the system itself that came under fire, and the answer, accordingly, was cast as one of improving and tightening up on the specific technologies of killing, rather than engaging more critically with the wider concept. Just as major corporations routinely deflect questions of institutional integrity by publicly censuring and making examples of individuals – racist cops, embezzling accountants, incompetent managers (Slapper and Tombs 1999; Reiner 2000), or employing various techniques of neutralization (Cohen, 1993), questions regarding the institutional integrity of capital punishment were deflected by replacing one method of execution with another. Given the continued overwhelming support for capital punishment in the state of Florida, and across much of America, it might even be conjectured that the death penalty re-emerged in its new guise of lethal injection stronger than ever: more constitutional, more humane and, in stark contrast to the scarred bodies of Tafero, Medina and Davis, relatively untarnished.

Conclusions

Like crime narratives more generally, execution narratives are structured and inflected in various ways that encourage 'seeing' through the eyes of the state and, in the midst of a proliferating and frequently punitive 'victim culture', through the eyes of victims or their loved ones. More particularly, they are routinely subject to various influences, not always pulling in the same direction, but often mutually reinforcing none the less, which serve at once to minimize the humanity of the individual facing death – the 'absolute other' – whilst maximizing the humanity of the institutions and processes that deliver it. Even when faced with the horrific spectacle of prisoners bleeding profusely or catching fire, coverage of two of the three botched executions considered here positioned the news reader in a way that constrained a deeper 'witnessing' of the violence involved in state killing, and did much to ensure that the integrity of the institution, if not the method, remained intact.

The altogether more critical tone adopted in the reporting of Medina's execution cautions against seeking to make sense of crime news production by locating it within overly deterministic (modernist) theoretical frameworks (Brown 2003; Greer 2003). Manufacturing news is not simple and straightforward, but complex and frequently unpredictable. Its impact is even more so. The Medina case illustrates how press representations created a mediatized space in which discussion shifted beyond the merely technological and engaged a more substantive conversation about the wider constitutionality of state killing. The importance of such examples of resistance to the normalization of capital punishment, particularly when considered alongside the highly organized and relatively high-profile abolitionist movement in America and globally, should not be overlooked. But nor can their role in shaping public perceptions about the death penalty be taken for granted.

Critical scholars have argued for decades that the presence of oppositional discourses in mainstream news media, whilst giving the impression of open and democratic debate, actually helps maintain the dominant conceptual categories that in the end subvert counter-definitions to marginal status (Marcuse 1964; Hall et al. 1978; Herman and Chomsky 1994). Reflecting the late-modern proliferation in communication technologies, more recent accounts endorse a less monolithic, conspiratorial understanding of media production, suggesting that in a 'multimediated world' a broader range of outlets does enable a wider diversity of views and interests to find resonance (McRobbie and Thornton 1995). But for all its sophistication, this approach can overstate the diversity of representation that actually occurs. Speciality magazines and Internet chat circles permit diversity, of course, but 'the main thrust of representation hinges around the major media chains' (Young 2005: 104, emphasis added; Leblanc, 1999). In the mainstream American press, as this chapter has illustrated, reportage may both reinforce and challenge the normalization of capital punishment. But whilst the legitimacy of state killing may come under serious and sustained criticism from time to time, the overall, cumulative message can still be one of political support and cultural reinforcement.

Moreover, as in the cases of Tafero and Medina, representations often fall short of promoting a critical dialogue which problematizes the legitimacy of the death penalty. Rather, they amount to a struggle over the proper norms within which executions may legitimately take place. Calls from anti-death penalty organizations and other commentators that criticize the technology rather than the wider practice of state killing implicitly validate restructuring and improvement over outright abolition. At best, these calls can challenge the administrative status quo and force the state to reconsider the methods it uses to deliver death. At worse, they may serve ultimately to reinforce the cultural hegemony of capital punishment in the USA and, with a cruel irony, to buttress the legitimacy of the very institution they seek to condemn.

Notes

1   Earlier versions of this paper were presented at the Law Schools of Sydney University and Macquarie University, Australia. The author would like to thank participants at both universities, and Carolyn Strange at Australian National University, for their helpful comments.
2   Executions involving America's most prolific killers make for high-profile coverage because serial and mass murderers are newsworthy in and of themselves, at times achieving a kind of celebrity status. They form part of a much wider mediatized phenomenon which may peak and trough over years, periodically capturing and recapturing the popular imagination from arrest and trial, through sentencing and incarceration, to execution and beyond. These executions offer closure and the restoration of some kind of moral order, not only to the victim's loved ones, but also to the wider audiences who may avidly have followed the case in the media throughout. The media construction of executions involving America's most prolific and infamous killers forms part of research which is currently ongoing.
3   In the Tafero and Medina executions, the problem was traced to the sponge placed against the condemned man's head, and used to conduct electricity. In the case of Davis, some suggested initially that the electrocution had caused bleeding from the mouth, throat and chest. The autopsy revealed that, probably due to the combined effect of tight leather straps and medication thinning the blood (the medication was unrelated to the execution), the condemned suffered a nose bleed.

4 This chapter presents a straightforward discourse analysis of the press representation of botched executions. Whilst making the most of available resources at the time of writing, there is a strong case for the development of a more ethnographic approach to this type of research which involves – at the least – interviews with journalists, sources and others involved in the news production process.

5 All press quotes on the Medina execution are taken from articles appearing on 26th March 1997.

References

Bedau, H. (1997) *The Death Penalty in America: Current Controversies*. New York, NY: Oxford University Press.

Brown, S. (2003) *Crime and Law in Media Culture*. Buckingham: Open University Press.

Caputi, J. (1987) *The Age of the Sex Crime*. London: Women's Press.

Chibnall, S. (1977) *Law and Order News*. London: Tavistock.

Cohen, S. (1993) 'Human Rights and Crimes of the State: the Culture of Denial', in *Australia and New Zealand Journal of Criminology*, 26(1): 87–115.

Ferrell, J., Hayward, K., Morrison, W. and Presdee, M. (eds) (2004) *Cultural Criminology Unleashed*. London: Cavendish.

Ferrell, J. and Websdale, N. (eds) (1999) *Making Trouble: Cultural Constructions of Crime, Deviance and Control*. New York, NY: Aldine de Gruyter.

Foucault, M. (1979) *Discipline and Punish: The Birth of the Prison*. Harmondsworth: Penguin Books.

Foucault, M. (1977) *Discipline and Punish: The Birth of the Prison*. London: Allen Lane.

Garland, D. (2001) *The Culture of Control: Crime and Social Order in Contemporary Society*. Oxford: Oxford University Press.

Garland, D. (2002) 'The cultural uses of capital punishment', in *Punishment and Society*, 4: 459–87.

Girling, E. (2004) 'Looking death in the face: the Benetton Death Penalty campaign', in *Punishment and Society*, 6: 271–87.

Greer, C. (2003) *Sex Crime and the Media: Sex Offending and the Press in a Divided Society*. Cullompton: Willan Publishing.

Greer, C. (2004) 'Crime, media and community: grief and virtual engagement in late modernity', in J. Ferrell *et al.* (eds) *Cultural Criminology Unleashed*. London: Cavendish.

Greer, C. (2005) 'Crime and media: understanding the connections', in C. Hale *et al.* (eds) *Criminology*. Oxford: Oxford University Press.

Greer, C. and Jewkes, Y. (2005) 'Extremes of otherness: media images of social exclusion', in *Social Justice*, 32(4): 20–31.

Hale, C., Hayward, K., Wahadin, A. and Wincup, E. (eds) *Criminology*. Oxford: Oxford University Press.

Hall, S., Critcher, C., Jefferson, T., Clarke, J. and Roberts, B. (1978) *Policing the Crisis: Mugging, the State and Law and Order*. London: Macmillan.

Herman, E. and Chomsky, N. (1994) *Manufacturing Consent: The Political Economy of the Mass Media*. New York, NY: Pantheon.

Hillman, H. (1993) 'The Possible Pain Expected During Execution by Different Methods', *Perception*, 22: 745–53.

Hood, R. (2002) *The Death Penalty: A Worldwide Perspective* (3rd edn). Oxford: Oxford University Press.

Jenkins, P. (1994) *Using Murder: The Social Construction of Serial Homicide*. New York, NY: Aldine de Gruyter.

Jewkes, Y. (2004) *Media and Crime*. London: Sage.

Leblanc, L. (1999) 'Punky in the middle: cultural constructions of the 1996 Montréal summer uprisings (a comedy and four acts)', in J. Ferrell and N. Websdale (eds) *Making Trouble: Cultural Constructions of Crime, Deviance and Control*. New York, NY: Aldine de Gruyter.

Lynch, M. (2005) 'Supermax Meets Death Row: Legal Struggles around the New Punitiveness in the US', in J. Pratt, D. Brown, M. Brown, S. Hallsworth and W. Morrison (eds) *The New Punitiveness: Trends, Theories, Perspectives*. Cullompton: Willan.

Maguire. M. and Pointing, J. (eds) (1988) *Victims of Crime: A New Deal?* Milton Keynes: Open University Press.

Marcuse, H. (1964) *One-Dimensional Man*. Boston, MA: Beacon Press.

McRobbie, A. and Thornton, S. (1995) 'Rethinking "moral panic" for multi-mediated social worlds', in *British Journal of Sociology*, 46: 559–74.

Reiner, R. (2000) *The Politics of the Police* (3rd edn). Oxford: Oxford University Press.

Reiner, R. (2002) 'Media made criminality: the representation of crime in the mass media', in M. Maguire *et al.* (eds) *The Oxford Handbook of Criminology* (3rd edn). Oxford: Oxford University Press.

Reiner, R., Livingstone, S. and Allen, J. (2000) 'No more happy endings? The media and popular concern about crime since the Second World War', in T. Hope and R. Sparks (eds) *Crime, Risk and Insecurity*. London: Routledge.

Sarat, A. (2002) *When the State Kills: Capital Punishment and the American Condition*. Princeton, NJ: Princeton University Press.

Schlesinger, P. and Tumber, H. (1994) *Reporting Crime: The Media Politics of Criminal Justice*. Oxford: Clarendon Press.

Slapper, G. and Tombs, S. (1999) *Corporate Crime*. London: Longman.

Sparks, R. (1992) *Television and the Drama of Crime: Moral Tales and the Place of Crime in Public Life*. Buckingham: Open University Press.

Thompson, D. (2000) 'Death and its details', in S. Prince (ed.) *Screening Violence*. London: Athlone Press.

Young, J. (2005) 'Moral panics, Margate and Mary Poppins: mysterious happenings in south coast seaside towns', in *Crime, Media: Culture: An International Journal*, 1: 100–5.

Zimring, F. (2003) *The Contradictions of American Capital Punishment*. Oxford: Oxford University Press.

Chapter 7

'Buried alive': representations of the separate system in Victorian England

Helen Johnston

Between the end of the eighteenth and the beginning of the nineteenth century there was a significant change in punishment and an increased use of imprisonment as a main area for the disposal of offenders. Broadly, the prisons of the eighteenth century that were characterized by neglect and disorder were replaced by the drab, functional and regulated prison of the nineteenth century. By the mid-nineteenth century the 'prison had assumed an unmistakable appearance' (McGowen 1998: 71). This chapter will discuss representations of one area of this transformation – known as the separate system – between 1820 and the early 1860s, using literary sources and newspaper articles from this period. The aim is to examine how these representations reflected, or shaped, public anxieties concerning imprisonment in nineteenth-century England. This chapter will use three main sources: two case studies from Charles Dickens's work; a factual piece from *American Notes* concerned with the operation of the separate system in Philadelphia and the main character's visit to the 'model' prison in the fictional work *David Copperfield*; and newspaper reports from *The Times* during the 1840s and 1850s. Dickens' work as a social commentator and novelist was widely read and, by publishing his work serially, he reached a far wider audience than just those readers who could afford broadsheet newspapers or hardback novels, and he perhaps even created a new reading public. This also encouraged other leading authors such as Thackeray, Trollope and George Eliot to serialize their novels in the periodicals of the time (Wilson 2003). One commentator said after his death that 'No other Englishman had attained such a hold on the vast populace' (Wilson 2003: 336). In his early journalistic career he edited *Bentley's Miscellany* and the *Daily News* and later in his career, his own weekly magazines appeared: *Household Words* and *All the Year Round*, all of which contained essays on social problems such as crime and punishment as well as fictional pieces (Collins 1962). Dickens wrote a number of factual and fictional pieces concerning imprisonment (debtors' prisons appear frequently in his novels, for example, in *Little Dorrit* or *Great Expectations*). However, this chapter is just concerned with criminal prisons and will only consider his writings on the separate system.

Pratt argues that, during the nineteenth century, the 'prison was still a highly contested site – it was not then the exclusive secretive property of penal bureaucracies that we can recognize it as today. At that time, official discourse was only one of a range of competing voices proclaiming their own version of "the truth" about prisons' (2004: 72). It is to these 'competing voices' that we shall now turn in a discussion of various viewpoints on the operation of the separate system and how attitudes began to change by the late 1840s. Ultimately this led to the decline of the use of the separate system as a reformatory method. Increasingly media representations focused on the prison as a means of deterring offenders, and there was also considerable public anxiety over the end of transportation and a moral panic about 'garotting' which resulted in a more severe prison regime, particularly from the 1860s onwards.

Whilst this chapter does not intend to cover the orthodox and revisionist accounts of the 'birth' of the prison during this period (cf. Webb and Webb 1963; Ignattief 1978; Melossi and Pavarini 1981; Foucault 1991), it will first provide a brief outline of the key debates and concerns regarding imprisonment during the early nineteenth century to provide a context for further discussion about the ways in which popular literature and the media of the time constructed these issues.

Prisons and punishment in the nineteenth century

The end of transportation to America in the late eighteenth century had sparked the first government initiative concerned with imprisonment. Under the Penitentiary Act 1779 it was the government's intention to build one or more penitentiaries to hold those who previously would have been sent abroad. However, the penitentiary was never built and the problem was alleviated by the suitability of Australia as a convict colony (Webb and Webb 1963). Nevertheless, this was not a complete solution, as the hulks (prison ships) were overcrowded and costly, and a proper place of confinement was still required to hold convicts before they were transported. In 1812 the government set about the construction of Millbank penitentiary. Millbank opened in the summer of 1816 and when completed was one of England's most expensive public buildings (McConville 1981). The penitentiary was originally designed to hold 800 prisoners but, during construction, capacity was extended to 1,000, although it was never used to its full capacity. The penitentiary 'existed alongside the hulks and transportation and did not replace more than a fraction of their capacity' (McConville 1981: 138).

By the 1840s, things began to go wrong, for the harshness of the discipline and the severity of the regime had profound mental health implications resulting in a growing number of prisoners pronounced insane. Millbank's Committee resolved that long periods of separation were unsafe, and introduced a period of association after the first three months of confinement. Millbank's objectives were overhung with failure, and the Home Secretary decided to move the reformatory efforts to other institutions. The use of Millbank as a penitentiary was terminated in May 1843. It then became a convict depot where prisoners were assessed and sent to other institutions or to the hulks to await transportation (McConville 1981). Wilson (2002) argues that Millbank collapsed because it suffered from a crisis of legitimacy. It was 'unable to convince any of the audiences that it needed to satisfy that it could actually operate successfully. In short, it could not make the public, the prison staff, or the prisoners feel or believe that it was legitimate' (2002: 379).

Throughout the 1820s and 1830s, there had been a national debate over the benefits of two different systems of prison discipline. Some advocates favoured the separate system, under which the prisoners were held in single cells, where they would spend all their time working, eating or sleeping. Supporters of the system believed that the separation of offenders and the existence of a potent religious force were crucial in the process of recognizing sin, the precondition to the offenders' regeneration (Forsythe 1987). The prisoners were only allowed to leave the cell to attend chapel or to go to exercise, but in such circumstances they were instructed to have their faces covered, or may have been sent to separate airing yards to avoid any contact with other prisoners. The prison chaplain, therefore, had a central role in the operation of the separate system, spending much of his time conversing with, and instructing prisoners in their cells, 'hoping that through them the grace of God would flow so the heart would turn' (Forsythe 1987: 45).

The opposing system of discipline was that of the silent system. Under the silent regime, the prisoners would be able to work in association with other prisoners but they were to be silent at all times. A notable supporter of the silent system was Captain George Laval Chesterton, the Governor of Coldbath Fields House of Correction in Middlesex. Chesterton believed that prisoners should be kept in classified association (according to their gender and crime), and be subjected to hard labour, but that all communication between prisoners should be prohibited, leaving the prisoner to contemplate his or her guilt. Those who would defy the system would be automatically punished and with increasing severity the longer the defiance lasted. This theory had a less optimistic view of the possibility of reformation. But prisoners who showed special effort were rewarded with badges, financial rewards and an occupation (Forsythe 1987).

Both systems were based on the idea that first offenders or young offenders could be contaminated by more experienced criminals, and that prisoners should be silent, or separated from others, to allow reflection and repentance for their criminal behaviour. There were other reasons for using each method apart from ideas about reform. The separate system made a prison easier to manage and control which may have been an incentive, but the silent system was cheaper than its rival to enforce, as the structure of the building could remain unchanged (Forsythe 1987).

Contemporary commentators discussed the advantages of each system, some preferring one to the other. The first two Inspectors of Prisons, Reverend Whitworth Russell and William Crawford appointed by the government in 1835, were both strong advocates of the separate system and Crawford had visited the system in operation in America. They 'expended a considerable amount of energy on demonstrating the superiority of the so-called Separate system over the Silent system' and the Home Secretary, Lord John Russell saw the system through on to the statute books in the Prisons Act 1839 (Stockdale 1983: 216). This Act regularized the use of the separate system in all prisons across the country. It also gave considerable power to the inspectors, as no separate cell was to be used until certified as fit by one of the inspectors (Stockdale 1983).

By this time, the government had already begun its second major initiative and Pentonville Model Prison was opened in 1842 to hold 520 prisoners (McConville 1981). Pentonville had been built for the use of the separate system and the regime was one where, with the exception of exercise and chapel, every minute of the prisoners' day was spent in solitude in their cells. Once the prisoner was admitted, bathed, registered, 'distinguishing marks' recorded, given a medical inspection, prison uniform and had his head shaved, he was 'severed from the "outside"', allowed only one visit every six months, and permitted to write and receive one letter every six months (Ignattief 1978: 7). Even before Pentonville was opened *The Times* was expressing concern about the proposed regime, noting that 'the principle which this prison is meant to carry out in its greatest extent and rigour we must dissent in the strongest terms, as unnecessarily cruel, impolitic, and injudicious' (20 May 1841). It stated that, for the prisoners:

> Death can only relieve them; and if the system be carried too far, madness will seize those whom death has for the present spared. It will be well to look in time into the effect of this system, or, if other prisons be built on the same principle, a madhouse will be a necessary adjunct to a county prison (20 May 1841).

Dickens and the separate system

Dickens was strongly against the separate system and after a visit in March 1842, he wrote a scathing critique of the use of the separate system at Cherry Hill, the Eastern Penitentiary in Philadelphia, which had been hailed as the 'international showplace' for the system (Collins 1962). The critique of the separate system appeared in *American Notes*, an account of his travels in America, and was also timely, as the work was published six months before Pentonville prison opened. As Collins notes Dickens was 'conspicuous...for his passion for dramatising and commenting upon the topic issues of the day' (1962: 2). Three thousand copies of *American Notes* 'were sold in Philadelphia inside half an hour – some sign of the furore it created' (Collins 1962: 122).

Dickens argued that the system was 'cruel and wrong' and the intentions of those who devized the system may have been rooted in kindness, humanity and reformation, but these gentlemen did not know what they were doing. He maintained that:

> very few men were capable of estimating the immense amount of torture and agony which this dreadful punishment, prolonged for years, inflicts upon the sufferers; and, in guessing at it

myself, and in reasoning from what I have seen written upon
their faces, and what to my certain knowledge they feel within,
I am only the more convinced that there is a depth of terrible
endurance to it which none but its sufferers can fathom, and
which no man has a right to inflict upon his fellow creature
(Dickens 1842: 153–54).

In particular, Dickens was concerned with the psychological effects of
the system on the prisoners. He goes on:

I hold this slow and daily tampering with the mysteries of the
brain to be immeasurably worse than any torture of the body;
and because its ghastly signs and tokens are not palpable to the
eye and the sense of touch as scars upon the flesh, because its
wounds are not upon the surface, and it extorts few cries that
human ears can hear, therefore I the more denounce it, as a
secret punishment which slumbering humanity is not roused up
to stay. I hesitated once, debating with myself, whether, if I had
the power of saying 'Yes' or 'No', I would allow it to be tried
in certain cases, where the terms of imprisonment were short;
but now, I solemnly declare that with no rewards or honours
could I walk a happy man beneath the open sky by day, or lie
me down upon my bed at night, with the consciousness that
one human creature, for any length of time, no matter what, lay
suffering this unknown punishment in his silent cell, and I the
cause, or I consenting to it in the least degree (1842: 154).

After a brief discussion of the physical structure of the building,
Dickens focuses on the dull and quiet regime, the occasional muffled
sound, the prisoners' lack of contact with the outside world, with
family or friends, and the hoods placed over the heads of prisoners
like 'an emblem of the curtain dropped between him and the living
world' (1842: 155). He describes the prisoner as a 'man buried alive;
to be dug out in the slow round of years; and in the meantime dead
to everything but torturing anxieties and horrible despair' (1842:
156). Indeed, Dickens uses this metaphor again in a later novel.
Collins (1962) argues that the memories of the visit to Philadelphia
are clearly one of the roots for *A Tale of Two Cities* published in 1859.
The original title of the book was *Recalled to Life*, but later this became
the title of Book One, and the password used by Mr Lorry 'on his
way to dig someone out of a grave' as he travels to Paris to rescue
Dr Manette from his long imprisonment in the Bastille. 'Eighteen

years!' he thinks. 'Gracious Creator of the day! To be buried alive for eighteen years!' (Collins 1962: 133).

Dickens continues his critique of the separate system by describing some of the prisoners he spoke with on his visit. In the short accounts of a number of these prisoners, Dickens describes how the prisoner 'gazed about him – Heaven only knows how wearily!' (1842: 158) or how his:

> heart bled for him; and when the tears ran down his cheeks, and he took one of the visitors aside to ask, with his trembling hands nervously clutching at his coat to detain him, whether there was no hope of his dismal sentence being commuted, the spectacle was really too painful to witness (1842: 158).

Of this prisoner he wrote: 'I never saw or heard of any kind of misery that impressed me more than the wretchedness of this man' (1842: 158–9). One female prisoner was asked by one of Dickens' companions if she was happy in the prison. She:

> struggled – she did struggle very hard – to answer, Yes; but raising her eyes and meeting that glimpse of freedom overhead, she burst into tears, and said, 'she tried to be; she uttered no complaint; but it was natural that she should sometimes long to go out of that one cell; she could not help *that*' she sobbed (1842: 162).

Later in the piece, Dickens reveals his support for the silent system, commenting that the separate system, 'in its superior efficiency as a means of reformation, compared with that other code of regulations which allows the prisoners to work in company with out communicating together, I have not the smallest faith' (1842: 170). Indeed, he argues that instances of reformation that had been described to him, he believed, could have been 'equally well brought about by the Silent System' (1842: 170). This brief section of the work is the only time in which Dickens offers any alternatives to the separate system to the reader.

However, Dickens was an advocate of the silent system and was friends with both Chesterton, the Governor of Coldbath Fields House of Correction, and Lieutenant Augustus Frederick Tracey, RN, Governor of Tothill Fields House of Correction. He preferred the silent system as he regarded it as more punitive and he extolled 'the virtues of hard and unrewarding labour' (Ackroyd 2002: 214).

Pentonville 'model' prison

When Pentonville first opened, convicts had spent 18 months in solitude, but this was later reduced to 12 and then 9 months. *The Times* commented in 1843 that, although Pentonville:

> has only been opened so short a time, and the prisoners have been carefully selected from the various gaols in point of health, two have become insane this year,...It is remarkable that insanity only occurs in the Penitentiary and Model Prison, under Government inspectors, and not in magistrates' prisons (25 November 1843).

The reduction in solitude resulted from complaints that the chaplain's preaching was producing 'morbid symptoms' in the prisoners. During the mid-1840s there was a sense of anxiety and hostility in public opinion, principally due to the high rates of insanity (McConville 1981). As Ignattief notes: 'men came apart in the loneliness and the silence...one prisoner became convinced that the hand pushed food through the trapdoor was trying to poison him' (1978: 9). At a coroner's inquest into the death of a prisoner at Pentonville, the coroner called the prisoners from the cells either side of the deceased's cell as witnesses. Reverend Whitworth Russell (Inspector of Prisons and one of the commissioners of Pentonville) who was also present stated that the prisoners 'do not know even that they had a neighbour'. The coroner replied:

> Never mind. Out of doors there is strong feeling against this place, and some persons can hardly find terms vehement enough to use in speaking of it. In a case of this kind it is a pity that any juryman should go away dissatisfied on any points as to the death for want of testimony; therefore, if anything is wrong – let us ascertain it at once (*The Times* 12 December 1843).

By the end of the 1840s, 'Pentonville had sunk under the weight of public disapproval', and it became a convict depot differing little in objectives from Millbank (McConville 1981: 209). The changing tide of feeling was foreseen by Commissioner Russell at the inquest quoted above, when he commented that 'Whatever the public may now think of this prison, I am much more afraid that by and by they will say that the inmates are too well treated here rather than not well enough' (*The Times* 12 December 1843).

Alongside the government initiatives, there also existed local prisons administered by local magistrates, to which prisoners serving shorter sentences were committed. After the Gaols Act 1823, which introduced the disciplinary regime of classification, and the Prisons Act 1835, establishing the inspectors, local prisons were increasingly subject to government policy and pressure to conform to uniform prison practices, a process which culminated in their nationalization in 1877.

However, the extent to which the separate system was fully implemented in all local prisons, particularly before mid-century, is unclear. Even at Preston House of Correction where the chaplain John Clay had been advocating the system since the late 1820s, a corridor of separate cells did not appear until 1843 (DeLacy 1986). In Shropshire, the magistrates at Shrewsbury prison were proactive in experimenting with the separate system, beginning before it was regularized with a small number of separate cells in 1837 but the system was only gradually adopted and conversion of the whole prison was not achieved until the 1860s (Johnston 2004).

The model prison and the model prisoner

In the work *David Copperfield* published in 1849/50, Dickens uses a fictional piece to criticize the operation of the 'model' prison. At the end of the text Copperfield is invited by Mr Creakle, previously David's schoolmaster and now a Middlesex magistrate, to visit the 'model' prison, a prison that seems to be based on Pentonville. There are a number of critical themes that can be identified within this relatively short part of the book which reflect some of the public anxieties regarding Pentonville and the philosophies of punishment prevalent during this period. The first critical comment by Copperfield is when he refers to the structure and grandeur of the 'immense and solid building, erected at vast expense' (1849/50: 693). Copperfield remarks:

> I could not help thinking, as we approached the gate, what an uproar would have been made in the country, if any deluded man had proposed to spend one half the money, it had cost, on the erection of an industrial school for the young, or a house of refuge for the deserving old (1849/50: 693).

Here the obvious criticism is that such vast sums of money would be better spent on the 'deserving' in society rather than on prisoners.

This point also reflects concerns about 'less eligibility', the notion that conditions in prison should be worse than the living conditions of those honest, poor people outside prison. In fact, this is a theme continuous throughout the piece. This is shown more obviously in the comments regarding the 'comfort' of prisoners. Here Copperfield states that he 'might have supposed that there was nothing in the world to be legitimately taken into account but the supreme comfort of prisoners, at any expense, and nothing on the wide earth to be done outside prison doors' (1849/50: 694). This comment may also reflect a concern that prison was seen as the only solution to crime and the lack of alternatives to prison with regard to reforming offenders or combating wider social problems.

Dickens then begins his criticism of the separate system itself. With regard to the system, his criticism reflects a number of widespread concerns of the period. First, he questions whether the prisoners are in fact completely separated and unknown to each other. Some commentators maintained that prisoners were still able to converse with each other, despite claims to the contrary by magistrates and governing bodies of prisons at the time. In fact, Dickens later states in the piece that it is widely known that prisoners do know each other and are able to converse with each other.

Secondly, he notes widespread concerns about prisoners' ability to deceive chaplains and magistrates with regard to their moral and religious transformation under this disciplinary regime. Before meeting the 'model prisoner' who has been selected for 'show' at the end of their visit, he questions how the evidence of penitence is shown and uses words such as 'foxes' to describe the 'histories of cunning' of such prisoners. However, he notes that the prison officers are not so easily deceived and are fully aware of what really goes on. Here he also criticizes the magistrate Mr Creakle and makes a number of negative comments about the poor way in which the man treated his wife and daughter in the past, despite his tenderness to prisoners.

Thirdly, he examines the question of the prison diet, reflecting again the public concern regarding 'less eligibility'. Here he is reflecting widely held beliefs that the diet in prison is better and more plentiful than that eaten by the honest labouring poor. Copperfield asks:

whether it occurred to any body, that there was a striking contrast between these plentiful repasts of choice quality, and the dinners, not to say of paupers, but of soldiers, sailors, labourers, the great bulk of the honest working class community: of whom not one man in five hundred ever dined so well (1849/50: 694).

Criticisms of both the prison diet and the general living conditions in prison during this period were widespread. It was frequently held that the poor, or those held in workhouses, would commit some small offence to get themselves committed to prison, where the diet was better, and medical conditions could be treated. Across the country, people were committed to prison after destroying their clothes in the workhouse, or smashing windows in such institutions to get committed to the local prison where the diet and conditions were thought to be better. DeLacy (1981) shows in her study of nineteenth-century Lancashire that during the winter months imprisonment was attractive to some sections of the population because the terms of imprisonment were short and combined with adequate food and free medical care. Indeed, William John Williams, Inspector of Prisons stated in 1837 that:

> One of the most serious and increasing obstacles to good discipline is the common practice of tramps and prostitutes, when infected with foul diseases, (not admitted into public infirmaries), committing some slight offence for the purpose of obtaining medical treatment in prisons. Their committals are generally for one or two months to hard labour, which they seldom or never under-go, often-times passing the entire of the term in hospital; and many of the females are scarcely discharged a month, ere they return again for surgical care. Such prisoners are more disorderly in behaviour, more pernicious in example, and more difficult to control, than any other class (quoted in DeLacy 1981: 184–5).

In touching on the question of 'less eligibility', Dickens is thus reflecting widespread concerns with regard to prison conditions and how they compared with the living conditions of the honest working classes. Robert Hosking, Governor of Pentonville prison in 1857, wrote to *The Times* defending the prison diet. Hosking stated that statements in a recent letter in the newspaper 'might lead some of your readers who are uninformed on the subject to suppose that the convicts in Pentonville Prison are actually rioting in gluttony'. He then set out the daily allowance of food for all prisoners, except those on punishment, as '3/4 pint of cocoa, with 10oz. of bread for breakfast, 4oz of boiled meat, 1/2 pint of soup, 1lb potatoes, and 5oz

of bread for dinner and 1 pint of gruel and 5oz of bread for supper'
(*The Times* 8 January 1857). Wilson (2002) argues that the attack on
prison food by Dickens is just one element of his dislike for the
separate system, but it seems to be much more than this as prison
diet was a particularly contentious issue during the period. Prison
inspectors stressed that criminals should not leave prison suffering
from ill-health physically or mentally, through the lack of proper
food, and it should not be extravagant or luxurious, but it 'was not
to be made an instrument of punishment' (Tomlinson 1978: 18).

This concern is still prevalent in contemporary society as
demonstrated in recent newspaper and media discussions – for
example, reports comparing the amount of money spent on children's
school meals to that spent on meals for prisoners (*Guardian* 6 October
2003), or in references in the popular press to prisons as 'holiday
camps' (Jewkes 2002; see also Chapter 9, this volume). Indeed, Sparks
discusses claims that prison regimes had become insufficiently austere
during the early 1990s, and the subsequent calls for harsher prison
discipline, that 'unwittingly but not accidentally reiterate the severe
stance that underlay so much of the nineteenth-century penal (and
Poor Law) ideology' (1996: 74).

Copperfield and the party of visitors are then introduced to the
'model prisoner'. The prisoner is first seen through the cell peep-hole
conscientiously reading his bible. Of course, Number 27, the 'model'
prisoner turns out to be Uriah Heep. Heep is the villainous clerk
who earlier in the book tried to take over Mr Wickfield's company
and blackmail his daughter into marriage. We learn that he is now
awaiting transportation for life for fraud, forgery and conspiracy
against the Bank of England. He expresses his penitence and replies
when asked if he is comfortable that he is far 'more comfortable here,
than I ever was outside. I see my follies now, sir, that's what makes
me comfortable' (1849/50: 695). The prisoner in the cell next door
turns out to be Mr Littimer, the former servant of Steerforth, who has
been convicted and sent to prison for robbery.

At the end of the visit to the prison, Copperfield reflects on the
events and states that:

> It would have been in vain to represent to such a man as the
> worshipful Mr Creakle, that 27 and 28 were perfectly consistant
> and unchanged; that exactly what they were then, they had
> always been; that the hypocritical knaves were just the subjects
> to make that sort of profession in such a place; that they knew
> its market-value at least as well as we did, in the immediate

service it would do them when they were expatriated; in a word, that it was a rotten, hollow, painfully suggestive piece of business altogether (1849/50: 699).

The extract thus returns to the notion of deception, that the cunning of the prisoners will serve them for a better life when they were transported to the Colonies after obtaining a good recommendation from the prison.

Yet the extract does not reflect the sympathy and compassion for the prisoners shown in earlier commentary in *American Notes*; rather it is a piece in which the system is regarded as useless in reformation and the prisoners merely 'play the system' to their advantage. But this fictional piece was written nearly ten years after *American Notes* and, as discussed earlier, attitudes towards this type of disciplinary regime in prisons had begun to change. Indeed, Dickens is certainly trying to make a point by including this section, as Collins (1962) argues he has to revive a character from 50 chapters earlier in order to do this – Mr Creakle – and notes that this is the only contemporary matter included in the novel. Thus, by the late 1840s and early 1850s, the separate system was increasingly coming under attack and public opinion was changing; some contemporaries argued that it was Dickens 'more than anyone else who brought about this change' (Collins 1962: 140).

As Walter Clay (son of Reverend John Clay, Chaplain of Preston House of Correction and advocate of the separate system) remarked:

The controversy about prison-discipline, which revived in 1847, increased the next year, grew vigorous in 1849, and culminated in 1850. By degrees, almost the whole press, which had been generally favourable to the plan of separation in 1847, veered round into brisk hostility. Early in 1849 *The Times* began to fulminate; presently the *Daily News*...in the spring [of 1850] Carlyle flung 'Model Prisons' at the belaboured system; and in the autumn Dickens, in the final number of *David Copperfield*, gave it the unkindest cut of all (Clay 1861 cited in Collins 1962: 156).

As a result of the adverse media coverage, by the 1850s 'enthusiasm for the separate system was beginning to wane' (Henriques 1972: 84). It was argued that separation was not absolute; that prisoners could recognize each other and wrote graffiti on chapel partitions.

The system was also being misused by magistrates who did not understand the aims of the system, and who introduced hard labour as punishment, which led to cruelties such as those uncovered at Birmingham Borough Gaol in 1853 (Henriques 1972) and at Leicester Gaol (Webb and Webb 1963). An investigation into the death of 15-year-old Edwards Andrews at Birmingham Gaol revealed the severity of the prison regime and a number of suicides (Roberts 1986). This scandal was later the basis for the novel by Charles Reade, *Its Never too Late to Mend* published in 1856 (see also Anderson 2005).

There were also concerns about the mental health of prisoners under the separate system. Some commentators still defended Pentonville or the separate system more generally. Robert Ferguson, writing in the *Quarterly Review* in 1847, thought that the separate system did not tend to deteriorate the prisoner's mind. He felt that a 'very strong impression on the nervous system is made, and it requires careful watching to regulate it, but we believe that with such watchfulness it is not only controllable, but essential to that change of mind which reforms character' (1847: 184–5). This was a view shared by some of the chaplains who were strong defenders of the system, such as Whitworth Russell, Joseph Adshead, John Burt and John Field (Henriques 1972).

But others were beginning to question the use of the system. Joseph Kingsmill, the senior chaplain at Pentonville, later described convicts who were suffering from a range of mental illnesses ranging from insanity to 'a sort of indescribable nervous or hysterical condition' (cited in Henriques 1972: 86). This was a view shared by John Clay, who realized that there was evidence of emotional disturbance in prisoners held under the system and began to see that 'separation was an instrument to be used with caution, and that it must be broken by periods of (silent) association' (Henriques 1972: 86).

The demise of the separate system

After the dramatic decline in transportation to Australia in the early 1850s another solution had to be found to house convicts in this country. Pentonville, Millbank, Perth were used and the government rented cells in local prisons, but it had already been decided that 12 months' separate confinement was the maximum that convicts could endure. Public works were the most obvious solution although onshore institutions would have to be built to replace the hulks. The

Chairman of the Directors of Convict Prisons, Joshua Jebb, estimated that a four-year sentence was the minimum to be served, and this was to consist of one year in separate confinement and three years on public works (Tomlinson 1981). Five establishments were built or adapted between 1847 and 1874. These were Portland, Dartmoor, Portsmouth, Chatham and Borstal.

The first Penal Servitude Act 1853 introduced the sentence of penal servitude alongside that of transportation. Four to six years' penal servitude represented seven to ten years' transportation, six to eight years' penal servitude represented ten to fourteen years' transportation, but those sentenced to fourteen years to life were still sent abroad (Tomlinson 1981). Thus during the 1850s and 1860s media representations focused on prison conditions and regimes, and whether the prison was able to sufficiently to deter the offender. *The Times* argued that the question of prison discipline still remained unsolved after the end of transportation. It summed up some of the concerns of the period when commenting that they 'would wish to see a prison as a place of punishment, – not punishment as understood by the authorities of Birmingham or Leicester Gaols, but still of a character severe enough to deter evildoers from a repetition of the offences which may have brought them there' (13 October 1853).

Yet there were still concerns about less eligibility with regard to the use of labour in prisons. *The Times* was against the use of unproductive hard labour, such as the crank calling its use 'cruel and oppressive … and so utterly without result to the public'. But the newspaper still noted the great objection to prisoner labour was that it was 'unfair to the honest labourer to bring him into competition with the labourer who is fed, lodged and clothed at the expense of the State' (13 October 1853). The article concluded that the 'time has surely come when half-a-dozen men of average ability might organize a system of prison industry which should not drive the prisoners to suicide, which should not interfere with the industry of the country, and which should yet be productive of a beneficial result' (*The Times* 13 October 1853).

The second Penal Servitude Act 1857 reduced the minimum sentence of penal servitude to three years and abolished the sentence of transportation. However, throughout the period there were problems with the system. Public anxiety about convicts resulted in pressure for adequate and deterrent punishment (Tomlinson 1981). In the early 1860s, the legitimacy of the system was questioned by a number of disturbances in convict prisons. The most notable incident was at Chatham convict prison where a large-scale riot broke out involving over 800 men and control of the prison was only restored after military intervention (Brown 2003).

In 1862 there was a series of incidents often credited as the first 'moral panic' in London after a number of garottings, which were thought to have been carried out by convicts on tickets-of-leave (an early form of parole). A number of commentators have discussed the 'creation' of this panic around street violence in terms of deviancy amplification by the media (Davis 1980; Tomlinson 1981; Sindall 1987, 1990; King 2004). This outbreak of newspaper reporting of street violence does seem to have resulted in more severity in both convict and local prison policy (Davis 1980; Sindall 1990). Although Bartrip (1981) argues that the end of transportation and the concern over dealing with serious and persistent offenders in Britain was the more significant event influencing the change in penal policy. However, it is likely, as Davis notes, that the end of transportation 'forced the public mind to think of convicts' but the 'garotting panic...focused criticism and aroused public opinion to an unprecedented pitch' (1980: 196–8).

A Royal Commission was set up and, in 1864, a further Act concerning penal servitude was introduced. This Act increased the minimum sentence to five years for the first conviction and seven years for any subsequent convictions. Stricter controls were implemented on the ticket-of-leave system and the photographing of convicts began to be used to trace repeat offenders (Tomlinson 1981). The new system of penal servitude was to be administered by Edmund Du Cane who hoped it would be 'the last and most dreaded result of a heinous offence against life or property, short of capital punishment' (Parliamentary Papers 1865, cited in Tomlinson 1981: 141).

In 1865, a new Prison Act introduced greater severity into local prisons, a policy favoured by the Carnarvon Committee of 1863. This Act put into effect a deterrent approach of 'hard labour, hard board, hard fare' where long hours of hard labour, strict diet and harsh living conditions would achieve the discipline in prison it was thought necessary. This regime was more rigidly enforced after 1877 when the nationalized local prisons came under Du Cane's control (McConville 1998). Thus the Acts which followed this period of public concern were primarily concerned with introducing more deterrent and severe conditions into the prison system and although the prisoners were still held in separate cells the reformatory aims of the separate system were lost.

Conclusion

The literary and media representations of the separate system during this period reveal a number of conflicting viewpoints and concerns as to its use within the nineteenth-century prison. On the one hand there was concern about the mental health of prisoners and the number of cases of insanity under the system. On the other hand the system did not want to be seen as soft. The concerns of the public were rooted in notions of less eligibility with regard primarily to the diet in prison but also in relation to productive prison labour, general living conditions or the expense of these institutions. Despite the defence of the system by leading prison chaplains and the inspectors of prisons, by the late 1840s the separate system was increasingly coming under attack. Whether the system was effective in preventing first-time and young offenders from 'contamination', or even if it was successful in properly separating the criminal, were amongst some of the concerns frequently voiced in newspapers and by leading social commentators like Charles Dickens. However, there was also a concern with legitimacy, the prison should not be abusive to inmates and those in charge should be accountable for their actions in the operation of the prison system. The demise of the separate system as a reformatory method led to media representations that focused on whether the prison deterred offenders and how this could be better achieved. The media also highlighted public anxieties over the end of transportation and concerns about public safety and, combined with the decline of the separate system, led to a severely deterrent regime from the 1860s in both local and convict prisons that lasted until the end of the nineteenth century.

Acknowledgements

The author would like to thank Yvonne Jewkes, Paul Mason and John Locker for comments on earlier drafts of this chapter.

References

Ackroyd, P. (2002) *Dickens*. London: Vintage.
Anderson, S. (2005) '(Re)presenting scandal: Charles Reade's advocacy of professionalism within the English prison system', in B.S. Godfrey and

G. Dunstall (eds) *Crime and Empire 1840–1940: Criminal Justice in Local and Global Context*. Cullompton: Willan Publishing.

Bartrip, P. (1981) 'Public opinion and law enforcement: the ticket of leave scares in mid-Victorian Britain', in V. Bailey (ed.) *Policing and Punishment in Nineteenth Century Britain*. London: Croom Helm.

Brown, A. (2003) *English Society and the Prison: Time, Culture and Politics in the Development of the Modern Prison, 1850–1920*. Woodbridge: Boydell.

Collins, P. (1962) *Dickens and Crime*. London: Macmillan.

Davis, J. (1980) 'The London garotting panic of 1862: a moral panic and the creation of a criminal class in mid-Victorian England', in V.A.C. Gatrell *et al.* (eds) *Crime and the Law: The Social History of Crime in Western Europe since 1500*. London: Europa.

DeLacy, M. (1981) '"Grinding men good?" Lancashire's prisons at mid-century' in V. Bailey (ed.) *Policing and Punishment in the Nineteenth Century*. London: Croom Helm.

DeLacy, M. (1986) *Prison Reform in Lancashire, 1700–1850 – a study in Local Administration*. Manchester: Manchester University Press.

Dickens, C. (1842/1906) *American Notes*. London: Collins.

Dickens, C. (1849/50/1994) *David Copperfield*. London: Penguin.

Ferguson, R. (1847) 'Pentonville prisoners', *Quarterly Review*, 82: 175–206.

Forsythe, W.J. (1987) *The Reform of Prisoners 1830–1900*. London: Croom Helm.

Foucault, M. (1991) *Discipline and Punish – The Birth of the Prison*. London: Penguin Books.

Henriques, U.R.S. (1972) 'The rise and decline of the separate system', *Past and Present*, 54: 61–93.

Ignattief, M. (1978) *A Just Measure of Pain: The Penitentiary in the Industrial Revolution 1750–1850*. London: Macmillan.

Jewkes, Y. (2002) *Captive Audience: Media, Masculinity and Power in Prisons*. Cullompton: Willan Publishing.

Johnston, H. (2004) 'The transformations of imprisonment in a local context: Shrewsbury prison in the nineteenth century.' Unpublished PhD thesis, Keele University.

King, P. (2004) 'Moral panics and violent street crime 1750–2000: a comparative perspective', in B.S. Godfrey *et al.* (eds) *Comparative Histories of Crime*. Cullompton: Willan Publishing.

McConville, S. (1981) *A History of Prison Administration 1750–1877. Volume One*. London: Routledge & Kegan Paul.

McConville, S. (1998) 'The Victorian prison, 1865–1965', in N. Morris and D.J. Rothman (eds) *The Oxford History of the Prison – The Practice of Punishment in Western Society*. Oxford: Oxford University Press.

McGowen, R. (1998) 'The well-ordered prison: England, 1780–1865', in N. Morris and D.J. Rothman (eds) *The Oxford History of the Prison – The Practice of Punishment in Western Society*. Oxford: Oxford University Press.

Melossi, D. and Pavarini, M. (1981) *The Prison and the Factory – Origins of the Penitentiary System*. London: Macmillan.

Pratt, J. (2004) 'The acceptable prison: official discourse, truth and legitimacy in the nineteenth century', in G. Gilligan and J. Pratt (eds) *Crime, Truth and Justice – Official Inquiry, Discourse, Knowledge*. Cullompton: Willan Publishing.

Roberts, D. (1986) 'The scandal at Birmingham Borough Gaol 1853: a case for penal reform', *Journal of Legal History*, 7: 315–40.

Sindall, R. (1987) 'The London garotting panics of 1856 and 1862', *Social History*, 12: 351–9.

Sindall, R. (1990) *Street Violence in the Nineteenth Century: Media Panic or Real Danger?* Leicester: Leicester University Press.

Sparks, R. (1996) 'Penal "austerity": the doctrine of less eligibility reborn?', in R. Matthews and P. Francis (eds) *Prisons 2000*. London: Palgrave.

Stockdale, E. (1983) 'A short history of prison inspection in England', *British Journal of Criminology*, 23: 209–28.

Tomlinson, M.H. (1978) '"Not an instrument of punishment": prison diet in the mid nineteenth century', *Journal of Consumer Studies and Home Economics*, 2: 15–26.

Tomlinson, M.H. (1981) 'Penal servitude 1846–1865: a system in evolution', in V. Bailey (ed.) *Policing and Punishment in Nineteenth Century Britain*. London: Croom Helm.

Webb, S. and Webb, B. (1963) *English Prisons under Local Government*. London: Frank Cass.

Wilson, A.N. (2003) *The Victorians*. London: Arrow.

Wilson, D. (2002) 'Millbank, the panopticon and their Victorian audiences', *Howard Journal*, 41: 364–81.

Chapter 8

Undermining the simplicities: the films of Rex Bloomstein

Jamie Bennett

Introduction: prisoners, offenders and the media

From Jack the Ripper to O.J. Simpson and Dr Caligari to Dr Lector, crime and criminal justice have come to dominate the news and entertainment media. This is now so central to our daily experiences that it has been argued that 'The fascination with criminal activity and law enforcement is at the very heart of popular culture' (Schlesinger and Tumber 1994: 6). This trend, it has been suggested, has had a serious impact on society: trivializing and sensationalizing crime (Krajicek 1998), increasing fear out of proportion to reality (Altheide 2002), undermining the jury system (Hargreaves 2003), perpetuating the interests of powerful political or economic groups (Chomsky 1991) and promoting a conservative or even retrogressive agenda in criminal justice policies (Wykes 2001; Wilson 2003).

Prisons in particular are secret, hidden worlds largely unknown to the public. For many, the closest they will get to prisons is through the media and therefore this is critical in shaping their views:

> [P]eople use knowledge they obtain from the media to construct a picture of the world, an image of reality on which they base their actions. This process, sometimes called 'the social construction of reality', is particularly important in the realm of crime, justice, and the media (Surette 1997: 1; see also Levenson 2001; Wilson and O'Sullivan 2004).

Prison officials have been poor at allowing access and are sceptical about the media (Schwartz 1989; Turnbo 1994; Levenson 2001; Kirby 2003). Quantitative research on news stories shows that corrections are poorly covered (Ericson *et al.* 1991; Chermak 1998). The content of these stories is often exceptional events such as riots, escapes and release of dangerous prisoners, with little considered analysis of day-to-day operations (Chermak 1998; Levenson 2001). The result of this is that most people do not know that 75,000 people are in UK prisons; in fact they can't even fathom a guess at how many there are (Roberts 2002), let alone have accurate knowledge about how they get there, what happens to them inside and what happens after they are released.

In this information vacuum, many people will obtain their main information about prisons from media representations (Gillespie *et al.* 2003). This will be central to the social construction of reality. Professor David Wilson has suggested that 'ultimately when we present an image of prison we shape the public's expectation about what prison is like, and what happens inside, of who prisoners are and what they have done' (2003: 28). These views have been further developed, suggesting that media depictions of prisons shape views by providing an insight into a world that the general public know little about: they provide a benchmark for acceptable treatment of prisoners, translate academic and political concerns into digestible narratives, expose perspectives often at odds with official descriptions and create empathy with prisoners and staff (Wilson and O'Sullivan 2004).

Despite the power of the media to shape public views about prison and offenders, this responsibility has not always been sensitively handled (Nellis 1981; Zaner 1989; Levenson 2001). However, in more than 30 years of documentary film-making, Rex Bloomstein has produced powerful and enlightening films covering the criminal justice system in the UK. These films have gone beyond the simple media portrayal and provided a closer look at reality of criminal justice. This chapter introduces the context of Rex Bloomstein's work and art, then explores the major themes in his films about the criminal justice system in the UK (for further writings, see also Bennett 2003a, 2003b, 2004a, 2004b).

Introducing Rex Bloomstein

Bloomstein was brought up by a working-class family in East London, and decided he wanted to become a documentary film-maker after seeing the influential film *7-Up* (1963). He left school at 16 to take up a short-lived post with Lew Grade's ATV. Following this he spent several years learning the trade in sponsored commercial documentaries until he landed a post with the BBC in 1966. He eventually gained an attachment and directors training with the documentary department, where he made *The Patient is the Family* (1969) about family therapy. However, he resigned in 1970 when no permanent post became available. From here, Bloomstein entered the world of independent documentary film-making, a world he has never left.

His earliest independent films included a number of entries in *Day in the Life* series (1970), such as *The Launch*, about the launch of a super tanker in Newcastle; *The City*, a day in the life of Sheffield; *The Candidate*, about the selection of a Labour Party candidate; and *The Auction*, a day in the life at Sothebys. Stirred by his sense of iniquity, arising from his humble origins, Bloomstein soon started to explore the marginalized and forgotten figures that populate much of his later work.

His first film about the criminal justice system was *The Sentence* (1976), the recreation of the sentencing of a petty thief in King's Lynn, a film that invited viewers to explore the reality of sentencing decisions. He followed this up with *Release* (1976), which followed newly released prisoner Charlie Smith and his attempts to resettle into the community, and *Prisoners' Wives* (1977), which examined the impact on those left behind. The natural next step was to film inside prisons, which he did for the first time in the 1979 film *Parole*. This described the parole process and featured interviews with four prisoners applying for early release, again confronting viewers with the complexity of decision-making with offenders. This was followed by the eight-part series *Strangeways* (1980), an intimate study of HMP Manchester that remains one of the most important films to be made on prisons, a film cited as an inspiration for a future Director General to join the Prison Service (Narey 2002). In 1983, *Lifer* was made, another important film, this time looking at the life-sentence process and the diverse people serving that sentence. The interviews filmed for this were also developed into a seven-part TV series, *Lifers* (1984). In 2000, Bloomstein made *Strangeways Revisited*, in which he returned to the prison he had documented 20 years before. His most recent film was *Lifer: Living With Murder* (2003), a follow-up to *Lifer* and *Lifers*, in which he spoke to some of those he first interviewed two decades ago.

During these years, Bloomstein also made a number of other documentaries that explore his concerns about international human rights, such as *Prisoners of Conscience* (1988), and Jewish history such as *Auschwitz and the Allies* (1982) and *The Longest Hatred* (1991).

The cinema of truth

Bloomstein was influenced by the *Cinema Verité* school (literally cinema of truth). This term has now become synonymous with a particular style of fictional film-making, using hand-held camera and naturalistic dialogue. Television programmes such as *Hill Street Blues* (1981–7) and *The Cops* (1998–2001) are typical examples. In documentary film, it has now metamorphosized into the ubiquitous docu-soap, a cheap and popular form of production more focused on creating everyday stars than illuminating their milieu or lives. However, this originally emerged as a distinct and exciting approach to film-making. In documentary, it was the result of the invention of portable sound recording, allowing film-makers to take to the streets to film the lives and thoughts of everyday people. It moved away from poetic films with soothing music and narrated voice-overs to a more spontaneous, direct form of cinema that was aesthetically more real and ideologically more democratic (MacDonald and Cousins 1997).

Bloomstein has remained loyal to *Verité*. His films focus on people in their environment, capturing genuine, spontaneous emotions. His philosophy seems close to that of the early *Verité* practitioner, the French film-maker Jean Rouch, who saw films as most effective both artistically and ideologically when dealing with marginalized people, challenging cultural myths: 'it is a question of throwing light on truth which is hidden from us by the particular prejudices and social values and conventions of our time' (Issari and Paul 1979: 80). Like Rouch, he uses the people he portrays both to tell their own personal stories and to illuminate the wider social issues raised by their plight. As Rouch himself commented:

> [I]t is a very strange kind of confession in front of camera where the camera is, let's say, a mirror, and also a window open to the outside. It may be the only way out for these persons who have some trouble, to open this window and to say to other people what their troubles are (Issari and Paul 1979: 73).

In this way, the films are a reflection of both individual stories and how they illustrate wider social issues; the social and human conditions.

125

It could be argued that, although Bloomstein's techniques are broadly based on the *Verité* approach, some, such as narration, inter-titles, the extensive use of interviews and occasionally, where access dictates, reconstruction, are directive and therefore the antithesis of this approach (Mamber 1974). However, an over-reliance on technique can obscure the fundamental philosophy of both these films and the *Verité* school. Bloomstein uses a variety of techniques in order to address real people, slowly unpeeling the lives and emotions, layer by layer, and allowing a more complex, nuanced picture to emerge. Communicating with this world and through it to the audience are the primary considerations. Technical and aesthetic dogmatism is secondary to this philosophical drive in his films and to the integrity of *Cinema Verité* (Schrader 1971).

By exploring issues that are important to us as citizens and a community and by giving voice to ignored and marginalized figures, Bloomstein illuminates a critical area. By showing crime and punishment through these individual stories, he goes beyond the headlines, allowing the subtlety and complexity to emerge. This is the truth, this is *Verité*.

Public perception and prejudice

Bloomstein's films often open with descriptions that capture the received wisdom of the subject and offer a challenge. In *Lifer* a title reads: 'A LIFE SENTENCE must be imposed for MURDER – and may be given for other crimes such as MANSLAUGHTER, ATTEMPTED MURDER, ARSON, ARMED ROBBERY, RAPE, BUGGERY and INCEST' (emphasis in original).

Confronting the viewer with these crimes evokes an emotional response, a gut feeling. In Bloomstien's words, 'when you think of a murder, rightly, you think of someone who has done a heinous crime. In our tabloid age these people usually become simply dehumanized monsters'. Such a view is hardly surprising when there is a disproportional emphasis on violent and sexual crime in news coverage (Reiner *et al.* 2003) and official reports scream about how 'the public are sick and tired' of serious offenders getting off lightly (Home Office 2002) despite the fact that serious violent crime is falling, detection improving and sentencing becoming increasingly severe (Tonry 2004). Bloomstein then sets about challenging this simplistic view, 'giv[ing] a sense of the complexity that underlines surrounds human action…undermining the simplicities' (this and other direct quotations from Bennett 2003a, 2003b).

In *Lifer*, he shows that those serving life sentences cover a great diversity of circumstances: cold-blooded executions, drunken mishaps, naïve accomplices, crimes of passion and revenge. He also shows the diversity of people, from intelligent and articulate people, disturbed and damaged individuals, the immature, unlucky and flawed personalities. They are also shown in a range of different stages, from the shock of early conviction through the long, slow road of acceptance and change through to release. He allows those people to speak for themselves in order to communicate how they ended up in that situation and how it has affected them and those around them. Simply in its scale and range, the film challenges any preconceived ideas, giving a depiction at odds with the tabloid view and building empathy. As one prisoner says at the end of the film, 'I hope the general public will see I haven't got two heads'.

This technique is also used in other films, such as *Parole* where it is revealed that 'In this year alone there are over three thousand prisoners serving their sentence outside the wall' and in *Release*, Charlie Smith is introduced as 'One of the tens of thousands of people released from prison each year'. *Prisoners' Wives* confronts the viewer with the extent of ignorance and neglect, revealing that 'No one knows how many wives, children and dependants there are of men in prison'. Again, the underlying purpose and aim of these films are to build a more complex picture that challenges the received wisdom.

Within the films the subjects themselves may also offer this challenge to stigmatizing stereotypes. In *Prisoners' Wives*, for example, Lorraine describes the reaction of other people: 'It's as if I've done it as well…It's like I'm involved…I'm to blame as well for what happened.' In *Lifer: Living with Murder*, Trevor describes how he cannot become a full member of the community. He challenges us to consider how we would respond to hearing that our next-door neighbour was a life sentence prisoner, how forgiving or accepting would we be? 'Ask yourself what you would think.'

A variety of techniques are deployed throughout the films to challenge perceptions. This may be in formal settings such as the solicitor in *The Sentence* who, in his summing-up, shows that commonplace crime is committed by people who are 'not so much a menace to society as a nuisance'. There are also more informal challenges to perceptions. One episode from *Strangeways* entitled *They*

Call us Beasts, follows the residents of the Rule 43 Unit, for those who are segregated for their own protection, either because of the nature of their offence (i.e. often sexual offences) or because they have been the victims of bullying. The film cuts between a group of prisoners and a group of staff discussing the residents. Whilst some seek to characterize all of them as 'beasts', others argue that some of them have been the unfair victims of bullying, so each individual should be taken at face value. Capturing this everyday discussion provides the moral context for the viewer, asking the questions and providing the perspectives that go beyond the label (for further discussion, see Mason 1995).

However, the most powerful tool used is by allowing these people to speak for themselves in long, largely uninterrupted interviews. Here they talk about who they are, what they have done, how they and others have been affected and their attempts to rebuild their lives. Bloomstein has described:

> That is the essence of my work, to present people as human beings and to try and reduce the happenings around so that you get a real sense of personality, of humanness ... How far can you go in really questioning, exploring, needling away at what they really feel, what their response really means?

This is a painful experience both for the viewer and the interviewee, but is a critical learning experience: 'It's this human capacity to reflect, and be able to articulate that reflection ... They paused, were sometimes silent, and told their distressing stories ... of course there were terrible, terrible revelations.'

In his films, Bloomstein avoids the easy answers, he confronts us with our gut reaction and deploys *Verité* techniques to look deeper and more sensitively at the people and issues. In doing so, a picture develops that does not match the common simplicities and challenges people to think again: 'The techniques that I have developed are designed to make you feel, and think, more about a particular theme or subject so you are no longer quite the same, you no longer have the same simple reaction to it – if you stay with it.'

Understanding the prison machine

The dynamic relationship between people and process is a central theme in Bloomstein's work. People with their unique individuality, character and fallibility contrasted with process and its rigorous requirement for conformity, uniformity and control. This is particularly important in criminal justice, with its monolithic bureaucracies, often hidden from public view. These films are educative in as much as they invite the viewer to understand how important decisions are made in the criminal justice process, but they are also ideological in that they ask questions about what the application of these processes says about the ethics of these organizations.

Lifer is the most extensive depiction of a criminal justice process in Bloomstein's work, but is also perhaps the most simple. It follows, in a way that makes it straightforward, the life sentence from remand and conviction through to release and recall. The film describes how this sentence works and, armed with this knowledge, the viewer can understand our approach to the most serious offenders. Given the scale, complexity and importance of the life-sentence system, this is an important achievement in itself.

On the face of it, *The Sentence* simply recreates a process. The sentencing of petty thief David Cross is re-enacted using all the same participants, lawyers, magistrates and clerks, saying all the same things they said at the original hearing. So, the film shows exactly what happens in the court. In this respect, it shows the external manifestation of the system. However, the film goes further and invites the audience to consider the real decision-making process. There are background and interviews with David, so the audience know about him and his history and there are interviews with the officials, who explain their roles and the main criteria they use in their decisions. In effect, the audience is given a toolkit to decide whether or not David should be sent to prison. In this way, the film moves the viewer from simple observer to a kind of participant-observer, actively considering these real-life decisions. In doing so, the viewer becomes inducted into the complexities of the criminal justice system. A similar technique is used in *Parole* where four prisoners are interviewed and then, after explanation of how the decisions are made, four similar cases are discussed and heard by the Parole Board. This approach offers a deeper educative function, giving direct insight into these decisions. By strengthening understanding in this way, Bloomstein offers the viewer the ability more closely to question these vital decisions, potentially democratizing the process and improving accountability.

Processes also reflect the values and culture of organizations (Schein 1985). At times, Bloomstein seems to use these not only to illustrate but also to challenge these values and cultures. In the first episode of *Strangeways*, entitled *The Human Warehouse*, the acute crisis facing the prison is laid bare. This eerily mirrors the findings of Lord Woolf's report a decade later following the worst series of riots in UK prison history, which started at Strangeways prison (Woolf and Tumin 1990). In this report, Woolf concluded that the main causes of the disturbances were:

- insanitary and overcrowded conditions;
- negative and unconstructive regimes;
- prisoners treated with a lack of respect;
- destructive effects on family relationships; and
- lack of independent redress for grievances.

One prisoner summed up this general failure of justice and fairness in the film: 'We've no rights in here.' The end of the episode shows prisoner applications to the Board of Visitors, independent monitors of prisons reporting directly to the Home Secretary. These applications are shown to be a sham; prisoners are marched in, forced to stand in front of the large Board seated around a table, their complaint is then responded to by the Governor and the Chair of the Board repeats this without any rigorous challenge and the still aggrieved prisoner is told that his next recourse is through a Kafkaesque petition to the Home Secretary. This process lacks the independence, fairness or transparency to give it credibility. It is a manifestation of the crisis faced by the prison.

The Human Warehouse also questions how the community has allowed the prison system to become dehumanized. Population pressures are described as forcing prisoners to be held in inhumane conditions. Prisoners are described as 'numbers' and the Governor of the prison describes it as the 'human warehouse' of the title. Bloomstein described the prison in process-like terms: 'Lock them, unlock them, feed them creating a sort of machine-like atmosphere in which people entered into, experienced and went out.' In simple terms, he said of the experience of imprisonment in Strangeways: 'It was a hell of an experience.' The drive to increase the use of imprisonment has forced the human element to be lost, the prison is shown as becoming a cold logistical procedure.

Understanding process, then, is central to these films. First, the films provide the awareness people need to act as informed citizens and invites them actively to consider the complexity of decision-making in the criminal justice system. Secondly, they show how the procedure and operation of institutions, including prisons, reflect beliefs, values and culture. With remarkable foresight, Bloomstein exposed the lack of fairness and justice in prisons that was to explode so catastrophically a decade later.

From prisoners to people

The *Verité* style was based on giving voice to everyday people. It is unsurprising then that people being interviewed or observed are fundamental to these films. Bloomstein always manages to find lucid, articulate subjects who can animate the critical issues as well as providing their own unique experiences. Occasionally, these individuals are so powerful that they overwhelm the subject, but the best of these human stories provide the most powerful examples of Bloomstein's art.

Release follows Charlie Smith, in the first few weeks following his discharge from Maidstone prison, facing familiar difficulties, with no family support, no job and no accommodation. However, Charlie is an exceptional and charismatic person, a dominating presence. Although he is a virtual destitute, he harbours ambitions to become a commercial designer. He hawks his prison-made models around various companies, throws his first commission back at the company when he does not get an unambiguously positive response and then finally lands a placement he hopes may lead to better things. This is an unusual and fascinating tale but that very quality means that it is not typical and cannot be generalized. In other films, unusual, extroverted and charismatic individuals are used, but are weaved into a larger canvass.

The three *Prisoners' Wives* films are perhaps the most effective in Bloomstein's canon, using the words and experiences of individuals with extraordinary results. The films look into the lives of three women: Eileen seen during her husband's trial and conviction; Lorraine, who gives birth to her and her husband's child alone whilst he serves a prison sentence; and Kathy who prepares for her husband's release. These women face problems that have social significance, including stigma or rejection (Eileen – '[There's] no pity towards the [wives]…even a bit of respect would help'), economic hardship (Kathy – '[It] feels like you're begging off everyone'), deteriorating relationships (Lorraine – 'I don't want to see him like that. I don't want to see him in there') and a lack of support (Kathy – 'Prison only really punishes the family…it's not like they make any effort to help the wife'). These women show, with their own words and actions, the issues faced by many partners of prisoners, illuminating issues often restricted to academic debate. On another level, these films also show in a more intimate way the emotional experiences of these three women. Lorraine is confused about her feelings towards her husband's offence. At one stage, she rejects his culpability: 'I don't think he did it.' However, at other times she seems to accept what has happened: 'It's done. There's now't we can do about that.' It is as if she is slowly working her way through her feelings and her reaction to what has happened, trying to come to some kind of equilibrium, but also fearing that this will be illusory: 'It seems like end of the rainbow-type thing.' In these films, both the social issues and the unique individual experiences are blended to create a rich work.

The combination of using everyday experiences to raise issues of wider social significance, but also showing the intimate, emotional drama of everyday life is typical of both Bloomstein and the *Verité* style. Like Rouch, Bloomstein uses his films to explore the world of marginalized figures and gives them an opportunity both to reflect on their own personality and to project wider issues. These films explore their human experiences and their social conditions.

Doing time or using time

The films of Rex Bloomstein have a sense of time. This is not only time in a passive sense that time ticks by, but also in the sense that people, processes and places change over time, or in some cases fail to change. This is most obvious in films like *Strangeways Revisited* or *Lifer: Living with Murder* where he goes back to interview the same people 20 years later. His films also reach back to give a sense of the history of individuals and reach forward to see their potential. In this way, he raises questions about how and why these people, processes and places change or do not. In Bloomstein's own words: '[T]here is something valuable about asking…can you change? How have you developed in your thinking? How has the system altered and what effect has this had on you?' In following life-sentence prisoners on the long road from conviction to release, *Lifer* and its follow-up give a sense of both time and its impact on individuals. This is not always a positive message. Some of the prisoners have made little or no progress in 20 years and still languish in prison. Some of those who have been released do not necessarily feel they have changed for the better. In the original film, one person who had been released from a life sentence and so could be said to be a 'success', says: 'I'm not a person any more. I've got the shape of a person but emotionally I'm hollow. There's just nothing there any more.'

In *Lifer: Living with Murder*, Steve is shown as a young man in 1983, constantly fighting the system. He states: 'If they can't control you physically, they use the drugs...and of course it affects you permanently.' The scene cuts to Steve now held in a secure hospital, aged beyond his years, mumbling and slurring to such an extent that he can only be understood through subtitles. He tells of how his quality of life has improved, how he can now go outside and how he can better control himself. However, the viewer is inevitably drawn into asking of this real-life clockwork orange: at what cost has this progress been made?

However, some prisoners do change and in *Strangeways Revisited* some of the positive actions of prisons and prison staff are shown to help some individuals to change. These are stories of 'hope and redemption' that are critical to success in the criminal justice system. Terry McDonald, who was in his thirties with a long institutional record in 1980, was shown making an escorted visit to his daughter in hospital after she was knocked over by a car. This incident helped to motivate him to start rebuilding his life with his family, outside crime. Norman Flavell also told of how he started to change his life when an officer in the segregation unit 'threw half an ounce on the bed, parked his arse' and confronted him with his options. This is an amazing story of how the casual humanity of some people can inspire change in others. This was one of Bloomstein's 'pockets of humanity...There are always humane things going on, a kindness here or there'.

At times, the past can dictate the present and the future. Paul Wood was an angelic-looking 16-year-old in the first series; the follow-up tells us that he was found dead in the Salford docks at 23. His sisters describe how, along with Paul, they had been physically abused by their father and how Paul had started to repeat this. He was violent towards them and to his wife: 'He was just like my dad.' The cycle of history was coming around. Vinnie Valente, a flamboyant hard-man in the original films, had hardly changed his ways, 18 months of freedom being his longest spell on the outside in 20 years. We see him in a pub, boasting of his exploits to young wannabes. Just when it seems that he is a lost cause, he reveals that he is due to give evidence in court against the care workers who abused him in a home as a child. This devastating revelation casts light on a hidden side, a hidden history that has perhaps shaped his life.

Bloomstein, and those he presents, are also acutely aware of the victims of their crimes, particularly those who have taken lives. For those, as the title of his latest film suggests, they live with murder. They live with the knowledge of what they have done. For some, like Trevor, it takes many years to acknowledge and when the realization dawns, they have pitifully small emotion with which to express it. For others, like Joyce, the guilt drives them to despair, attempted suicide and emotional breakdown. For her, there is a constant memory of the life taken: 'It's there all the time, but I just live with it…It's not something I'll ever forget.' These people are not just living with the life sentence, they are also living with murder.

Bloomstein is a prison reformer who, whilst recognizing that 'humanity' in prisons has improved, is clearly frustrated that 'For the majority, the punishment they receive will neither reform nor rehabilitate' (from *Strangeways*). More than that, he is disappointed that the rehabilitative ideal remains elusive over the last two decades: 'Much has changed, but one thing has not, over half of the adult men released from prison are reconvicted within two years' (from *Strangeways Revisited*).

Whilst for some people, a chance happening or a casual remark can be the spark that starts a change, for many others their problems are either not addressed or not recognized. For Bloomstein, too often time is just ticking by and life is too valuable for that.

Conclusion: the films of Rex Bloomstein

Rex Bloomstein has stood aside from the general trends in media coverage of serious crime. He has attempted to present a more complex and substantial depiction of the criminal justice system.

It has been identified that the media shape public views about prisons by providing an insight into a world that the general public know little about and have little direct experience of, they provide a benchmark for acceptable treatment of prisoners, translate academic and political concerns into digestible narratives, expose perspectives that are often at odds with media and official descriptions and create empathy with prisoners and prison staff (Wilson and O'Sullivan 2004). Bloomstein's films give substantial insights into this world not only through illustrating the criminal justice system, but by drawing the viewer into participating in complex decisions. They provide a benchmark for decent treatment, often highlighting how prejudice and insensitive procedures produce injustice and unfairness, also showing how positive treatment can be a catalyst for change in individuals.

He goes behind the headlines to show real experiences and exposes how decisions affect individuals, using their personal stories to raise issues of wider social significance. His long interviews undermine the simplicities of common depictions of offenders, showing them with all their ambiguity, complexity and fallibility, showing a less ideological, more empathetic picture of these marginalized groups.

It is in these ways that Bloomstein has built up a substantial body of work that delivers high standards of film-making craft and produces pressure for reform. Although these films have been made against a depressing backdrop of increasing prisoner populations, deafening political polemic on law and order and questionable media coverage, he has created and maintained an important media space for more considered and thoughtful reflection on these issues. The fact that such coverage is so rare only makes Bloomstein's work more important.

References

Altheide, D.L. (2002) *Creating Fear: News and the Construction of Crisis.* New York, NY: Aldine De Gruyter

Bennett, J. (2003a) 'The interview: Rex Bloomstein', *Prison Service Journal*, 148: 53–9.

Bennett, J. (2003b) 'The films of Rex Bloomstein', *Prison Service Journal*, 150: 41–5.

Bennett, J. (2004a) 'Lifer: Living with Murder (2003)', *Prison Service Journal*, 151: 62–4.

Bennett, J. (2004b) 'Life lessons: Rex Bloomstein's lifer films', in *Journal of Crime, Conflict and the Media*, 1: 43–54.

Chermak, S.M. (1998) 'Police, courts, and corrections in the media' in F. Bailey and D. Hale (eds) *Popular Culture, Crime, and Justice.* Belmont: West/Wadsworth.

Chomsky, N. (1991) *Media Control: The Spectacular Achievements of Propaganda.* New York, NY: Seven Stories.

Ericson, R.V., Baranek, P.M. and Chan, J.B.L. (1991) *Representing Order: Crime, Law and Justice in the News Media.* Milton Keynes: Open University Press.

Gillespie, M., McLaughlin, E., Adams, S. and Symmonds, A. (2003) *Media and the Shaping of Public Knowledge and Attitudes Towards Crime and Punishment.* London: Rethinking Crime and Punishment.

Hargreaves, I. (2003) *Journalism: Truth or Dare?* Oxford: Oxford University Press.

Home Office (2002) *Justice for All.* London: Home Office.

Issari, M. and Paul, D. (1979) *What is Cinema Verite?* Metuchen, NJ and London: Scarecrow Press.

Kirby, D. (2003) 'Prison life through a lens', *Prison Service News*, 215: 22–3.

Krajicek, D.J. (1998) *Scooped! Media Miss Real Story on Crime while Chasing Sex, Sleaze, and Celebrities*. New York, NY: Colombia University Press.

Levenson, J. (2001) 'Inside information: prisons and the media', *Criminal Justice Matters*, 43: 14–15.

MacDonald, K. and Cousins M. (1997) *Imagining Reality: The Faber Book of Documentary*. London: Faber and Faber.

Mamber, S. (1974) *Cinema Verite in America*. Massachusetts: Massachusetts Institute of Technology Press.

Mason, P. (1995) 'Prime time punishment: the British prison and television' in D. Kidd-Hewitt and R. Osborne (eds) *Crime and the Media: The Postmodern Spectacle*. London: Pluto Press.

Narey, M. (2002) 'Human rights, decency and social exclusion', *Prison Service Journal*, 142: 25–8.

Nellis, M. (1981) 'Notes on the American prison film', in M. Nellis and C. Hale (eds) *The Prison Film*. London: Alternatives to Prison.

Reiner, R., Livingstone, S. and Allen, J. (2003) 'From law and order to lynch mobs: crime news since the Second World War', in P. Mason (ed.) *Criminal Visions: Media Representations of Crime and Justice*. Cullompton: Willan Publishing.

Roberts, J.V. (2002) 'Public opinion and sentencing policy', in S. Rex and M. Tonry (eds) *Reform and Punishment: The Future of Sentencing*. Cullompton: Willan Publishing.

Schein, E.H. (1985) *Organisational Culture and Leadership*. Oxford: Jossey Bass.

Schlesinger, P. and Tumber, H. (1994) *Reporting Crime: the Media Politics of Criminal Justice*. Oxford: Clarendon Press.

Schrader, P. *Roberto Rossellini: The Rise of Louis XIV in Cinema* Vol. 6 No. 3 (1971) reproduced in Jackson, K. (ed.) *Schrader on Schrader and Other Writings* (Faber and Faber: London 1992).

Schwartz, J.A. (1989) 'Promoting a good public image: effective leadership, sound practices make the difference', *Corrections Today*, 51: 38–41.

Surette, R. (1997) *Media, Crime, and Criminal Justice* (2nd edn). Belmont, CA: West/Wadsworth.

Tonry, M. (2004) *Punishment and Politics: Evidence and Emulation in the Making of English Crime Control Policy*. Cullompton: Willan Publishing.

Turnbo, C. (1994) 'News at eleven', *Federal Prisons Journal*, 3: 47–50.

Woolf, H. and Tumin, S. (1991) *Prison Disturbances April 1990*. London: HMSO.

Wilson, D. (2003) 'Lights, camera, action', *Prison Report*, 60: 27–9.

Wilson, D. and O'Sullivan, S. (2004) *Images of Incarceration: Representations of Prison in Film and Television Drama*. Winchester: Waterside Press.

Wykes, M. (2001) *News, Crime and Culture*. London: Pluto Press.

Zaner, L. (1989) 'The screen test: has Hollywood hurt corrections' image?', *Corrections Today*, 51: 64–6, 95, 98.

Chapter 9

Creating a stir? Prisons, popular media and the power to reform

Yvonne Jewkes

Whilst not as prevalent as the TV detective, the world of prisons and prisoners has now permeated most television genres: sit-com (*Porridge*), 'serious' drama (*Buried, Oz*), light entertainment drama (*Within these Walls, Bad Girls, The Governor, Prisoner*), documentary (*Strangeways, Lifer: Living with Murder, Jailbirds, Prison Weekly, Feltham Sings*) and reality TV (*The Experiment, The Real Bad Girls*), to name but a few. Even soaps have got in the act and although scenes of incarceration are not featured as regularly as court rooms and police interview suites, characters in all the major British soaps have faced jail terms, most famously *Coronation Street*'s Deidre Rachid who, in 1998, won the backing of the Prime Minister during the 'Free the Weatherfield One' campaign. Whilst these programmes span multiple genres and are very different in style and purpose, their common mission to entertain (i.e. to maximize audience figures) is unquestionable. But to what extent is it the role of programmes such as *Porridge* and *Bad Girls* to inform and educate as well? If the backdrop is a prison, does television comedy, drama and light entertainment have a duty to encourage discussion and debate about imprisonment? Is it – as some have claimed (Wilson and O'Sullivan 2004) – the role of the popular media to advance the cause of penal reform? And if media producers do indeed have a mission to reveal the grim realities of life in prison, does it necessarily follow that audiences will be receptive to the message?

These questions will underpin the discussion that follows in three parts. The chapter begins by exploring three alternative ways of 'decoding' the classic BBC sit-com *Porridge*, locating the inmates of

Slade Prison within contemporaneous penal discourse and policy. The question of whether it is important or desirable for fictional television portrayals of confinement to be accurate and whether it is incumbent upon television writers and producers to encourage prison reform through their creative output will then be analysed using ITV's *Bad Girls* as an example of a television text that strives for realism as well as ratings. In the third and final section, the issue of whether mainstream entertainment media can set an agenda for prison reform will be set within the context of wider discourses of imprisonment – played out in the pages of the popular press – which serve to reinforce pejorative attitudes to prisons and construct prisoners as an undeserving underclass. Newspaper reporting of prisons provides an essential counterpoint to fictional representations in the broadcast media and it is important to remember that, whilst the vast majority of people have no direct knowledge of imprisonment, their mediated experience is wider than simply what they see on the television or cinema screen. It is within this broader framework that audience antipathy to prisoners will be explored.

Porridge: sheer grit or mere wit?

Of all TV programmes set in prison, the one generally cited as the source of most people's 'knowledge' about imprisonment is the BBC comedy *Porridge*; in fact, Wilson and O'Sullivan go so far as to cite *Porridge* as 'probably the major influence on the British public's understanding of prison today' (2004: 7). The series, which ran from 1974 to 1977, became an iconic stalwart of British comedy, with 21 episodes (including the pilot and two 'specials'), plus a sequel entitled *Going Straight*, a US version called *On the Rocks* (1975–6) and *Porridge* the feature film (1979). But whilst the antics of Fletcher, Godber, Grout, Mr MacKay and Mr Barrowclough made HMP Slade as much a part of the British mediascape as the Rover's Return or the Fawlty Towers Hotel, *Porridge* divides expert opinion concerning the extent to which it can be described as an accurate or realistic portrayal of prisons. Broadly speaking there are three divergent opinions concerning the importance and impact of Britain's most famous TV portrayal of a prison.

The first is the view that the prison setting is entirely immaterial. *Porridge* is a depiction of human relationships, particularly the friendship between old-time, persistent criminal Norman Fletcher (played by Ronnie Barker) and his cell-mate, naïve first-time offender

Lennie Godber (Richard Beckinsale). It is this relationship that lies at the heart of the programme and gives rise not only to some of the best one-liners but also much of the programme's warmth and depth. In this sense, *Porridge* is no different from many other British sit-coms (nor for that matter from prison-buddy movies such as *The Shawshank Redemption*). *Open All Hours, The Likely Lads, Steptoe and Son, Only Fools and Horses, Yes Minister* and *Blackadder* all have at their comic heart a dynamic between two men; one a confident, cunning, quick-witted, sophisticated or streetwise father-figure/mentor; the other a gullible or innocent, but likeable, dreamer. In sit-com, then, it is the former's ambition or the latter's romantic naivety that lands the pair in trouble and provides the comic potential for each episode as – in the classic tradition of narrative devices – they move from equilibrium, through conflict, to resolution. The success of *Porridge*, in this interpretation, lies in the fact that the action takes place in a highly restricted world where the focus is on dialogue and characterization (the writers of *Porridge*, Dick Clement and Ian La Frenais, had been trying to come up with a show that was essentially two men talking in a room for 12 years, since the *Hancock* episode 'The Lift' had demonstrated the comic potential of people stuck in a confined space; http://www.bbc.co.uk/comedy). To this extent, then, the series could have centred on any pairing of father (figure)-and-son or mentor-student and could arguably have been set in any constrained living space from a prison to a submarine. The other feature that *Porridge* shares in common with many other sit-coms is its gentle mocking of those who are pompous and/or in authority. Fletcher's good-humoured attempts to deflate Prison Officer MacKay's ego, get one over on the authorities or generally beat the system are echoed in other classic comedies, including *The Good Life, Dad's Army, Only Fools and Horses* and *Blackadder*.

An alternative viewpoint is that the prison is absolutely integral to the show, and that *Porridge* has grit beneath the wit. The writers visited Brixton, Wandsworth and Wormwood Scrubs prior to scripting the series, were meticulous in their use of prison slang (although it was, of course, toned down for pre-watershed broadcast) and came up with the idea of using real prisoners as extras. In this interpretation, *Porridge* has a great deal to tell us about a particular period in prison history – the early to mid-1970s – during which the 'welfare' approach, which emphasized care, rehabilitation and decriminalization, was giving way to the justice model which had a strong punitive edge (Matthews 1999). This dynamic was allegorically represented in the form of a 'soft' screw and a 'hard' screw; the benign and well-meaning

Mr Barrowclough, who always saw in his charges the potential for reform, and officious disciplinarian, Mr MacKay, who ruled his wing with an iron will and military disposition. The character of Fletcher also alludes to the principle that came to underlie penal thinking in the late 1970s–early 1980s – 'Nothing Works' (Martinson 1974). In brief, it was concluded at this time that rehabilitative efforts were having no appreciable effect on recidivism and were a waste of time and money (Matthews 1999). As we know from *Porridge*'s opening credits which are overlaid with the voice of his trial judge passing sentence, Norman Stanley Fletcher was a 'habitual criminal' well used to serving time. If we accept, then, that *Porridge* informs us about life in prison, we may be some way to understanding why this programme, and other cinematic and TV portrayals of prisons, are so popular. As others have observed, fictional media portrayals of prisons provide a window on to a fascinating but inaccessible world and their appeal is, in part, scopophilic (Rafter 2000; Mason 2003). And before we write off *Porridge* as having little to add to our knowledge of imprisonment let us not forget that humour, relationships and scoring 'little victories' over the authorities are incontrovertibly important aspects of the reality of any prison (Gardner, cited in Wilson and O'Sullivan 2004).

A third view is that *Porridge* has done prisons and prisoners a great disservice and set back penal reform by several decades. This argument is predicated on the belief that *Porridge* presents a cosy and unrealistic image of the prison system which makes the viewing public complacent about prison conditions and prevents them from challenging the reality of imprisonment, which includes an inexorably rising prison population and dangerous levels of overcrowding. In contrast to the gently comic world of HMP Slade, the 1970s was a time of shame and conflict within the prison system, remembered by many as an era of staff brutality, prisoner riots, rooftop protests, hunger strikes and the forming of radical prison organizations, not to mention endless lock-ups, little exercise and slopping out (Fitzgerald and Sim 1979). When asked in a radio programme what is missing from media portrayals of prisons, Benjamin Zephaniah, the poet and playwright, who has served time in prison, answered:

> I think we miss the boredom of it…most of the time, people just sitting around doing nothing. I was in a prison called Winson Green in Birmingham where we did nothing. We were banged up 23 hours a day. We were just let out to walk around a yard…And one thing I always think is missing is the smell

of the place – when you're in a room which was built for 1 or 2 people and you've got 4 or 6 people in there...We used to slop out so we used to have chamber pots, for want of a better word, and you've got the smell of 4 or 6 people's urine, the smell of masturbation, in one little room. I mean you can never capture that...' ('Start the week', *Radio 4*, 22 December 2003).

For another participant in the show, David Wilson, this mis-representation makes *Porridge* a 'failure' because it has given the British public a sense of what prison is like, but has ignored the reality of prisons, presenting them as merely a 'bit of a laugh' ('Start the week', *Radio 4*, 22 December 2003). It falls short, then, because it does not persuade us to think critically about prisons, but rather encourages us to believe that prison is something that we need not worry about (Wilson and O'Sullivan 2004). But whether we subscribe to the view that *Porridge* is harmless entertainment, or breeds dangerous complacency, or has something important to tell us about the evolution of penal reform, we are starting to uncover some of the complexities of assuming that the 'meaning' of any media text is fixed at the point of production. This theme will be further explored in relation to ITV's *Bad Girls*.

Bad Girls: good research?

Whilst *Porridge* might be regarded as constituting the 'baseline default representation of prison' for those growing up in the 1970s (notwithstanding that it has been repeated many times over the last 30 years and remains a regular feature of the TV schedules), it has been suggested that for the current generation 'this role is much more likely to be filled by *Bad Girls*' (Wilson and O'Sullivan 2004: 116). A soap-style drama, *Bad Girls* is in the same mould as *The Bill* and *Footballers Wives*: indeed, in a fabulous moment of postmodern, self-referential irony, a character from *Footballers Wives* turned up in *Bad Girls* doing time in HMP Larkhall for drugs possession. Wilson and O'Sullivan (2004) argue that *Bad Girls* has done more than most television dramas to present an accurate picture of prisons and to enhance public awareness and encourage debate about the problems facing inmates, staff and governors. However, if we continue this line of argument – that *Bad Girls* is a prime example of a fictional TV portrayal with a revelatory mission – we can begin to untangle some of the difficulties inherent in the notion that media texts influence public opinion or can act as a catalyst for penal reform.

It seems reasonably uncontroversial to state – as Wilson and O'Sullivan (2004) do – that *Bad Girls* is entertaining, informative and educational. However, their assertion that *Bad Girls* has done more than any other prison drama to advance the cause of penal reform is worthy of further critical reflection. Claims about any television programme having the power to affect audience opinion or behaviour are highly contestable and go right to the heart of debates about the power of the media to influence audiences. This is perhaps not the place for a detailed exposition of the 'media effects' literature (see, *inter alia*, Gauntlett 1995; Barker and Petley 2001; Jewkes 2004a; Kitzinger 2004) except to note that the extent and nature of media influence remain a thorny debate. It is now well established that media are integral to the processes of meaning-making by which we negotiate the semiotic uncertainties of our everyday lives, and that misrepresentations concerning the extent of certain types of crime and the effectiveness of the criminal justice system are bound to create a skewed picture of the 'problem' of crime and its solutions. Given that most of us will not serve time and do not have access to prisons, it seems reasonable to assume that our ideas about what prisons are like are informed by what we read in the press and watch on the screen. Yet the effects of fictional, dramatized portrayals on screen must not be overestimated. A general problem lies in the assumption that because a television series sets out to portray an unfamiliar world, or to bring 'issues' to the attention of an audience, viewers will all 'read' that text in similar ways, and will be willing to be informed and educated while they are being entertained. As any student of media studies knows, the idea of isolating a television, film or any other medium as a variable and ignoring all the other factors that might influence the viewer or reader, is considered too crude and reductive an idea to be of any epistemological value.

There's no doubt that *Bad Girls* takes prison issues seriously and, like one interpretation of *Porridge*, the series can be viewed as an example of 'art' mirroring 'life'. In congruence with the most pressing problems facing prison ministers, the Prison Service and HM Inspectorate of Prisons over the last two decades, the programme's storylines have included prison breakouts, protests, suicide, self-harm, alcohol and drug abuse, AIDS and hepatitis, and bullying. All these issues also feature on a *Bad Girls* website (www.badgirls.co.uk), where plotlines are fleshed out with reference to real prison practices and policy. The fact that this resource is compiled in conjunction with criminologists and psychologists at the Centre for Crime and Justice Studies, King's College London, lends further credibility to the programme makers' claims for authenticity. *Bad Girls* has also tackled broader political issues such as prison privatization, the rising female prison population, overcrowding, inmate segregation, the use of mother and baby units, and policies concerning the removal of children from their mothers in custody. To this extent the series, which initially aired in 1999, reflects developments in penal policy that emerged in the 1990s with the 'New Right' ideology of the Conservatives which resulted in tougher sentencing policies and more offenders being imprisoned (Dunbar and Langdon 1998). One of the key engineers of this hard-line policy in the latter years of the Conservative administration was Michael Howard, Home Secretary from 1993 to 1997. The rapid drift to a law-and-order society that occurred under Howard's term of office meant prison reformers had to concede that, despite all evidence to the contrary, the Home Secretary strongly defended the efficacy of imprisonment as a criminal justice strategy, and believed that the more humane prison regimes become, the less effective they are as a deterrent. The 'get tough' rhetoric of that political era – variously termed 'authoritarian populism' or 'populist punitiveness' – thus extended to conditions inside prisons. Although the practice of slopping-out alluded to by Zephaniah above was abolished in 1991 following recommendations by Lord Justice Woolf, the new Home Secretary did not want to appear to be 'soft' on any aspect of penal policy and this was an era marked by significant expansion of the prison estate and the introduction of increasingly punitive security measures (Jewkes 2002).

When a new Labour government was elected in 1997, many reformers and prison sociologists hoped that a more liberal approach would be taken to prison policy. Alas, the rhetoric, philosophy and policies of Blair's government are not strikingly dissimilar to those of their predecessors and the Prime Minister is now competing for popular support with Michael 'Prison Works' Howard as Leader of the Opposition. As a result, prisons continue to be constructed in popular and political discourse within a very narrow framework, and issues surrounding women in custody have become especially concerning to prison reform groups. Between 1992 and 2002, there was a 184 per cent increase in the female prison population (www.prisonreformtrust.org.uk) as compared to 42 per cent for men. As the consultants from King's College London note, the backgrounds of many women in prison are predictably bleak: 25 per cent have been in public care; 20 per cent have spent time as an in-patient at a psychiatric hospital; 40 per cent have alcohol problems; 50 per cent are drug dependent; 47 per cent have no educational qualifications; 75 per cent have neurotic disorders; and over 50 per cent are on prescribed medication. In addition, over half the women in prison are victims of domestic violence and at least a third have experienced sexual abuse (www.badgirls.co.uk/lib/lib_wip/lib_wip6.html). These grim statistics – all too familiar undercurrents in the 'real' world of women's prisons where six vulnerable women took their own lives in a 12-month period between the summers of 2002 and 2003 at HMP Styal in Cheshire (*Guardian* 19 January 2005) – are dramatically reflected in *Bad Girls*. To this extent, then, the programme has succeeded in bringing to public attention some of the most depressing aspects of women's confinement. In addition, the series has educated the public regarding prison procedures that many might be unfamiliar with, including the personal officer system, sentence planning and pre-sentence reports.

But whilst these efforts are to be congratulated, it is debateable whether they actually have any positive effect with regard to putting prisons and prisoners on the agenda for public debate and political reform. Representations of life in confinement have to be 'sexed up' for a mainstream TV audience, and there is undeniably a great deal more drama, glamour and, yes, sex, in *Bad Girls* than might be found in an actual women's prison in the UK. Furthermore, whilst the programme makers strive to achieve a realistic demographic mix within Larkhall, non-white inmates and foreign nationals are none the less under-represented in comparison to their real-life counterparts (around 29 per cent and 20 per cent of the total female prison population respectively; www.homeoffice.gov.uk/rds). In addition, because the exigencies of TV drama require character development over a significant period of time, so that the audience can get to know characters, identify with them and believe in them, most of the inmates in *Bad Girls* are serving long or life sentences. This is at odds with the reality of women's imprisonment: two out of three women held in custody on remand do not receive a prison sentence when they go to court and, when convicted, the majority of women serve short sentences (the average sentence length for women in custody in 2001 was 10.4 months; www.prisonreformtrust.org.uk).

So, although the fictional HMP Larkhall provides an interesting backdrop to the action and gives rise to numerous stories that could only happen in a prison, *Bad Girls*, like *Porridge*, is essentially character driven and may thus engage viewers at a relatively superficial level. Like many viewers of soap and light drama, fans of *Bad Girls* may regard the show as escapism, and will care that it is a realistic portrayal of a prison only to the extent that they expect any other dramatic TV portrayal to be realistic (take by way of example *Midsomer Murders*, a small cluster of archetypal idyllic English villages which witness at least one murder a week). The fact that Shed, the production company behind *Bad Girls*, set out to create a programme that was 'a powerful and accessible way of educating the public' about the over-representation of women in prison and 'a way of reaching different audiences to those traditionally targeted by prison reform and the criminal justice agencies' (www.badgirls. co.uk) tells us nothing about how audiences receive and interpret the message, nor about the relationship between raised awareness and prison reform.

People are not blank slates who approach a television programme without any pre-existing opinions, prejudices or resources and, whilst the media may act as a conduit for the reinforcement of what we already believe, it is much rarer that they challenge our pre-existing 'knowledge' (Kitzinger 2004). Consequently, it is likely that individuals who have strong views about particular social issues will watch programmes that match their agenda and confirm the correctness of their priorities, whilst the same material will be avoided by individuals who disagree with, or do not care about, the issues raised therein (Surette 1998, Chapter 2, this volume). However noble their intentions, then, programmes with a revelatory or reforming mission may only provoke strong and lasting reactions in viewers who are already thus motivated, and raising public awareness is not the same as changing people's opinions. A further difficulty inherent in making a causal link between text and effect is, if we accept the possibility that public opinion is informed by storylines in soaps and dramas, it is arguably more likely to be a drip-drip effect over a very long period of time than a sudden impact that turns viewers' attention to issues of penal reform. Most of us may be affected by an issue we see on television for the duration of the programme, and perhaps for a short time afterwards, but we inhabit an increasingly diverse and fragmented media environment in which there is a constant flow of images, and television is the most disposable of mediums. It is therefore much more difficult to make the kind of impact in 2005 that, for example, *Cathy Come Home* reputedly did in relation to homelessness in 1966 when there were only three television channels and the programme was watched by a quarter of the population (www.bfi.org.uk). Whilst it might still be morally justified to hold the belief that media producers should strive to create realistic representations of prisons, it is a view that does not hold up to scrutiny given the economic and structural determinants of media production in the twenty-first century. What is beyond doubt is that one of the primary objectives – perhaps the *only* real objective – of *Bad Girls* is to deliver audiences to ITV's advertisers. To that extent, the emphasis of this issue-led drama is always going to be on the drama rather than the issue. A 'realistic' representation of prison – given the boredom and tedium described by Benjamin Zephaniah above – is simply not going to make good TV.

The problem, then, with much criminological research into media representations of prisons (and other criminological concerns, for that matter) is that it lacks a fundamental grounding in media theory and ignores the last 20 years of audience research which, whilst producing its fair share of cultural dead ends and reinvented wheels (Philo and Miller 1997; Morley 1998) has, none the less, alerted us to the complexities of the producer–consumer dynamic. All too often, criminologists fail to address the subtleties of media meanings, the polysemy of media texts (that is, they are open to multiple interpretations), the unique characteristics and identity of the audience member, or the social and cultural context within which the encounter between media text and audience member occurs. Even in its very earliest and simplest form, the encoding–decoding model pioneered by Stuart Hall (1973) urged scholars to attend to the need for a reconfiguration of the recognized model of communication which implied transmission of a fixed message from producer to receiver, to one that emphasized the social and symbolic complexities involved in the process of encoding (when a producer invests a text with a 'preferred meaning'), and the process of decoding (when a consumer may impose his or her own 'negotiated' reading and interpretation of that text, or may take an 'oppositional' position, resisting or entirely rejecting the preferred meaning; Hall 1973; cf. Kitzinger 2004). The media's influence on an individual's agenda of social problems is seldom direct: more often, influence is mediated through multiple social networks and is secondary to other factors such as age, gender, occupation and income (Shaw and McCombs 1977; Surette 1998). Consequently, the possible readings of any media text are as subtly nuanced as the unique experiences of the individual viewers and the contexts within which they are watching it. That is not to say that there are millions of different interpretations of the message, but rather that there are potentially numerous divergences in the extent to which the audience member believes the message, and limitless other factors that may come into play.

The issue of media 'effects' is thus complex and contested. Effects – if they occur at all – may be subtle and diffused, and 'influence' is not the same as 'action'. Charities and other organizations often utilize soaps to improve public knowledge, and research by Gillespie and McLaughlin (2002, 2003) has found that the public gleans as much information from TV dramas and soaps as from factual programmes. It is therefore plausible that *Bad Girls* has brought the problems associated with women's incarceration highlighted above to the attention of a wider audience than would otherwise have been aware of them. However Gillespie and McLaughlin also found that public understanding of sentencing and punishment is limited (compared to their knowledge about crime and policing, for example), and that tabloid newspapers are most influential in shaping public attitudes, which tend to be overtly punitive and inclined towards the view that the criminal justice system is over-lenient and ineffective. Furthermore, the media's ability to change behaviour or galvanize the public into action is notoriously unsuccessful (witness safer sex, anti-drugs and anti-smoking campaigns) and, even if it was possible to harness public interest in prisons to any tangible degree, it does not necessarily follow that those in power will take notice unless, like Tony Blair's support of *Coronation Street*'s Deidre, it is an uncontroversial matter that generates good publicity.

In general, prison reform is not considered a political vote winner because, quite simply, the public don't care very much about the welfare of prisoners. To influence prison reform a programme would have to shock viewers out of their indifference (difficult to do in documentary and journalistic formats, never mind drama) and there is simply not the widespread public interest in prisoners that there is in other groups of people. Even programmes that have succeeded in creating a political furore about scandals in other areas – such as the BBC exposés *MacIntyre Undercover* (1999) which revealed a culture of abuse and neglect in a private care home, and *The Secret Policeman* (2003) which uncovered racism amongst new police recruits – failed to make care homes or racist police officers a 'popular' cause, shocking as their messages were.

Nonces and narks: prisoners in the popular press

The discussion so far has revealed that there are a number of difficulties with the assumption that TV light entertainment can be blamed for the relative lack of public outcry at Britain's current record high prison population. Wilson and O'Sullivan ask whether the popular media have systematically *misinformed* audiences as to the nature of prison and, somewhat contentiously, they argue that *'Porridge* may have contributed to public complacency' (2004: 24). Their recurrent theme is that *Porridge* has failed because it presents a sanitized, comic version of confinement, which allows the public to sidestep the reality of incarceration and absolves them from concerning themselves with the grim reality of confinement at Her Majesty's Pleasure. But not only does this imply that media fiction assumes a primary status (when compared to, say, news reporting), it also suggests that the programme is interpreted identically by all those who have watched it over the last 30 years. A further important consideration not elucidated by Wilson and O'Sullivan concerns the complexity of a stratified society in which prison inmates are frequently regarded as the lowest of the low; the underclass of contemporary Britain. Television consumption cannot be extrapolated from wider anxieties about crime and the effectiveness of punishment, and it is important to remember that there are contradictory versions of reality which arise from the material fact of conflicting power and interests, just as there are contested interpretations of media texts (Philo and Miller 1997). Mediated explanations of crime are by no means monolithic, but it is now widely accepted that the popular press tap into and reinforce cultural fears of 'otherness', and that it is often the truly powerless, rather than the truly evil, who are most fervently demonized and stigmatized (Greer and Jewkes 2005).

Put simply, prisoners are viewed as society's detritus by large segments of the British press's readership and thus frequently induce a lazy contempt amongst journalists. On the whole, the grim and frequently inhumane conditions of their incarceration only reach public attention if accompanied by a sound bite from a statement by Her Majesty's Inspector of Prisons in language that will appeal to the popular press. There are exceptions, of course. Generally, the 'quality' press are better at reporting on prison conditions than the tabloids, and the *Guardian* deserves praise for its investigative reports and editorials (including those by Erwin James, written whilst he was serving a 20-year sentence) which have brought numerous 'unpopular' prison issues to the attention of its readers, amongst them overcrowding, racism amongst inmates and prison staff, drug addiction, mental illness and suicide (www.guardian.co.uk/prisons). But in the tabloid press, coverage of these issues is sparse and, on the whole, newspaper reporting tends to concentrate on notorious inmates who have committed particularly heinous crimes such as paedophilic/sexually motivated murder (Peter Sutcliffe being one example who is still a regular in the press 25 years after his conviction for the murder of 13 women). Another standard narrative device is that of characterizing prisons as 'holiday camps' in which inmates enjoy perks and privileges they do not 'deserve' (Jewkes 2002). Such stories fuel the tabloid media's view of a criminal justice system which is soft on crime and which prioritizes the requirements of offenders over those of victims. Although such narratives might be dismissed as a trivialization of prison issues they serve further to stigmatize a population which is already at the margins, and which rarely has a right of reply.

At the same time, more serious issues such as prisoner suicides and assaults are rarely reported in those newspapers with the highest circulation figures. An acquaintance with the processes of news selection and production helps us to understand why most assaults and deaths in custody are not considered newsworthy. Suicides and attempted suicides usually only reach the pages of the popular press if the story conforms to several cardinal news values – e.g. it concerns a particularly notorious ('celebrity') inmate, thus meeting the required 'threshold' for inclusion, and is reduced ('simplified') to an event that was both 'predictable' and therefore preventable (Jewkes 2004a). The suicides of Fred West, Harold Shipman, and the attempted suicide of Ian Huntley are all notable examples. The more general trend, however, is for prison suicides to go unreported, and few newspaper readers may be aware that there were 95 self-inflicted deaths in prisons in 2004 (the same figure as in 2002 and just one more than in 2003), including 13 women and one 14-year-old, who is not included in the Home Office statistics, as he died in a privately run secure training unit, but who is believed to be the youngest person to die in British custody (www.howardleague.org/press). Meanwhile, abuses and assaults inflicted on prisoners by staff or by other inmates are generally reported only when an official inquiry has taken place. Like crime news more generally, the appearance of a story about an assault or act of abuse in prison is dependent upon editorial judgements being made about the victim, with some victims being considered more worthy than others (Jewkes 2004a). And, again, in common with wider media constructions of victims, a story will always be considered more newsworthy if the victim's relatives are prepared to use the media and make themselves part of the story (Jewkes 2004a). But, aside from a few notable examples where a family campaigns tirelessly to keep a case in the public eye (as have relatives of Zahid Mubarek, murdered by his racist cell-mate at Feltham Young Offenders Institution in March 2000), most assaults and abuses remain hidden behind prison walls.

That the press unfailingly get themselves in a lather about incidents which are atypical and which lend themselves to sensational reporting, whilst ignoring the mundane reality of assaults and deaths in custody, is indicative of the media's inclination to pander to the most voyeuristic and punitive emotions of the audience. For all the cynical treatment of high-profile prisoners at the hands of the British tabloid press to whip up support for more restrictive penal policies, and the success of the familiar portrayals of prison in sit-coms such as *Porridge*, not to mention the adrenalin-charged, yet ultimately unchallenging, episodes of *Bad Girls*, there is only one conclusion to be drawn. When it comes to 'real' or 'realistic' representations of imprisonment, which many inmates experience as brutalizing, dehumanizing and intolerable, public indifference prevails and some of the worst atrocities go unnoticed and unchecked. Whilst the statistics on prisoner self-harm and suicide provide graphic evidence of the damage that prisons do to some of society's most vulnerable members, the popular view of prisons as holiday camps offering an array of 'luxuries' such as in-cell television and gourmet cuisine to an undeserving and dangerous underclass continues to circulate (Jewkes 2002). Meanwhile, other, more disturbing trends in incarceration (the inexorably rising numbers of women and children behind bars, the accusations of institutional racism and systematic neglect that have been directed at adult prisons and YOIs alike, the HMIP report that some prisons are effectively being run amid a culture of fear and brutality by inmate gangs and so on) are failing to make an impact on the collective public consciousness.

If we look at contemporary television and newspaper output as a whole, we cannot avoid the conclusion that the representation of prisons and prisoners in the media is negligible and, when visible, contradictory. No wonder, then, that prisons remain shrouded in a certain amount of mystique and mythology. What is arguably needed, then, is a more reflexive approach to studying the relationship between media constructions of prisons, public perceptions of prisoners and imprisonment, and opportunities for prison reform. Recent research has suggested that the media's framing of a social issue can help the audience to think about solutions to problems and act as a forum through which pressure can be brought to bear on policy-makers, but that such influences are not free-floating; they operate amongst a plethora of pre-existing cultural resources and prior experiences and through a nexus of demographic predispositions including gender, ethnic and sexual identity (Kitzinger 2004).

Media influence appears to be most compelling when either the audience member has prior knowledge or experience of the subject being portrayed, or has some other means of empathizing with the issue or with the protagonists involved (hence the use of highly emotive language in media reports about many social problems including crime). But prison inmates present a problem in this respect. In her study of media framing of sexual abuse against children (particularly in the cases of Cleveland and the Orkneys), Kitzinger (2004) found that media influence was most powerful amongst victims/survivors of child sexual abuse, for whom the media served to confirm the criminality of what had happened to them and give public voice to what had hitherto remained a very private issue. Other, non-victimized, audience members found the ability to relate to stories about children being forcibly taken from their homes by social workers on the basis that they presumed (erroneously in some cases) that the parents alleged to have abused their children were innocent. This ability to empathize with fellow parents supports Gillespie and McLaughlin's (2002, 2003) finding that media content has a more significant impact on audience members if they can, in some way, 'identify' with the person on screen (see also Chapter 2, this volume). But for so long have the press and television media – underpinned by punitive political rhetoric and policy – constructed prisoners as stigmatized 'others' that the possibilities for empathy have closed down to all but those who have experienced incarceration, or have some other relevant experience on which to draw.

Any sort of 'deeper knowledge' of individual prisoners is precisely what is missing from most print media, where sympathy, empathy or understanding are simply not options (Jewkes 2004b). Presented by the popular press as a 'breed apart', many prisoners are judged within a moral framework which stimulates sentiments of revulsion and repugnance whilst simultaneously reinforcing populist ideas about punishment (Gillespie and McLaughlin 2002). As countless followers of Durkheim have demonstrated, one of the primary functions of the media is publicly to censure deviants in order to give strength to the group as a whole (Becker 1963; Cohen 1972; Ericson *et al.* 1987). In the context of those who transgress the legal and moral boundaries of society and find themselves in custody, this means confinement within institutions resonant with symbolic moral disapproval, and then further censure by a media industry who strive to achieve public consensus. Against this backdrop, TV portrayals that seek to educate and reform may do little to challenge the prevailing views of the tabloid-reading, channel-hopping majority for whom prisons remain full of bad girls, nonces and narks.

References

Barker, M. and Petley, J. (eds) (2001) *Ill Effects: The Media/Violence* (2nd edn). London: Routledge.

Becker, H. (1963) *Outsiders: Studies in the Sociology of Deviance*. New York, NY: Free Press.

Cohen, S. (1972) *Folk Devils and Moral Panics: The Creation of Mods and Rockers*. London: MacGibbon & Kee.

Dunbar, I. and Langdon, A. (1998) *Tough Justice: Sentencing and Penal Policies in the 1990s*. London: Blackstone.

Ericson, R., Baranek, P. and Chan, J. (1987) *Visualising Deviance: A Study of News Organisations*. Buckingham: Open University Press.

Fitzgerald, M. and Sim, J. (1979) *British Prisons*. Oxford: Blackwell.

Gauntlett, D. (1995) *Moving Experiences: Understanding Television's Influences and Effects*. Luton: John Libbey.

Gillespie, M. and McLaughlin, E. (2002) 'Media and the making of public attitudes', *Criminal Justice Matters*, 49: 8–9.

Gillespie, M. and McLaughlin, E. (2003) 'Media and the shaping of public knowledge and attitudes towards crime and punishment', *Rethinking Crime and Punishment* (available at www.rethinking.org.uk).

Greer, C. and Jewkes, Y. (2005) 'Extremes of otherness: media images of social exclusion', *Social Justice*, 32.

Hall, S. (1973/1981) 'Encoding and decoding in the television discourse', in S. Hall *et al.* (eds) *Culture, Media, Language: Working Papers in Cultural Studies 1972–79*. London: Hutchinson.

Jewkes, Y. (2002) *Captive Audience: Media, Masculinity and Power in Prisons*. Cullompton: Willan Publishing.

Jewkes, Y. (2004a) *Media and Crime*. London: Sage.

Jewkes, Y. (2004b) 'Media representations of criminal justice', in J. Muncie and D. Wilson (eds) *Student Handbook of Criminal Justice and Criminology*. London: Cavendish.

Kitzinger, J. (2004) *Framing Abuse*. London: Pluto.

Martinson, R. (1974) 'What works? Questions and answers about prison reform', *Public Interest*, 35: 22–54.

Mason, P. (2003) *Criminal Visions: Media Representations of Crime and Justice*. Cullompton: Willan Publishing.

Matthews, R. (1999) *Doing Time: An Introduction to the Sociology of Imprisonment*. London: Macmillan.

Morley, D. (1998) 'So-called cultural studies: dead ends and reinvented wheels', *Cultural Studies*, 12: 476–97.

Philo, G. and Miller, D. (1997) *Cultural Compliance: Dead Ends of Media/Cultural Studies and Social Science*. Glasgow: Glasgow University Media Group.

Rafter, N. (2000) *Shots in the Mirror: Crime, Film and Society*. Oxford: Oxford University Press.

Shaw, D.L. and McCombs, M. (1977) *The Emergence of American Political Issues: The Agenda-Setting Function of the Press*. St Paul, MN: West.

Surette, R. (1998) *Media, Crime and Criminal Justice*. Belmont, CA: West/Wadsworth.

Wilson, D. (2003) 'The perception and the reality of crime.' Paper presented to the NACRO conference 'Crime watching: crime, public perception and the media', British Library, London, 19 November.

Wilson, D. and O'Sullivan, S. (2004) *Representations of Prison in Film and Television Drama*. Winchester: Waterside Press.

Chapter 10

The violence of images: inside the prison TV drama *Oz*

Brian Jarvis

Although official statistics suggest that crime rates are falling, the past decade has witnessed an explosive proliferation in images of crime in the US media.[1] Cop shows such as *Crime Scene Investigation*, *Law and Order* and *NYPD Blue* rule the ratings alongside 24/7 media coverage of real-life crime stories. In combination with political rhetoric about a domestic 'War on crime' and a global 'War on terror', the visual culture of crime has helped to forge a climate of fear. The crime drama promotes anxiety; however, it also provides partial reassurance with its conventional narrative trajectory of crime–detection–punishment. That punishment provides closure to the crime narrative may begin to explain why, in the midst of the media crime wave, there are so few prison stories. The prison drama complicates ruling narratives by hinting that punishment is not the end so much as the beginning of a new story. During a period when the US prison population has soared, from around 744,000 in 1985 to over 2,000,000 in 2002, popular culture has effectively colluded with the 'experiment in mass incarceration' and ensured that inmates remain disappeared. The few successful prison films made during this incarceration boom, such as *The Shawshank Redemption* (1994) and *The Green Mile* (1999), have tended to be set in earlier eras and television has consistently shunned the contemporary prison-industrial complex. In the context of unprecedented lockdown there is an urgent need for representation and television is arguably the most influential instrument for what Henry Giroux terms 'public pedagogy' (1998). The TV prison drama is in prime position to teach by taking its viewers inside this closed and secretive institution.

The HBO prison drama *Oz* (1997–2003) promised to do precisely this by offering 56 episodes of life inside the fictional Oswald State Penitentiary. The action centred on an experimental unit within 'Oz', nicknamed 'Emerald City' and run by Tim McManus, a psychologist and white, middle-class liberal committed to progressive penology. 'Em City' was a low-security environment which permitted free interaction of inmates outside their Plexiglas cells and offered numerous opportunities for counselling, education and recreation. McManus frequently found himself at odds with the prison's African-American warden, Leo Glynn, who favoured an 'old school' approach focused on security issues rather than rehabilitation. The prisoners included representatives from various racial, ethnic and ideological factions: African-American Muslims and homeboys, Aryan Supremacists and bikers, Italian-American wiseguys and Irish-American shysters all engaged in endless internecine warfare. *Oz* was a commercial success: the longest-running series on HBO with audience figures over 4 million for season premieres. It also won awards and praise within the media for its realistic representation of prison life. 'Realism', however, is a notoriously slippery term. This essay will begin by addressing issues of genre and ideology to determine whether *Oz* managed to 'keep it real'.

Hard-boiled or hyperreal?

> Where is the cinema? The American city seems to have stepped right out of the movies. To grasp its secret you should not, then, begin with the city and move inwards towards the screen; you should begin with the screen and move outwards towards the city (Baudrillard 1989: 43).

> Toto, I have a feeling we're not in Kansas anymore (*The Wizard of Oz*).

Before they turned their attention to prison drama, the team behind *Oz*, Tom Fontana and Barry Levinson, were responsible for *Homicide: Life on the Streets* (1993–9), a cop show that was also much praised for its hard-boiled realism. In an episode entitled 'The documentary', a chase scene culminated in a suspect accidentally running into the shooting of a crime film and surrendering to the uniformed actors in front of a bemused director (Barry Levinson 'playing himself'). The scene was inspired by an incident involving a criminal, on the run from the Baltimore Police Department, accidentally running into the shooting of *Homicide: Life on the Streets* and surrendering to the uniformed actors in front of the bemused director Barry Levinson. What does it mean to describe an image as 'real' in the context of hypermediated spaces? Can popular culture represent the 'reality' of prison life when perceptions of prison are largely constructed within popular culture? According to Baudrillard, the American city seems to step 'out of the movies' so perhaps, to grasp the secrets of Emerald City, we need to begin with screen.

Most of the inmates in *Oz* were transferred from the vaults of the Hollywood prison film: good guard and bad guard, artist and animal lover, fresh fish and old lifer, weasely narc and wily escapologist. The fidelity *Oz* displayed in depicting various factions in Emerald City was largely to filmic sources: the Black Muslims recalled Spike Lee's *Malcolm X* (1992), the gangstas belonged to New Jack Cinema, the wiseguys were inspired by the Scorcese œuvre whilst the Latinos were prompted by *American Me* (1992) and *Blood in, Blood out* (1993). The prison staff were similarly familiar: Sister Peter Marie, for example, is clearly modelled on Sister Helen Prejean in *Dead Man Walking* (1995).[2] These stocky characters tended to follow formulaic plotlines. For most inmates prison is about time: the waiting and the boredom of the stretch. Commercial television, of course, cannot afford to devote air time to images of prisoners languishing or quietly doing their bids. Instead, *Oz* offered a steady stream of melodramatic contrivances as predictable as (and including) the last-minute stay of execution.[3]

'Emerald City' was then a fantasy world, but perhaps the choice of place-name signposts some ironic self-consciousness of this fact. *Oz* relied primarily on a quasi-documentary *mise-en-scène* – hand-held cameras, naturalistic sets and minimalist make-up – but spliced this approach with bursts of expressionistic excess and postmodern self-reflexivity. Emerald City could unexpectedly be transformed into a war zone or a nightclub. Each episode included a lyrical metacommentary by a wheelchair-bound African-American prisoner, Augustus Hill, delivered from within a revolving Plexiglas box which double framed the shot by foregrounding the 'box' on which *Oz* was watched. Although the box was suspended in the heart of Emerald City it went unseen by the other inmates who were often preoccupied with watching TV and watching reports of themselves on TV. Film crews, photographers and journalists appeared regularly in Emerald City and a fashion magazine was granted permission to shoot prisoners on death row. The centrepiece to the final episode of

Oz was a prisoner production of *Macbeth* which ended in a bloodbath as 'real' weapons were substituted for props.

Although Emerald City was then the setting for some habitual cinematic cliché, it also displayed a degree of self-consciousness and managed to correct some of the offences committed by mainstream prison films. Whilst Hollywood tends to offer exclusive focus on individuals, the ensemble cast and serial format of the TV drama allowed some recognition of prison as a social institution. Mainstream prison film is preoccupied with life on one side of the bars in its romanticized depiction of the prisoner-hero, but *Oz* tracked a network of relations, of shifting alliances and antagonisms between inmates and prison staff over seven series. During a period which has seen a massive rise in the incarceration of African-Americans, Hollywood has continued its preoccupation with Caucasian prisoners (and the occasional black buddy to salve the liberal conscience).[4] Conversely, the demographics in *Oz* proved more inclusive with a high percentage of storylines devoted to those racial and ethnic minorities who are the majority inside.

Irrespective of race or ethnicity, healthcare issues are of vital importance in prisoners' lives. Generally low standards of healthcare in the US prison system are compounded by overcrowding, poor hygiene and catering, high levels of smoking and drug use, STDs and unprotected sex, enforced physical inactivity, incidents of violence and macho attitudes. Whilst these issues are practically unheard of in Hollywood dramas they were broached in *Oz* alongside storylines that would not have been out of place in a medical drama.[5] However, unlike the majority of those inside US prisons, the inmates at Oz benefited from a fully resourced medical facility. Emerald City was a state-of-the-art installation: high-tech and relatively commodious, gleaming kitchens, well stocked libraries and even a suite of rooms set aside for conjugal visits. The spectator's prison tour of polished Plexiglas pods in *Oz* should not obscure the bigger picture in a system characterized by crumbling infrastructure in overcrowded low-tech dungeons.

Screening violence

When *Oz* was applauded for its 'realism' this label was not referring primarily to the built environment, nor to aspects of social geography such as demographics and healthcare. 'Realism' was largely a euphemism for the ceaseless displays of violence that were the series' distinguishing feature. A preoccupation with violence was evident from the outset in a credit sequence which foregrounded images of fighting, murder and electrocution. In the opening scene of the opening episode, 'The routine', a new inmate was stabbed the moment he arrived in Emerald City. Following this inaugural act of violence, in swift succession, a gay prisoner was severely beaten in the showers, an AIDS patient was suffocated and a fresh fish was raped and had a swastika branded on his backside. 'The routine' climaxed with a prisoner being beaten unconscious by guards, then drugged, doused in lighter fluid and burnt to death.

During the subsequent 55 episodes there were so many murders (almost 100) that Emerald City seemed like a death camp. Following burning and suffocation in the opening instalment, *Oz* included deaths by stabbing (with shanks, razors, fingernails and a crucifix), electrocution (in the chair, by hairdryer in a hydrotherapy tub and a camera flash cube inserted in the mouth), poisoning (by foods, drugs, gases and HIV-infected blood), execution (by lethal injection, hanging, firing squad and a proposed stoning), strangulation, crushing and several comparatively mundane shootings. The number of murders in *Oz* was massively outweighed by incidents of non-fatal violence. Stabbing was easily the most common of these (and there were four separate incidents in one episode, 'Cuts like a knife', alone). The sadistic ingenuity of the series was manifest in multiple mutilations that included the removal of penises, eyes and tongues and attacks involving rats, dogs and boiling grease. This DeSadean carnival featured numerous scenes of self-mutilation: prisoners scarring their own faces, arms and hands and even attempting, on one occasion, to cut out their own gums.[6] Unsurprisingly, suicide, the definitive act of self-violence, was also routine in *Oz* and one might conjecture that many acts of apparently other-directed violence were expressions of covert death wishes.

According to Department of Justice records, in the recent era there have been approximately 50–60 murders and 8,000–9,000 incidents of serious violence per annum throughout the entire US prison system.[7] *Oz* concentrates all its violence in one wing of a single prison. Although Emerald City departs from official statistics, it might be argued that this ultra-violent milieu simulates the lived experience of many prisoners who feel continually vulnerable to attack. *Oz* perhaps managed to recreate the structures of feeling within US prisons, but was far less effective at analysing their contexts and causes. The cycle of violence was interrupted by the metacommentary of Augustus Hill. However, his occasional hints at connections between race, class, capital, prison and other institutions remained entirely secondary to the spectacle of violence.[8] This spectacle involved a reductive homogenization that was disconnected from relations of power: there was no real differentiation between violence against women, or racial and sexual minorities, or institutional violence. One particularly prominent example of this myopia concerns racial violence. Despite the fact that Emerald City's mouthpiece was African-American and racially motivated violence was conspicuous, *Oz* did very little to connect race to a wider social context. The so-called 'War on drugs' is a covert offensive against the African-American community with prison as the front line. As Angela Y. Davis has argued, it is no coincidence that the waning of the rehabilitative ethic in US corrections has accompanied a dramatic rise in the numbers of non-white prisoners (2001: 36). The late twentieth century witnessed a renaissance in the representational regime that flourished in the late nineteenth-century American South: a discourse that disseminated notions of habitual black criminality and proposed prison as biological destiny for an incorrigible race.

In the absence of sustained attention to broader social contexts, structural causes and possible solutions, *Oz* could only mirror media images of violence and their associated demonologies. Hypersaturation results in banality, a 'waning of affect' (Jameson 1991: 27) and the 'production of moral indifference' (Bauman 1999: 65). This is the violence of images: its conversion of the reality of violence into spectacle. As Mark Seltzer has argued: '[t]he fascination with scenes of a spectacularized bodily violence is inseparable from *the binding of violence to scene, spectacle, and representation*' (1998: 129). In the postmodern prism of Emerald City, even the image of violence is shattered into images of images. During a fight between a Latino gang and an African-American, a prisoner was murdered by having his head smashed through a television screen. This might be read as an exemplary moment. Screen violence can screen the reality of violence in its various forms. The spectacle of fighting and murder obscures the underlying structural violence of social inequality and the crime of transferring public resources from welfare to warfare.

Body talk

This is not to suggest that prison violence itself is insignificant. Despite the fact that over 75 per cent of US prisoners are doing time for non-violent offences, violence inside is compulsory, compulsive and mandatory to the masculine code. Foucault contended that punishment is not primarily directed at the offender so much as the potentially guilty (1995: 208). Prison violence repeats this dynamic: aggression is often not primarily directed at the victim so much as those who might victimize the aggressor. Violence might be a defensive gesture and can also be tied to codes of prestige and honour. What appears to be senseless barbarism can be what Erving Goffman called 'a status bloodbath' (1961: 78).[9] The wounds inflicted in these rituals can be worn as proudly as prison tattoos. The marks of battle do not signify weakness but, rather, inscribe the prisoner's body with signs of masculine agency and resistance to the will of others. Wounds and wounding play a vital role in the culture of machismo.

Rather than escaping the binary logic of the patriarchal gender system, prisons reproduce asymmetrical relations of power *in extremis* by casting some inmates as 'super-males' and others as 'bitches'. Within these polarized extremes, prison subculture constructs a dominance hierarchy which *Oz*, with its ensemble cast, was able to reproduce. At the top are the alpha male gang lords and leaders of powerful religious factions: in *Oz* this included Simon Adebisi (the homeboys), Chico Guerra (*El Norte* Latinos), Nino Schibetta (the wise guys), Vern Schillinger (the Aryan Brotherhood), Jazz Hoyt (the bikers) and Kareem Said (the Black Muslims). The second tier is occupied by gang members, 'stand-up guys' and merchants (figures like Ryan O'Reilly who establish connections to powerful figures and access to contraband). Moving down the hierarchy one finds various marginalized males without gang affiliation, often from middle-class backgrounds, who get involved in prison programmes and try to do their bid quietly. At the bottom of the heap is an underclass that consists of Queens, snitches and sex offenders.

The dominance hierarchy is fiercely regulated by violence and cemented with shame. In 'Subject honour, object shame', a study of macho subcultures, Roger Lancaster has commented on 'the peculiar power of stigma to regulate conduct and generate effects' (2002: 47). In prison, stigma has an extravagant force that inmates seek to disavow and pass down the pecking order. The unpredictability of violence and what Lancaster terms the '*stickiness* of shame' make the hierarchy profoundly unstable (2002: 51). One's position in the ranking is constantly in jeopardy and in need of consolidation. In *Oz*, Peter Schibetta goes from respected wise guy to 'Adebisi's Bitch' in the space of one night and is never able to remove the stigma of having been sodomized. Once a prisoner is 'turned out' he will find it virtually impossible to ascend the hierarchy and there are many other ways to lose 'jizz' (respect).

As well as enduring the disciplinary gaze of the authorities, the prisoner will be subjected to surveillance by his peers searching for signs of weakness. The performance of masculinity in this theatre of punishment involves learning certain lines. One might expect the script to be limited given that masculinity is typically *dumb* and prison is an institution that rewards reticence (there are many subjects you do not talk about, many people you do not talk to and the penalties for snitching are severe). However, given the amount of 'free' time and enforced sociality of prison life there is a high volume of conversation. Whilst many Hollywood prison dramas are practically silent movies (Clint Eastwood's typically taciturn performance in *Escape from Alcatraz* (1979) exemplifies this), *Oz*, like all soap operas, was overflowing with gossip. In prison society information is one of the most precious commodities and the residents of Emerald City spent much of their time 'working the corners', 'running someone's tags' and getting 'plugged in'.

Oz represented prison society as chatty, but also underscored the extent to which the most crucial communications involve body talk. The prisoner's body is the key prop in the masculine masquerade. Comportment is crucial: inmates have to learn how to 'walk the walk' rather than hugging the walls and how to 'front up' by returning a glare rather than averting the eyes. The body inside is largely stripped of those commodities through which consumers on the outside are encouraged to define themselves and is continually called forth to present itself to the authorities and other inmates. *Oz* highlighted the vulnerability of the prisoner's body and the absence of private space with images of Plexiglas pods (regularly searched), communal showers and toilet facilities, pat downs, strip searches and body cavity checks allied to the constant threat of assault at the hands of inmates and guards. Emerald City may have been voluble, but violence and wounding were the master discourse and as Elaine Scarry (1985) contends, the body in pain threatens to erase language.

In prison, masculine subjectivity is thus irrevocably sutured to the body. Deprived of control over other aspects of their life, inmates often seek to compensate by exercising control over the corporeal. As Don Sabo (2001) has argued, sports are one of the most conspicuous features of US prison society. Prison sports can be a means of building a body that exudes a masculine aura thus improving prestige and deterring attacks. At the same time it can be deployed by prison authorities to defuse tension and encourage compliance. This dual status was reflected in *Oz* which regularly featured shots of prisoners performing callisthenics in their cells and weightlifting in the gym as well as basketball and boxing competitions arranged by McManus.[10]

Sports in Emerald City exemplified the dialectical relationship which exists between space and the social construction of the body. Inside, the body *is* building. The prisoner must become a prison, must model himself on a structure which itself is modelled on hegemonic definitions of masculinity. The prison/er must be solid, must have an imposing facade, must be heavily defended against attack and maintain tight control over what goes in and comes out. The rock-hard muscles are a fetish that seek to transform flesh into tumescent stone, body into armour. If one is not the impregnable phallus they are left open to penetration. Images of penetration formed a key visual cluster in the iconography of *Oz*: from the close-ups in the opening credits of a prisoner getting an 'Oz' tattoo, to shots of skin perforated by needles, knives, fingernails, the ingestion of poisons, glass and various foreign objects and scenes of bodily invasion during cavity checks.[11] Although Emerald City was crowded with images of hard-core macho physiques, ultimately the prisoner's body was rendered profoundly permeable.

Camp Oz

The most feared form of penetration in prison, one addressed repeatedly by *Oz*, is rape. The Federal Bureau of Prisons estimates that 9–20 per cent of inmates are the victims of sexual assault.[12] 'Turning out' is crucial to the dominance hierarchy and erotic economy of prison. Typically, this practice involves the threat or actuality of gang rape to transform a new inmate into a 'punk' or 'bitch'. The coerced sex slave can be loaned or sold and is expected to perform domestic duties such as laundry, cleaning the cell and making drinks whilst the 'Daddy' assumes responsibility for protecting his bitch from other inmates. Dominant males may try to establish superiority by stealing their rival's punk, or even kidnapping and turning out a gang member.

'Turning out' and 'hooking up' takes place within a culture of queer-bashing. Prisons are thus home to the strange bedfellows of widespread homosexual activity and virulent homophobia. This marriage is underwritten by a contract that defines heterosexuality as the preserve of the penetrative subject irrespective of the partner's gender.[13] The homosexual–homophobic dynamic takes place within a broader context of intense homosociality. Prison life maximizes the necessity of forming associations and mitigates against forming full friendships. It is risky to get too close to certain prisoners (rival crews, snitches, sexual deviants) and prisoner–guard friendships are strictly taboo. Inmates come and go and are reassigned cells, blocks and prisons on a regular basis. At the same time, isolated from family, one can find a surrogate in the companionship of other inmates with whom you spend considerable time. In these circumstances intense bonds can form based on shared experience, intimate communication and trust.

The prison career of Tobias Beecher, inmate no. 97B412 in Emerald City, offered a fascinating example of the interplay between sexual violence, homosexuality, homophobia and intense male bonding. As a white, middle-class lawyer with no prison experience prior to his conviction for vehicular manslaughter whilst drunk, Beecher fit the profile of a potential rape victim. This was perhaps underlined by a choice of surname which has distinct echoes in US history. The sisters Catherine *Beecher* and Harriet *Beecher* Stowe were leading social reformers in the mid-nineteenth century associated with abolition, prison reform and equal rights for women. Beecher's family name echoed an era when southern white men feared the ravaging of their women folk by 'buck Negroes'. In the modern slave ship, however, white men now fear for themselves. On arrival at Em City, Beecher is put in a cell with a muscular Nigerian prisoner, Simon Adebisi, who promises he will make him his bitch. This scenario might appear to reinforce crude racist stereotypes, but official statistics suggest that the majority (70–80 per cent) of prison rapes involve black aggressors and white victims. Black resistance to sexual slavery and eagerness to be 'master' rather than sexual 'bitch' has roots that stretch back into the era from which Beecher's name is borrowed.

Beecher is rescued by another inmate, Vern Schillinger, who helps arrange for a cell transfer. Unfortunately, Schillinger is revealed to be the leader of the Aryan Brotherhood and on Beecher's first night he is sodomized and his arse is branded with a swastika. Subsequently, as Schillinger's bitch, Beecher is expected to perform 'wifely duties' and is subjected to ritual humiliations (cleaning jackboots with his tongue and dressing up in drag). The feminization of the victim here, alongside entrapment, enforced silence and constant fear all mimic domestic abuse. The cycle of abuse is broken abruptly when Beecher goes berserk and shoves broken glass into Schillinger's eye. A second act of vengeance involves beating Schillinger unconscious with weights in the prison gym before defecating on his face. Following his Oedipal blinding of the 'Daddy', Beecher uses his anus, the focal point of Schillinger's aggression against him, in a gesture of symbolic deterritorialization. When another prisoner, Jim Robson, attempts to force Beecher to perform oral sex he castrates him with his teeth. Despite being sent to 'the Hole' for these attacks, Beecher's remasculinization is completed by a symbolic repossession of both phallus and anus.

Following his remasculinization, Beecher attempted to protect other vulnerable inmates from sexual predators and engaged in a torrid long-term romance with another inmate (Chris Keller). Although it took until the third season, the recognition of consensual sex between inmates in *Oz* none the less constituted a breakthrough. With its acute division of inmates into sexual subjects and objects, prison can reproduce the patriarchal gender system *in extremis*, but *Oz* hinted at how this can also be a site which reveals the inherent instability of the 'heterosexual matrix' (Butler 1990: 151). The tidy symmetries of the hegemonic gender system – male and female, heterosexual and homosexual – are undermined inside by libidinal alchemies. The use and abuse of bodies in prison foregrounds sexual, social and semantic slippages that extend beyond the prison walls. The prison bitch is marginalized and yet occupies a central position in grounding the cult of masculinity. The 'He-Man' system disavows the queer other and yet is dependent on it for meaning and potency. Sociology and psychology deploy the concept of 'situational homosexuality' to explain erotic relations in single-sex environments (boarding schools, the military and certain religious institutions). Alternatively, we could argue that prison society underlines the practice of 'situational heterosexuality' on the outside. The traversals of traditionally stable categories in *Oz* allowed a peep behind the door to the prison house of prescriptive sexual identities. Rather than an exotic deviation from the norm, prison society exemplifies the intricate algorithms attendant upon all relations of power and desire.

Masculinity in crisis?

In its representation of prison sexuality, *Oz* introduced the basis for a critique of patriarchy. However, the series failed to sustain an investigation of the connections between patriarchy and penal culture. In place of an unequivocal assault on male violence as regressive and pathological, *Oz* offered a deeply contradictory account of modern masculinities. In this respect it belongs alongside a wave of cultural productions that swelled during the 1990s and have been diagnosed by critics as symptoms of a 'crisis in masculinity'. In 'Are you a man or a mouse?' Homi Bhabha proposes that the 'manifest destiny of masculinity' has recently been rewritten (1995: 57). The underlying causes of this rewriting are economic. The postwar era has seen an international relocation of the manufacturing base outside advanced industrial nations such as the USA and the concomitant rise of an information economy and consumer society. This shift from the production of goods to the service sector has impacted on hegemonic definitions of masculinity. The male body, traditionally privileged as authoritative agent of production, has increasingly been 'feminized' as a receptacle for conspicuous consumption. In *Stiffed: The Betrayal of the American Male*, Susan Faludi (2000) proposes that this development, alongside increasing unemployment, has produced large numbers of 'angry white males' deprived of traditional sources of male sociality and uncertain about their role in society. The transition to flexible Fordism appears to have been accompanied by a switch to 'flexible patriarchy': the core of masculinity has become less fixed with greater emphasis for middle-class males on diverse roles. This is the context within which to view the depiction of masculinity in *Oz*. The TV prison drama offered the nostalgic recreation of an 'authentic', virile and primal masculine community. In Em City, unlike the soft suburbs, real men have not been domesticated: their dwellings are not colour co-ordinated and cluttered by soft furnishings; cappuccino makers and designer clothing are replaced by shanks hidden in faded denim.

The changing economic status of American men has been accompanied by a series of social and historical developments that have accentuated the alleged 'crisis in masculinity'. White heterosexual males in the USA have had their authority challenged at home and overseas: the loss of the war in Vietnam, the advances for minority and subaltern classes (women, racial and ethnic groups, gays and lesbians), identity politics and political correctness. In paranoid response to these challenges, a master narrative has emerged about an alleged loss of mastery. In *Marked Men: White Masculinity in Crisis*, Sally Robinson (2000) underlines the crucial point that, whilst this cohort continues to monopolize economic and political power, the cultural sphere has witnessed a marked rise in narratives of white male victimhood. Robinson notes that these narratives are often conflicted and perversely aim to perpetuate the conditions they protest. In *Taking it Like a Man*, David Savran diagnoses this dynamic as fundamentally sadomasochistic:

[There is] a new cultural fantasmatic in fiction, film and real-life: a new masculinity involving a relentless flirtation with pain, injury, and death, it goes beyond heroism and bravery to a kind of self-torture...the emergence of a particular kind of masochistic male subjectivity – dubbed reflexive sadomasochism by Freud – which has become hegemonic in American culture over the course of the past twenty years (1998: 163).

The new fantasmatic is two-faced. The relatively soft face of the 'white male backlash' (Savran 1998: 4) is the men's movement and various groups inspired by Robert Bly's influential polemic *Iron John*. The hard face, however, involves a resurgence in crypto-fascism that includes the paramilitary right, numerous militia factions, Aryan supremacists and the Patriot movement. Both hard and soft faces feed off disenchantment, primarily amongst white working and lower middle-class males, about a sense of lost status at the hands of women, racial minorities and 'sexual deviants'.

The prison narrative has always been an arena in which Caucasian males can be envisaged as down-trodden victims rather than oppressors. *Oz* repeats this practice as it reflects and responds to developments in *fin-de-siècle* masculinity. The repeated drama of prisoners 'taking it like a man', enduring ever-greater levels of pain and suffering, the endless insistence on *proving* and *displaying* masculinity must be read as indices of a sense of entrapment *outside*, in a feminine sphere of domesticity and consumption. For all its violence, Em City is in fact a sanctuary: a televisual equivalent of the Iron John retreat far away from the world of women, consumerism and domesticity, where what Bly mystically termed the 'deep masculine' can be recovered. At the same time, however, *Oz* offered to take the spectator beyond the disenchantment of Iron John by flirting with his dark Nietzschean twin, the *Übermensch*. *Oz* displayed the key signatures of the fascist personality as outlined by Klaus Theweleit (1989) in his seminal study, *Male Bodies: Psychoanalyzing the White Terror*: the valorization of violence and warrior masculinity, the stylized brutality, the insistence on the triumph of the will, thinking with the blood and intense misogyny.[14] In this respect *Oz* belongs alongside cult postmodern buddy films, such as *Pulp Fiction* (1994) and *Fight Club* (1999), which beneath their patina of social critique are essentially consonant with a fascist formula that valorizes violence as cleansing ritual, bodily pain as the path to bonding and the feminine as deadly problematic.

Beneath a patina of liberal critique, *Oz* combined its fascist leanings with a strong streak of fatalism. Em City was devised and designed in accordance with the rehabilitative ethic. The Perspex cells reflected the panoptic desire for *transparency* and the inmates were given countless opportunities to reform in a state-of-the-art facility: support groups and prison councils, educational and self-help programmes and access to a supportive staff that included a psychologist (McManus), a counsellor (Sister Peter Marie), a priest (Father Makurda), a performing arts co-ordinator, a sympathetic nurse and a librarian. However, over six years and almost 60 episodes, McManus' experiment to get people to 'learn to live together' was an unequivocal failure. This emphasis on the failure of rehabilitation offered implicit sanction to current practices and new-right criminological thinking with its emphasis on the redundancy of social engineering and prioritization of security over prisoners' 'souls'. *Oz* thus mirrored the planned obsolescence of the prison-industrial complex and in its latter stages conservative fatalism threatened to assume cosmic proportions. One of the prisoners, Idzik, became a doomsday prophet who offered a metaphor for the void into which the politics of *Oz* ultimately fell:

> Eventually, all the gas, all the heat, all the light will dissipate, the galaxies will grow cold and still...So don't you see? Everything that we do, the plans we make, the hopes we have, they're futile...Life is a waste of time. So, that's why I'm counting on you to kill me. You will, won't you?

Prison drama in the age of terror

Although *The Wizard of Oz* was released on the eve of the Second World War, it was canonized during the Eisenhower 1950s by endless reruns on television. The nostalgic reassurances offered by Fleming's film were especially warming during the early days of the cold war as the state fabricated paranoia on both domestic and international fronts about the Red Menace. At the close of the century the state was once again working assiduously to manufacture a culture of fear. On both domestic and international fronts the rhetorical wars on crime and terror have legitimated massive expansions in the machinery of state oppression and terror at home and overseas. In this era, *Oz* does not offer the sanguine reassurances of its musical predecessor, but instead relishes a millennial fatalism. With its endless cycle of arbitrary ultra-violence and labyrinthine caries, cabals and conspiracies, *Oz* was prison drama for the age of terror. In American popular and political culture the individual and the national body have often been mapped on to each other. In *Oz*, the body was repeatedly subjected to random terror attacks, its boundaries were painfully penetrated and sovereignty proved impossible to maintain.

The prison and the prison drama are sites with the potential to teach us what E.P. Thompson termed 'history from below' – the past from the perspective of the marginalized, the oppressed and the defeated (1986: 12). These inside spaces can offer access to maps of power and pleasure not easily seen on the outside. Following Foucault, the analysis of prison can be seen as the key to unlocking the metastasis of carceral practices on the outside. In this context, *Oz* is especially disappointing. As public pedagogy, the main lesson taught in Emerald City was fear. In place of enlivening democracy, *Oz* capitulated to reactionary impulses by flirting with fascism and fatalism. In place of progressive social critique, *Oz* offered the violence of images, the involutions of intertextuality and postmodern navel-gazing. In place of a look at the realities of life inside, *Oz* took its audience over the rainbow.

Notes

1 The *Sourcebook of Criminal Justice* statistics shows a steady increase in the 'total crime index' (offences known to the police) from 1960 (3,384,200) to 1990 (14,475,613). In the following decade, however, the figure drops (reaching 11,877,218 by 2002).

2 The language spoken by these characters was similarly hackneyed. The inmate vernacular consisted of 'hacks' and 'prags', 'bids' and 'counts', 'shanks' and 'shakedown' that were imported from prison film and showed little awareness of racial and ethnic variants to contemporary prison vernacular. *Oz* also repeated the Hollywood formula in respect of age. Prison dramas tend to focus on mature adults rather than the 15–24-year-old cohort who make up the majority of the prison population. In this respect the prison drama matches its generic kissing cousin the war film. The arrival of the kid on the cell block, or in the platoon, disguises the fact that *most* inmates and soldiers are 'kids'.

3 The following example is not untypical. An old lifer persuades a guard to buy a lottery ticket in the hope that his winnings will secure a rare South American herb that will cure a dying grandson. With Dickensian subtlety, the guard then buys and runs off with the winning ticket before returning with a guilty conscience the very day that the prisoner learns his grandson has died.

4 African-Americans account for approximately 12 per cent of the national demographic but almost 50 per cent of the prison population.

5 These storylines included subjects such as coping with terminal illness, male breast cancer, drug testing, mental illness and AIDS. AIDS is approximately ten times more prevalent inside the US prison system than outside. Early episodes of *Oz* spent time on an AIDS ward and addressed the issue of assisted suicide. In subsequent series, however, ethical and epibidiological concerns were eclipsed by subplots that lent themselves to HIV hysteria (such as using infected blood as a weapon). In recognition of the increased incidence of pharmaceutical companies using inmates as guinea pigs, a plotline in *Oz* introduced a drug that caused rapid ageing. Prisoners were given the 'option' of chemically accelerated decrepitude instead of serving their full sentence. Of those who volunteered, one died and the remainder experienced extreme side-effects. *Oz* also tackled the increasingly urgent issue of mental illness in prison. One consequence of the switch from welfare to warfare in US public policy has been a dramatic rise in the numbers of people in prison who ought to be housed in mental health facilities. Problems are exacerbated by increasing emphasis, especially in SHUs, on segregation and prolonged solitary confinement. *Oz* hinted at this crisis by featuring characters with severe mental illnesses (such as Cyril O'Reilly) alongside others who experienced visual and auditory hallucinations, forms of traumatic disorder and SHU syndrome.

6 This feat was attempted by a member of the Aryan Brotherhood on discovering that he may have been the beneficiary of a gum transplant from an African-American donor.

7 One could of course challenge the accuracy of these figures since they are compiled by authorities with a vested interest in maintaining the appearance of control. An obvious ruse for massaging these figures involves failing to include 'accidental' deaths and recording others as 'unknown causes'.

8 Hill's commentary offers only a superficial critique of the violence and perhaps its more significant function is to provide an alibi for the viewer's sadistic pleasures. These monologues fulfil a function similar to that served by the voice-over in conventional Hollywood war movies. The trite maxim, 'war is hell', is repeated to disguise the emotional investment of film and viewer in two hours of exhilarating bloodshed and violence.

9 For example, internecine warfare in the Hispanic gang results in one inmate (Alvarez) allowing another (Guerra) to stab him in the shoulder as a means of ending a long-running feud. Many of the violent encounters in *Oz* were, at root, a means of maintaining status and repaying debts.

10 The official boxing competition in Emerald City took place alongside unofficial 'death matches' arranged by the guards. The inspiration for these scenes may have been notorious events at Corcoran State Prison in

California. Guards placed rival gangs in the yard at the same time and placed bets on who would win the inevitable fights. The prisoners were then shot at for failing to stop fighting on command. Between 1988 and 1996 this resulted in over 50 shootings and seven fatalities.

11 The motif of ingestion in *Oz* might be read as a microcosm of the prisoner being swallowed into the 'belly of the beast' (to quote the title of Jack Henry Abbott's prison novel). In one scene this ingestion was symbolically reversed in dirty protest as a guard swallowed some of an abject cocktail containing blood-piss-shit-semen-and-vomit thrown into his face by an inmate.

12 Independent groups, such as Stop Prisoner Rape, underline the upper figure in this estimate. There is, however, good reason to believe that even 1 in 5 may be an underestimate. Many victims of sexual assault do not report incidents from fear of reprisal and stigma. On the outside, some victims of prison rape have argued that the authorities tolerate certain levels of sexual violence to help manage and manipulate the Gen Pop.

13 The daddy protects his bitch, but the passive partner simultaneously protects his abuser by assuming the stigma of homosexuality. The practice of having sex with feminized men whilst retaining one's heterosexuality is of course well established in cultures where homophobia is less pronounced than the USA.

14 Although Sister Pete played the conventional female role of ministering angel, she stands alongside a troupe of depraved women that included Officer Claire Howell who routinely assaulted inmates both physically and sexually and lodged false claims of sexual harassment against McManus; Nurse Grace who sedated inmates and then killed them; and a mother, one of the first casualties on death row, who murdered her own daughter.

References

Baudrillard, J. (1989) *America*. London: Verso.

Bauman, Z. (1999) *In Search of Politics*. Stanford, CA: Stanford University Press.

Bhabha, H. (1995) 'Are you a man or a mouse?' in M. Berger *et al.* (eds) *Constructing Masculinity*. New York: Routledge.

Butler, J. (1990) *Gender Trouble: Feminism and the Subversion of Identity*. London: Routledge.

Davis, A.Y. (2001) 'Race, gender, and prison history: from the convict lease system to the supermax prison', in D. Sabo *et al.* (eds) *Prison Masculinities*. Philadelphia, PA: Temple University Press.

Faludi, S. (2000) *Stiffed: The Betrayal of the American Male*. Pymble, NSW: Perennial.

Foucault, M. (1995) *Discipline and Punish: The Birth of the Prison*. New York, NY: Vintage.

Giroux, H. (1998) 'Public pedagogy and rodent politics: cultural studies and the challenge of Disney', *Arizona Journal of Hispanic Cultural Studies*, 2: 253–66.

Goffman, E. (1961) *Encounters: Two Studies in the Sociology of Interaction*. Oxford: Macmillan.

Jameson, F. (1991) *Postmodernism, or the Cultural Logic of Late Capitalism*. Durham, NC: Duke University Press.

Lancaster, R. (2002) 'Subject honour, object shame', in R. Adams and D. Savran (eds) *The Masculinity Studies Reader*. Oxford: Blackwell.

Robinson, S. (2000) *Marked Men: White Masculinity in Crisis*. New York, NY: Columbia University Press.

Sabo, D. (2001) 'Doing time, doing masculinity: sports and prison', in D. Sabo *et al.* (eds) *Prison Masculinities*. Philadelphia, PA: Temple University Press.

Sabo, D., Kupers, T.A. and London, W. (eds) (2001) *Prison Masculinities*. Philadelphia, PA: Temple University Press.

Savran, D. (1998) *Taking it Like a Man: White Masculinity, Masochism and Contemporary American Culture*. Princeton, NJ: Princeton University Press.

Scarry, E. (1985) *The Body in Pain: The Making and the Unmaking of the World*. Oxford: Oxford University Press.

Seltzer, M. (1998) *Serial Killers: Death and Life in America's Wound Culture*. Oxford: Routledge.

Theweleit, K. (1989) *Male Bodies: Psychoanalysing the White Terror. Vol. 2*. Minneapolis, MN: University of Minnesota Press.

Thompson, E.P. (1986) *The Making of the English Working Class*. Harmondsworth: Penguin.

Chapter 11

The anti-heroines of Holloway: the prison films of Joan Henry and J. Lee Thompson

Steve Chibnall

In Britain before World War Two, the fiction film was firmly regarded as a medium of popular entertainment. It was not expected, and certainly not encouraged, to stray into areas of social and political controversy. If it did, its duty was to support prevailing mores and arrangements, and never to mount a challenge to public policy (Richards 1984). Prisons and penal policy were particularly sensitive fields for cinematic treatment. The sort of critique offered by *I am a Fugitive from a Chain Gang* (Mervyn LeRoy 1932) in the USA was simply unthinkable in Britain. Draconian censorship by the BBFC and acute suspicion from the Home Office had restricted prison subjects to convicts on the run, foreign jails and a single Will Hay comedy. Although a number of prison memoirs appeared in the 1930s, their filming was heavily discouraged (Nellis 1988: 6–7). After the war, the spirit of social reconstruction fostered by the new Labour government allowed film-makers a little more latitude in tackling social issues. The subject of false imprisonment was raised by Cavalcanti in *They Made me a Fugitive* (1947) and *For them that Trespass* (1948), and the Home Office and the Prison Commissioners began to offer tentative co-operation, first to the Crown Film Unit for its drama-doc *Children on Trial* (1945), and then to Anatole de Grunwald to make the first British drama of prison life, *Now Barrabas was a Robber* (1949).

If penal institutions for men had received some cinematic exploration by the early 1950s, the subject of women in prison remained largely untouched. Although there were more than a dozen treatments of the theme by Hollywood between 1929 and 1952 (Parish 1991; Zalcock 1999), there was no depiction of a British penal institution for women until 1948 when David Macdonald filmed Arthur la Bern's *Good Time Girl*, partly set inside a girls' reformatory. Two other British films had told the stories of incarcerated women, but both were set in France: Brian Desmond Hurst's *Prison without Bars* (1938) and Frank Launder's *2000 Women* (1944). The first glimpse inside an adult women's prison had to wait until 1953 when the governor of Holloway offered limited co-operation for the opening scenes of Jack Lee's *Turn the Key Softly*. By then, the women-in-prison subgenre had been given a new currency by the critical and popular success of Warner Bros' *Caged* (John Cramwell 1950) which secured three Academy Award nominations for its uncompromising dissection of brutality and sexuality behind bars.

Late in 1952 the promising British film-maker, J. Lee Thompson, noticed a new bestseller from Victor Gollancz. The book was concerned with conditions in Britain's penal institutions for women, and was creating a storm of protest from the prison service and headaches for Conservative Home Secretary, David Maxwell Fyfe. It may be a worn-flat cliché but it was to be the book that changed Lee Thompson's life. He told the tale very simply:

> I read the book called *Who Lie in Gaol* by Joan Henry and I went to [Associated British's studio head] Robert Clark and said 'We've got to buy this book'. And I went to see Joan Henry and I fell in love with her, and I divorced my wife for her, and we eventually married. Before we married I made *The Weak and the Wicked*, which was the film of her book. It became a huge hit.[1]

The film was not only a hit, it was effectively the first intervention by cinema into the debates surrounding British penal institutions for adult women.

Joan Henry was a novelist and ex-debutant whose life had taken an unusual turn for a woman of her class. The gambling debts she had incurred had led to a fraud conviction and, after spending eight months of 1950 in Holloway and the new 'open' prison at Askham Grange in Yorkshire, and at the insistence of her literary agents, she reluctantly wrote a memoir of her experiences. Although *Who Lie in Gaol* is a first-person account, it is intended to be 'the story of any woman, innocent or guilty, who has the misfortune to go to prison' (Henry 1952: 7).[2] The opinions about the penal system expressed in the book are, for the most part, liberal humanist, but they are coloured by personal loss and discomfort:

During the first week in prison, the average prisoner forms a revulsion against authority that in normal circumstances would take a lifetime of mismanagement to acquire; a revulsion born of bitterness and self-pity, and nurtured by being in the power of uneducated people, who for the most part should not be in charge of animals, far less human beings. The majority of women in prison are weak characters who have become victims of circumstance (Henry 1952: 48).

Henry goes on to condemn the way in which Holloway Prison fosters 'a life that saps initiative and encourages lethargy' (1952: 120), and to contrast its corrosive effects with the more positive results of the progressive regime at Askham Grange (Lewis and Crew 1997). The book was bound to arouse controversy on its publication in the midst of the 'cosh boy' panic in the autumn of 1952, providing a rallying point for liberal consciences. Lee Thompson immediately saw its dramatic potential, and his boss, Robert Clark, quickly snapped up the film rights.

Henry's book, with its muted plea for better conditions, never matched the intensity of *Caged*, but the screenplay would emphasize the comedic passages of Henry's book and sandpaper some of the rougher textures of what was already a somewhat sanitized account, particularly in the reporting of speech. Prison officers could not be referred to as 'screws' and sanitary towels could not be mentioned. Nor could there be any explicit suggestion of lesbianism, although the book had identified 'unnatural practices' between women (including prison officers) as 'a very difficult problem for the prison authority' (Henry 1952: 83). Lesbian desire could only be suggested, as it had been in *Caged*, through the biases of a brutal prison officer.

The summer of 1953, with its mood of patriotic fervour stoked up for the coronation of Elizabeth II, was not the most auspicious time to show the Home Office a screenplay which was critical of a national institution like the prison service. Unsurprisingly, official approval was withheld. Luckily, the progressive Roman Catholic governor of Askham Grange, Mary Size, had recently retired and, despite fears for her pension, she agreed to act as adviser on the film. The *Daily Mirror* (17 August 1953) congratulated Associated British on a 'bold and provocative' project, and on some intriguing casting: not only Glynis Johns as Joan Henry (changed to Jean Raymond for the film), but the opportunity given to Diana Dors to extend her acting range in drab prison garb. Dors' first 'deglamorization' became *The Weak and the Wicked*'s key publicity motif. She plays one of 'the weak', Betty, an impressionable young woman who is in gaol because of misplaced loyalty to her larcenous boyfriend. The part is a highly sanitized version of the book's Betty Brown, a young recidivist with two young children, tuberculosis and venereal disease (Henry 1952: 14). Worries about offending the Home Office and the Censor combined with the problems of interpreting the personality of a literary narrator to make the Jean Raymond character rather blander than Joan Henry would have liked: 'I felt it made me seem awfully sort of goody-goody, when I wasn't the least bit goody-goody.'

For Jean Raymond and, by implication, hundreds of other women, prison is the consequence of a wilful and self-centred recklessness which blinds her to danger, and the random selection of fate. In the film both are represented by a spinning roulette wheel. However, as Marcia Landy (1991: 454) argues, there are deeper well-springs to the misfortune of Jean and her fellow inmates which have their origins in gender relations. Clearly, Betty is in gaol because of her attachment to an inappropriate male who has manipulated her, but Jean's downfall results from her lack of commitment to her medical man, Michael (John Gregson), denying her destiny as a colonial wife and chancing her freedom at the gaming tables. Part of the rehabilitative role of prison is to end her selfishness and help her to appreciate the importance of her romantic duty. As she confides to the kindly prison chaplain: 'I want to help Michael to forget all the unhappiness I have caused him. I want to make him a good wife.' What preoccupies the prison inmates is not the loss of freedom or even sexual satisfaction but a loss of role, of the supportive relationships to men which allow them to make sense of themselves as women. In prison, even the tangible fruits of their heterosexual relationships, their babies, are taken away nine months after birth (mostly for adoption by respectable couples). The women are reduced to an unnatural and undesired state of individualism, and their reactions to the savage environment in which they find themselves locate them on a continuum on which femininity and recidivism are posed as polar opposites. The line between compassion and selfishness is the one which separates 'the weak' from 'the wicked'. It is this realization which will ultimately make Cambridge drop-out and inveterate gambler Jean into a woman who is truly marriageable. This, presumably, is the reason why Michael has abandoned his job in Rhodesia and is waiting in his sports car when Jean is released.

Henry distanced herself from this trite ending, blaming the conceptions of commercial film-making shared by Lee Thompson, fellow scenarist Anne Burnaby and Associated British. In her analysis of *The Weak and the Wicked*, Marcia Landy prefers to sidestep the unpalatable sexual and cultural politics of the film's conventional closure. Instead, she emphasizes the way in which the film successfully explores women's relationships to each other in the context of 'resistance to the status quo', exemplified in the Jean and Betty friendship (Henry 1952: 455). However, although the film depicts heterosexual bonding as a site of tension and disappointment and makes efforts to explore the redemptive qualities of relationships between women, the elements of sisterhood which Landy celebrates are ultimately offered only as moderating considerations in the recommendation of women's selfless commitment to stable relationships with men. *The Weak and the Wicked* may be more a discursive than a didactic text, with its rhetorical flourishes largely concentrated on the inhumanity of prison regimes, but its radicalism stops just short of the toleration of sisterhood over patriarchal marriage. One only has to observe the type of labour which the film appears to endorse as therapeutic in the open prison – consisting as it does of dressmaking, rugmaking, leather work, knitting and cleaning – to appreciate that the world for which these women are being 'fitted' is a primarily domestic one. The impression persists that prison – open or closed – is a means of punishing and re-educating women for their gender transgressions as much as for their infringements of the law. Marriage may be, as one middle-aged inmate describes it, an act of 'martyrdom', but it is ultimately the only route to a state of grace.

Just as prison may help women to refocus on their gender obligations, so, the film suggests, it may also assist bringing greater understanding between them. In the process of imprisonment it is evident that some of the barriers of class, temperament, and cultural awareness which atomize women in everyday life are dissolved. A sense of commonality is a by-product of communal incarceration. The airs and graces of Mrs Skinner (Mary Merrall), 'a British subject born in Salisbury', cut no ice in the melting pot of the prison where the screws enforce a universally harsh regime and wealth is a packet of cigarettes. Gentlewoman and hard-hearted harridan share the same predicament, and under such abnormal conditions, as the Governor of the Grange (Jean Taylor-Smith) assures us, 'ill assorted pairs' can be 'valuable to each other'. Mutual aid, rather than opposition, is what is advocated. Although the brutality of prevailing prison conditions may be deplored, overt resistance to authoritarian regimes is not endorsed, and is even subtly coded as un-British when it is depicted.[3] Jean and Betty's transfer to 'a prison without bars' which the film's rhetoric advances as the future of imprisonment suggests the system's ability and motivation to reform itself.

Lee Thompson's socialist beliefs show through in the film's treatment of class and its advocacy of mutuality and trust, just as Anne Burnaby's talent for comedy writing is apparent in some of the flash-back sequences which extend and embroider Joan Henry's original text. The most whimsical of these comic episodes, the arsenic-and-old-lace tale of poisoning featuring the comic talents of Sybil Thorndike and Athene Seyler, has all the macabre gentility of Ealing but its position within a social problem drama caused raised eyebrows amongst the critics. The *Daily Mail*'s Fred Majdalany (3 February 1954) summed up the feelings of most when he suggested that the film's 'gay revue sketches' were hardly 'the right substitutes for the starker details of the book'. Left-wing critics in particular thought the film much too 'nice'.[4] It was left to Caroline Lejeune (*Observer* 7 February 1954), however, to relate the concerns about realism and sentimentality to the issue of essentialism in gender representation. She argued that the film's unintentional effect was 'to make crime committed by women seem a bit of a freak, a loveable eccentricity or lark, or at the very worst, an error of judgement'. The film might more accurately have been titled 'The Weak and the Weaker' because wickedness (at least amongst prisoners) is largely absent from its Christian Socialist discourse. Malevolence and maliciousness are traits largely confined to the custodial staff, and to the system of incarceration which disciplines and punishes with a minimum of compassion.

Critical opinion may have deplored the genre compromises and sanitized representations of *The Weak and the Wicked* but audiences responded positively to its shrewd populism. The commercial success of the film would enable Henry and Lee Thompson to develop something far more radical for their next collaboration: a film that would make a strategic intervention in the debate about penal policy. The genesis of *Yield to the Night* is recalled by Joan Henry:

> [Lee] was against capital punishment like me, and he said 'I've always wanted to write a book or a play about a man in a death cell'. I said, 'Well, I couldn't write about a man, but I might be able to do that about a woman.' So he really gave me the idea, and then I showed him a plan.

Lee Thompson was insistent that, if the story was to present an effective case against the death penalty, there should be 'no mitigating circumstances' to the woman's crime. Henry threw herself into the project. 'I wrote the book in six weeks, very, very quickly,' she remembered, 'and I was in tears most of the time and had quite a lot to drink ... I felt that it was me almost.' The book was published in 1954 in the aftermath of a royal commission which had been given the brief of recommending more humane means of execution but had suggested in its report that the 'real question now is whether capital punishment should be abolished or retained' (Hopkins 1964: 214). The subject of Henry's novel was clearly a timely one, and Lee Thompson was desperate to turn it into a film. He wanted to evoke the same elegiac sadness, the same nobility of suffering, the same feeling of persecution and martyrdom as Carol Reed's *Odd Man Out* (1947). It would be Lee Thompson's *Odd Woman Out*, the long journey into night of a shop girl who, in Reed's phrase, 'had done something wrong for the right reasons' (cited in Wapshott 1990: 179). The executives remained to be convinced, but the sudden box-office potential given to the project by a highly publicized murder which closely resembled the fictional events in *Yield to the Night* eventually won them over.

Henry's novel is the first-person narrative of Mary Hilton, a sexually-adventurous shop assistant who deserts her dull husband to pursue an affair with a night-club pianist. Their relationship, however, is blighted by her lover's obsession with Lucy, a rich society woman. When unrequited love leads him to suicide, Mary avenges the death by shooting her ex-rival, and spends three weeks in the condemned cell at Holloway prison awaiting execution. Those events were uncannily paralleled by the case of Ruth Ellis, a young night-club manager and model who shot her faithless lover David Blakely on Easter Sunday 1955 and was herself executed in Holloway that July (Hancock 1993). The two narratives are so similar that *Yield to the Night*, with its attractive blonde protagonist, is often mistaken for a Ruth Ellis 'bio-pic', even though the book was published the year before she fired the fatal shots in Hampstead[5]. Just how closely life imitated art can be seen in the following comparisons: in both cases a brooding obsession with an unreliable man results in a young woman being driven to a residential part of London where she fires a volley of bullets into her victim who dies in the full view of bystanders.[6] Both women have recently experienced a failed marriage, both kill people from a higher social class, are summarily convicted and spend three Sundays in Holloway before execution.

Lee Thompson strenuously denied any connection between the Ruth Ellis case and his own film, to the extent that he came to believe the film was finished *before* the execution of Ellis. Joan Henry believed that the film was being shot at Elstree when the Ellis execution took place. In fact, Ruth Ellis was hanged on 13 July 1955, three months before *Yield to the Night* went before the camera. The script for the film, held in the BFI library, is dated 9 August. This is *not* to suggest that the film is actually based on the Ellis case, but that its makers spent so long refuting the idea that they were cashing in on the notoriety of a real crime that it distorted the sequence of events in their memory. The accusation of exploitation dogged the film from the very beginning. The hanging of Ruth Ellis is a milestone event in the abolition of capital punishment because the adverse public reaction ensured that she would be the last woman to be executed in Britain.[7] In February 1955, two months before Ellis killed Blakely, an anti-hanging bill was defeated in the House of Commons by 31 votes. A year later, Sidney Silverman's Abolition Bill passed its first reading. By that time, *Yield to the Night* was in the can and almost ready to make its own contribution to a fierce ongoing debate.

From the beginning, the film had been conceived by Henry and Lee Thompson, unashamedly, as a propaganda drama in the campaign against hanging. In the wake of serious doubts about the conviction and execution of Timothy Evans, melodramas about innocent men battling to avoid execution were beginning to be filmed: *Eight O'Clock Walk* (Lance Comfort 1953) and *Time without Pity* (Joseph Losey 1957). But by eschewing the portrayal of a wrongly convicted innocent in favour of a calculating killer, Henry and Lee Thompson hoped to mount a more comprehensive argument for abolition. As Lee Thompson told *Kinematograph Weekly* (10 November 1955): 'We are not making this film a special case. If hanging is essential to our civilization then the heroine of our picture deserves to hang. If anything, we're loading the dice against the girl; she is not really a sympathetic character.' If the film could evoke revulsion, for the execution of even an unrepentant murderer, then the grounds for retaining the death penalty would be severely undermined.

The success of this argument hinged on the studio's acceptance of the book's bleak and gloomy ending, with Mary Hilton going to her death. The profound sadness in the audience that this would provoke was vital to subsequent protest against the death penalty, but had always been considered commercial suicide by British movie executives. Lee Thompson was determined that *Yield to the Night* would not pull its final punch, but Joan Henry remembered 'terrible trouble at Elstree' with the director standing firm: 'Lee said before the film started, 'They're going to try to make me have a happy ending, but I'm not going to. I'll shoot the ending first'.' The glib closure of *The Weak and the Wicked* was now to be resisted at all costs.

When an additional screenwriter, John Cresswell, was imposed on Henry and Lee Thompson, the reaction was defensive, as Henry recalled: 'Lee tried to strangle him at one of our meetings at [producer] Kenneth Harper's flat. He never came back again.' The incident gives an insight into the passion and intensity with which Lee Thompson approached the filming of *Yield to the Night*. As the project progressed his demand for creative control became more insistent – not least in the casting of the film. Diana Dors was the controversial choice to play Mary Hilton. After her supporting role in *The Weak and the Wicked*, Dors was offered the chance to transcend her public persona and demonstrate her dramatic prowess alongside established 'serious' actress Yvonne Mitchell. The casting would underline Mary's worldliness as well as attracting enormous publicity to the film.

Shooting on *Yield to the Night* began in late October 1955 at Elstree. Without Home Office co-operation, the claustrophobic 'death cell' was designed by Robert Jones from information bought from a prison officer at Pentonville.[8] The dreadful verisimilitude of her surroundings and the film's costumes had a profound effect on Diana Dors. As she told reporter Maurice Wiltshire: 'I keep telling myself this is only a film. But it's no good. I shudder every time I have to go into that cell, even though it's only a film set. I think it's the clothes. I keep thinking about the wretched women who have to wear them' (*Daily Mail* 3 November 1955). Moreover, Dors' husband, Dennis Hamilton, had recently persuaded her to abort the child she was carrying, a decision she experienced as a 'blight on our conscience', and in these circumstances, her role as a condemned murderer, can be seen as a form of atonement (Dors 1959: 139).

Associated British's publicity strategy was again to market the contrast between the two Dianas, to discover the real woman beyond the nyloned veneer. This approach may have stimulated in its audience fantasies which would only handicap the film's attempts to win sympathy for its protagonist. After all, a film that shows a beautiful woman being punished (a key component of the women-in-prison genre), whatever the motivation of its creators, offers wish fulfilment to misogynists, and retributive satisfaction to women who feel threatened by feminine display. Her marketing as Britain's first Hollywood-style 'sex bomb', and her scandalous private life, marked out Diana Dors as a prime object of vindictive fantasy (Harper and Porter 1999: 73). Her 'come-uppance' in *Yield to the Night* would offer succour to critics of both Americanization and sexual licence, although they might find themselves recoiling from the sadistic spectacle of a 'blonde bombshell' stripped not to her nubile flesh but to her emotional bone and clinging desperately to life. There is something distinctly embarrassing about viewing Dors in this condition. We almost feel we should turn away to allow Diana to paint her face and cantilever her bosom, to reconstruct the 'glamour babe' persona on which her confidence and sense of self appears to rest. Without it, there is no sparkle in her eyes, the light within has been extinguished just as she craves the switching off of the bulb which continuously illuminates her cell. The electric light, of course, symbolizes both Mary's own life and the surveillance which she is constantly under, both from her warders and, extra-diagetically, from the film's audience. As in Michael Powell's *Peeping Tom* (1960) we, the audience, are obliged to watch the moments leading up to death and invited to acknowledge our complicity. But, whereas Powell shamelessly implicates us in a lurid Eastman colour fantasy, Lee Thompson offers us a monochromed realism which intensifies our discomfort with the role of voyeur. Our unease is expressed in the way the camera continually shuns the direct shot, preferring to adopt a furtive, sheltered position, behind furniture, low to the ground, or (quintessentially scoptophilic) peering though the cell window. Merciless in its interrogation, it records every nuance of Mary's relationship to her environment as if gathering data for an ergonomic study. 'I know every mark and blemish in this cell', Mary's voice-over tells us, and Gilbert Taylor's camera shows us with microscope clarity, 'every crack in the walls; the scratches on the wooden chairs; the place where the paint has peeled off the ceiling; and the door at the foot of the bed, the door without a handle'. Mary remarks that she knows it 'better than any room I've ever lived in' and it begins to have the same oppressive familiarity for the audience.

But what *Yield to the Night* shows us with the greatest clarity is the collapse or dislocation of human relationships in the face of death. Lee Thompson uses the metonym of eye contact to express eloquently the emotional disengagement which prefigures death. When Mary's mother (Dandy Nichols) visits and tells her she cannot look the signatories of the reprieve petition in the face it is evident that Mary cannot meet the gaze of her mother. In a shot which becomes a rhetorical trope of the film, her profile on the left of the frame is contrasted with the full face of her conversational partner on the right – a 'two shot' which quotes the dual-angle police 'mug shot'. This compositional practice complements the use of hands and feet as signifiers. In her bath, for example, a disengaged Mary is seen in profile whilst her fingernails are clipped by a gaoler. She has not requested this service and it may be read as a metaphor for the submission of her feminine vanity to the disciplinary regimes of the prison as well as for the curtailment of her growth (life). There is also constant reference to the condition of feet and shoes, from Mary's heightened awareness of one of her warder's 'flat, sensible shoes with iron studs in the soles' (illustrated in hyper-real close-up), to her problems with a blister on her own foot.[9] The blister 'matters', she is told, and clearly the condition hobbles her, just as prison restricts her bodily freedom and shackles her to its routines. We are shown a close-up of Mary's bandaged foot and, in a scene where she angrily sweeps a chess set from its board, the camera creeps below the table to reveal the carpet slippers Mary wears. In stark contrast to her youthful, high-heeled pomp, this is the footwear of the aged, as if imminent execution had accelerated the ageing process. She is certainly cared for as the old or sick are cared for – her mattress is turned and she is weighed, bandaged, manicured and generally tended – by her uniformed companions who frequently talk distractedly amongst themselves. The banality of their conversations strikes an ironic counterpart to the profundity of Mary's situation, a difference of depth which is sometimes given visual expression in the use of deep-focus photography – notably when Mary is seen with a warder knitting in the foreground like a tricoteuse before the guillotine.

Yield to the Night begins and ends with the execution of a woman. The first takes three minutes of rapid-fire montage. The second is stretched over an almost unendurably poignant hour and a half. Without a word of dialogue and employing film-making techniques which were strikingly progressive for British cinema in the 1950s, the dynamic opening sequence shows the crime for which Mary Hilton will be incarcerated. With disquieting camera angles and compositions, the sequence eloquently expresses the distanciated state of mind of the protagonist and introduces the visual language and motifs which the rest of the film will use (Chibnall 2000: 84–6). These include mediated shots in which foregrounded objects break up the frame, distance the viewer from the action and register the intrusive and voyeuristic gaze; high, low and canted angle shots to disturb further the audience's complacent viewpoint; strong attention to geometric design within the frame with particular emphasis on verticals suggesting entrapment; keys and locks as emblems of a situation from which the protagonist craves release; and the detailed observation of body parts, used both to suggest a heightened state of consciousness and to express key states of mind.[10] When the full ensemble of technical expertise, acting talent and directorial sensitivity work together within the codes of the film's symbolic system – in the scene in which Mary learns that she will not be reprieved, for example – the effect is stunning (Chibnall 2000: 91–3).[11] The film's editor Dick Best agrees that it is 'tremendous in the way it's shot', adding, 'There was a power [...] *Yield to the Night* needed very little editing – it is nearly all single planned master shots'. Dors' performance registers every milestone of Mary's slow disintegration into abjection and paranoia, sensitively capturing her embittered anguish. In such an unbearable present with such an unthinkable future, it is inevitable that Mary should retreat into the past, and Lee Thompson uses the standard noir technique of flashbacks which reveal how his protagonist arrived at her doomed situation. The use of this narrative device allows us regularly to compare the two Dianas/Marys.

One might interpret the bonds that develop in this isolated and pressurized environment between Mary and her wardresses (particularly Yvonne Mitchell's McFarlane) as an alliance against a repressive masculine apparatus of justice. But there is little feminist solidarity in the death cell, only the contradiction between an embarrassed compassion and a collusion in the act of murder. As Mary puts it, her warders 'all have a funny look in their eyes – like I had once – but they're going to kill someone too; only this time it's legal'. They encourage her not to fight for life but to 'accept' her punishment, making it 'easier to bear'. Although there is a suggestion that McFarlane is as much a prisoner of circumstance as the woman she guards (Henry 1954: 65) and there is evident affection between them, McFarlane is ultimately part of the conspiracy against Mary: 'You're in league with the others; you want to kill me', she once rants at McFarlane, 'I hate you, I hate you all'. No, to interpret Mary's fate, as Marcia Landy (1991: 458) does, as 'a broader allegory of society's retaliation against female desire through all of its institutional channels' glosses over too many complexities and contradictions. Mary may have broken the bonds of domesticity and threatened patriarchal stability with her sexuality, but her wrath is directed principally against other women, and it is they who endorse her punishment.[12] Indeed, it was her sexuality which was implicitly offered as grounds for reprieve in the film's promotional campaign which was dominated by an alluring portrait of Diana Dors – lips full and open, eyes closing in ecstasy – accompanied by the largely rhetorical question: 'Would You Hang Mary Hilton?'[13]

I have argued elsewhere (Chibnall 1999) that the crisis of masculinity evident in so many British genre films in the 20 years following World War Two was marked by an unresolved ambivalence towards the sexually assertive woman. In *Yield to the Night*, that ambivalence is apparently resolved by the desexualizing of Dors/Hilton and the (justifiable?) homicide of the predatory Lucy, but resurfaces in the film's publicity which enlists male desire in the campaign against the noose. Perhaps is it not an inappropriate strategy for a film which laments the violent repression of libidinous impulses by a vengeful and puritanical state. Raymond Durgnat (1970: 165), in discussing the 'punitive streak' in British Puritanism which is exemplified by a 'fascination with the condemned cell', suggested that *Yield to the Night* appeared at 'a kind of junction of liberalism and severity'. He refers to an 'identification with suffering passivity' which, one might argue, is an inchoate state of social criticism. Lee Thompson and Joan Henry's film begins to move British cinema beyond sympathy for the underdog and into the realms of active critique. It opens the door not only to the liberal-humanist social problem films of Dearden and Relph, but also to the bitterness of *Look Back in Anger* (Tony Richardson 1959) and *Saturday Night and Sunday Morning* (Karel Reisz 1961). Dilys Powell also argued that *Yield to the Night* marks a transition point in the replacement of a strict morality by a less censorious one,[14] and perhaps it is not over-fanciful to see Mary's condemned cell as an image, not simply of an imprisoning social order, but also of the stifling restrictions imposed on British film-making. When the prison doctor (Geoffrey Keen) advises Mary to 'conform to the routine however hard and futile it may seem' he could be offering a credo to all toilers in a national film industry shackled by gentility, euphemism and banality. Either way, there is a compelling case for interpreting the overwhelming identification with Mary's suffering which the film encourages as a vital expiation of guilt before the slow acceptance of more progressive moral, regulatory and artistic frameworks. Or to express this idea of necessary catharsis more flippantly: Mary Hilton had to swing before the 1960s could.

In the end, we identify with a woman who atones for her sins without the customary remorse. Although she knows she has 'done wrong', she regrets nothing, is 'not ready to die', and rejects a hearty breakfast on the day of her execution. As she smokes her final cigarette[15] before praying with her gaolers she remains recalcitrant and, as the camera closes in on a neck that will soon feel the touch of hemp, she still refuses to endorse the legitimacy of her fate. When she is lead to the gallows she leaves with dignity,[16] and as she fixes the viewer with her eyes before moving into shadow, any lingering desire for retribution we might harbour is swept away by a profound sense of tragedy. And as contemporary audiences watched the final frames of the film with a bell tolling solemnly and the smoke coiling up symbolically from Mary's abandoned cigarette they would have needed no reminder of Mrs Bligh's prediction that the burden of Mary's sin would pass from her 'to those who have to go as usual about their daily business'. It is the final transfer of a film in which tragedy has been passed in a relay from one recipient to another. Its progress has been motivated by the dynamic set-up when obsession meets rejection – Jim's indifference to Mary's desire; Lucy's rebuff of Jim's infatuation; Mary's refusal to legitimate the pious ministration of her gaolers; and, ultimately, the audience's rejection of the obsessive rituals of a criminal justice system bent on retribution.

When *Yield to the Night* was shown at the Cannes film festival in 1956, continental critics were enthusiastic, but British reviewers were concerned about its sombre mood and the controversial nature of its message. However, the reviews that followed the film's opening at London's Carlton cinema on 13 June were predominantly laudatory. Most critics seemed genuinely amazed at the qualities Diana Dors had demonstrated in her performance and praised its tone of emotional understatement. It was, remarked Caroline Lejeune (*Observer* 17 June 1956), 'played with a decent reserve'. This same quality was valued in the film as a whole, and a number of reviewers contrasted its dignity with what Campbell Dixon (*Daily Telegraph* 16 June 1956) called 'the hysterical sadism' of an earlier French film about capital punishment, Andre Cayatte's *Nous sommes tous des assassins* (1953). Declaring *Yield to the Night* the 'most harrowing' film he had seen in years, Roy Nash (*Star* 15 June 1956) told readers that, although it was three days since he had seen the film, 'the faces of Miss Dors and the wardresses in the final scenes haunt me still'. Again, it was understated emotion which most affected him: 'without mawkishness, with an almost clinical restraint, it brings home the full grisly ghastliness of the death cell.'

It is curious that contemporary reviewers felt able to use so many of their favourite terms of appreciation – 'decency', 'restraint", 'dignity', 'reserve' – to describe a film which is certainly no *Brief Encounter* (David Lean 1945). Rather than endorsing the social mores which elevate institutional imperatives above the gratification of personal desires, *Yield to the Night* exposes, at the core of institutionalized order, an inhumanity which coarsens and corrupts the lives it touches. Gone is David Lean's cosy vision of a hearth and home which may be dull, but which offers loving security. In Lee Thompson's film the hearth is no longer a place of safety, but a venue for suicide by gas heater in a lonely bedsitter. Home is not a comfy armchair in suburbia but an austere prison cell. The family which *Brief Encounter* championed as the bastion of 'decent' social arrangements has all but disappeared in *Yield to the Night*,[17] Mary Hilton has done what *Brief Encounter's* Laura Jesson (Celia Johnson) could never bring herself to do; she has left the stifling confines of her marriage. In gaol, she grudgingly tolerates her husband's visits and is uncomfortable with her mother and brother. The comfort she receives is chiefly from strangers like Mrs Bligh, her visitor (Athene Seyler) and state functionaries like the warders who give care and companionship in a death cell ensemble which constantly mocks the family group.

It might be tempting to read these inversions as a warning about the dangers of abandoning the normative world of *Brief Encounter*, were it not for the perverse purposes to which its sober conceptions of love and duty are applied. In *Yield to the Night*, the state's representatives demonstrate their commitment to loving compassion by ensuring that Mary Hilton goes to the gallows in the best possible health, and to duty by their unwavering dedication to hanging her. In other words, the finest of ideals are put to the basest of ends: the extinction of a life which has long ceased to be a danger to others. What the film offers is not a critique of deteriorating moral standards amongst the wayward, glamour-conscious young, but an indictment of a continuing ethical failure by those older and more powerful. It rejects the hypocrisy of a state which punishes an act of revenge with its own, mortal vengeance.

Yield to the Night's polemic was an extraordinarily brave one by the conservative standards of 1950s film-making. British pictures of the era rarely deal with the institutionalization of violence, let alone attempt to enlist our sympathy for a convicted murderer. But *Yield to the Night* achieves its aims without overt didacticism, and with a visual sophistication and unity worthy of Michael Powell. J. Lee Thompson regarded it as 'very much one of the best' films of his career. It was, he said, 'always very close to my heart'. For this, he felt, much of the credit should go to Diana Dors. For Joan Henry, too, Dors' performance was her abiding memory of a film which had faithfully reflected the spirit and mood of her story: 'I can see her now, walking towards the door in the wall, and she looked really as if she was already dead.' Caroline Lejeune (certainly not the most sentimental of critics) remarked at the time that 'it is impossible for anyone with an imaginative turn of mind not to be moved' (*Observer* 17 June 1956), and the film remains the most disquieting and harrowing of experiences.

Yield to the Night was screened for Members of Parliament on more than one occasion, and Lee Thompson liked to think that 'it had some small part in removing the Death Penalty'. The direct influence of the film is harder to establish. The last execution of a woman (Ruth Ellis) in Britain took place a year before *Yield to the Night* premiered with a cautionary 'X' certificate.[18] The film was already an elegy for a departed method of dealing with the unruly female. Two days after its West End release, the House of Commons voted to retain the death penalty only for murders committed by prisoners already serving life sentences. When the Abolition Bill was debated by the Lords the following month, leading supporters Arthur Koestler and Gerald Gardiner QC arranged a special screening of Mary Hilton's ordeal for their lordships. Only six peers turned up to the National Film Theatre. Their reactions were mixed. One of them, 71-year-old Lord Burden voted for the bill whilst another, 28-year-old Lord Denham, voted against (*News Chronicle* 20 August 1956). Denham was in the majority and the bill was defeated in the Lords.

The death penalty lingered on into the next decade, but the moral order it symbolized was already being given its last rights by the time *Yield to the Night* was released. Bill Haley and Elvis Presley dominated the pop charts and Britain's nostalgic attempt to flex its muscles as a world power ended in the military fiasco of Suez. As crowds flocked to see Dors sans glamour, the mass-circulation tabloid *Tit-Bits* (16 June 1956) carried a front page pin-up of Diana in a strapless evening gown dramatically slashed to the hip. Inside, 'famous TV personality' Jeanne Heal assured her women readers that it was no longer necessary 'to keep on being British at all costs'. With the days of Empire-building over she suggested that 'we might now relax and enjoy ourselves in the manner of other people'. Rather than 'Why foreigners find *us* attractive', her piece might easily have been titled 'Yield to the Europeans', which, in a way, Lee Thompson's film already had: a British picture with a continental-style 'X' certificate: a British actress promoted like a foreign sex symbol; a British woman rejecting her dull husband and taking a younger lover and committing a continental crime of passion; and, finally, a British film-maker relishing what *Picturegoer* (30 June 1956) called 'cunning French-type direction'. Mary Hilton may never have escaped her prison cell, but her death was a significant moment of liberation for British cinema.

Notes

1 Interview with the author 10 April 1999. All subsequent quotations from Lee Thompson are taken from this interview.

2 The page number refers to the 1958 edition of the book published in London by Four Square Books.

3 The attack on the warder, which Jean intercepts, is by a woman of Latin appearance (Simone Silva).

4 For example, *Daily Worker* (6 February 1954), and *New Statesman* 13 February 1954).

5 *Dance with a Stranger* (Mike Newell 1985) *is* a bio-pic of Ruth Ellis.

6 The resemblance to the Ellis case was increased by moving the murder of Lucy from the interior of her flat to the street outside and reducing Mary Hilton's age from mid-thirties (the age of the book's author) to mid-twenties.

7 A Mass Observation poll published in the *Daily Telegraph* in January 1956 revealed that only 8 per cent of those asked actively approved of her execution (*Murder Casebook*, 11 1990: 375).

8 Camera maestro Gil Taylor improvised by using a lightweight Arriflex with a wide-angle lens to solve the problem of producing dynamic images in such a confined space (*Kinematograph Weekly* 10 November 1955).

9 Joan Henry had received treatment in prison for a foot condition, and the nursing sister who cared for her became the model for prison officer McFarlane. The close observation of hands and feet is taken directly from Henry's original novel.

10 The implications of this fragmentation of body parts in a feminist theory of representation are clearly significant, signifying the destruction and dehumanizing of the female body and a refusal to see women as complete individuals.

11 Harold Conway (*Daily Sketch* 15 June 1956) singled out this sequence and 'Miss Dors' expression of mute, numbed dread' as the film's most 'unforgettable moment', but although its dramatic power is undeniable, we should not rush to equate its performativity with authenticity. In the real situation, Ruth Ellis's reaction to being told by the governor of Holloway that she would not be reprieved was apparently that 'she had hysterics and lay on her bed screaming "I don't want to die" ' (Hancock 1993: 176).

12 Viv Chadder's discussion of Ruth Ellis suggests she may have been 'hung for her transgressive image' and goes on to refer to contemporary surveys which revealed that women were less inclined than men to pardon her (1999: 72–3).

13 Critic Dilys Powell returned to the same point when, recalling *Yield to the Night* on the television documentary series *Fifties Features* (1986): 'I just don't know whether people...thought it was a good idea for this

girl who looked so pretty, and had worn such lovely clothes, and had had such a jolly good time, whether they thought it was a good idea for her, in particular, to be hanged.' Physical attractiveness was also an important element in the opposition to Ruth Ellis's execution. It is significant that the death sentence passed only a few months previously on Mrs Styllou Christofi, a plain Cypriot woman in her fifties, elicited a far lower level of public protest.

14 Powell (*Fifties Features* 1986).

15 This final image of the smoking cigarette was not specified by the script of 9 August. It was added by Joan Henry after speaking to the prison officer who acted as an anonymous informant on the execution process.

16 Dignity was not necessarily present in the process of a real execution. Edith Thompson, for instance, had to be carried to the gallows in 1923 (*Murder Casebook*, 11 1990: 391). Joan Henry's prison officer informant told her that as the moment of execution approaches, most prisoners experience the need to urinate and defecate but would, if necessary, be dragged to the scaffold with their pants down. They were obliged to wear their own clothes so that prison garments would not be soiled. On 20 August 1955, the *Lancet* disclosed that condemned women were made to put on waterproof underwear on the morning of the execution (Koestler and Rolph 1961: 67). *Yield to the Night*'s audience are spared these realities, although the script of 9 August has Mary dressed for execution in her own clothes.

17 The film's sympathetic attitude towards the dissolution of marriage is probably a consequence of Lee Thompson's and Joan Henry's own desire to abandon previous relationships and to establish a new partnership with each other.

18 *Yield to the Night* was released by Allied Artists in the USA without a PCA seal of approval as *Blonde Sinner*. It was cut from 95 to 70 minutes with many of the prison sequences removed.

References

Chadder, V. (1999) 'The higher heel: women and the post-war British crime film', in S. Chibnall and R. Murphy (eds) *British Crime Cinema*. London: Routledge.

Chibnall, S. (1999) 'Alien women: the politics of sexual difference in British sf pulp cinema', in I.Q. Hunter (ed.) *British Science Fiction Cinema*. London: Routledge.

Chibnall, S. (2000) *J. Lee Thompson*. Manchester: Manchester University Press.

Dors, D. (1959) *Swingin' Dors*. London: World Distributors.

Durgnat, R. 1970) *A Mirror for England: British Movies from Austerity to Affluence*. London: Faber & Faber.

Hancock, R. (1993) *Ruth Ellis: The Last Woman to be Hanged*. London: Orion Books (first published in 1963).

Harper, S. and Porter, V. 1999) 'Cinema audience tastes in 1950s Britain', *Journal of Popular British Cinema*, 2: 66–82.

Henry, J. (1952) *Who Lie in Gaol*. London: Victor Gollancz.

Henry, J. (1954) *Yield to the Night*. London: Victor Gollancz.

Hopkins, H. (1964) *The New Look: A Social History of the Forties and Fifties in Britain*. London: Secker and Warburg.

Koestler, A. and Rolph, C. (1961) *Hanged by the Neck*. Harmondsworth: Penguin Books.

Landy, M. (1991) *British Genres: Cinema and Society 1930–1960*. Princeton, NJ: Princeton University Press.

Lewis, B. and Crew, H. (eds) (1997) *The Story of a House: Askham Grange Women's Open Prison*. Castleford: Yorkshire Art Circus and Askham Grange.

Nellis, M. (1988) 'British prison movies: the case of *Now Barabbas*', *Howard Journal*, 27: 2–31.

Parish, J. (1991) *Prison Pictures from Hollywood*. Jeferson, NC: McFarlane.

Richards, J. (1984) *The Age of the Dream Palace: Cinema and Society in Britain 1930–1939*. London: Routledge & Kegan Paul.

Wapshott, N. (1990) *The Man Between: A Biography of Carol Reed*. London: Chatto & Windus.

Zalcock, Bev (1998) *Renegade Sisters: Girl Gangs on Film*. London: Creation Books.

Chapter 12

Relocating Hollywood's prison film discourse[1]

Paul Mason

Introduction

The invisibility of punishment brought about by the birth of the prison has ensured that media representations of incarceration contribute, at some level and in some way, to public knowledge and comprehension of penal culture. The hidden environs of bars, cells, stairwells and razor wire are made visible in a spectacle of punishment offered by the prison narratives of the media. One such discourse is constructed by Hollywood, which in the last hundred years has produced over 300 prison films. One used to be able to write confidently about the dearth of analysis of the prison film: the puzzling lacunae of research on a considerable corpus of cinema. However, in recent years there has been significant growth in academic writing in the area (Kermode 2003; Mason 2003; Nellis 2003; O'Sullivan 2003; Jarvis 2004; Schauer 2004; Wilson and O'Sullivan 2004), ironic given the small number of prison films that have been made since 2000. It has been this increase in analysis that has prompted me to reassess the ways in which the prison film has been discussed, and in this chapter I wish to offer three things as part of a larger exploration of prison cinema (Mason forthcoming). Primarily I am interested in suggesting a framework for analysing the prison film, and argue that a useful epistemological structure takes account of genre theory but also Foucauldian discourse analysis and representation. Secondly, I wish to propose a cartographic account of Hollywood's prison film output without the constraints of the artificial taxonomies which unhelpfully punctuate many prison film chronologies. Finally, to illustrate how this framework might be applied, I offer some brief thoughts on one aspect of Hollywood's discourse on imprisonment which, I argue, continues to pervade its discursive regime of prison representations.

Prison films, genre and Hollywood

Much of the work carried out thus far on the prison film has either relied on a small number of films and then used them as a basis for sweeping commentary on the genre (for example, Cheatwood 1996; Rafter 2000; O'Sullivan 2001 and, indeed, some of my own work – Mason 1998, 2000) or used audiences merely as 'the rhetorical guarantor' (Hutchings 1995: 66) of the rightness of the analysis and failed to engage with real audiences at all, such as Wilson and O'Sullivan (2004). My analysis is predicated upon the recognition of genres as social constructions, subject to constant negotiation and reformulation, and thus in researching the prison film and its history 'it is necessary to include as wide a range of films as possible, while trying not to misrepresent the spectrum of audience conceptions' (Tudor 1989: 6). Nellis and Hale are right when they suggest that 'no other type of crime film – the gangster movie, the police procedure movie and the characteristically English murder mystery – has claimed such impressive credentials in its bid for genre status [as the prison film]' (1982: 6) and it is this 'bid' I wish to address first.

The term 'genre', despite being used in Hollywood production terms since the 1910s, came to prominence in writing on cinema some 50 years later 'to situate the *auteur* more systematically (and perhaps more credibly) within the Hollywood set-up' (Hutchings 1995: 60), engaging with an audience who saw that 'it is not a new Hawks or Ford or a new Peckinpah; it is a new western' (Buscombe 1970: 43). A trawl through the vast literature on genre theory proves both complex and contradictory. Indeed, the only facet of generic accounts that appears consistent is disagreement concerning terminology, application and ideology. Writing on genre can often be narrow, circular and indulgent, where its recurrent structuralism often excludes not only historical factors but also misinterprets industrial ones. Whilst Hollywood has undoubtedly minimized commercial risk through 'repetition with difference, similarity with variety' (Neale 2003: 54), there has been a tendency in some genre work to overstate the apparent symbiosis between Hollywood production and genre categories. With the perpetuation of genres often undertaken by critics not film-makers, Neale and Maltby concur in suggesting Hollywood is a 'generic cinema' (Maltby 2003: 99) rather than Ryall's contention that it is 'a cinema of genres' (1998: 327).

Despite these misgivings, and as Neale suggests, genre theory enables the 'exploration of the cultural values and ideological dilemmas central to American society' (2003: 162). In choosing to adopt genre theory for an analysis of the prison film, one is immediately faced with the problem of terminology and definition. The prison film is often lumped together in larger genres such as crime films, social problem films or juvenile delinquent and teenpics. I would argue, however, that to distinguish the prison film as a separate corpus of work offers the opportunity for, what Muncie and McLaughlin term, 'high definition, wide screen analysis' (2002: x). Naturally, there is a blurring at the edges: a venn-diagramatic overlap between genres, for as Jarvis suggests, whilst 'the classical prison film is either an escape or an execution drama; it is complemented by a number of sub-genres and hybrids' (2004: 166). Amongst these we can note the prison comedies, *The Slams* (Jonathan Kaplan 1973) and *Stir Crazy* (Sidney Poitier 1980), the prison musical, *Jailhouse Rock* (Richard Thorpe 1957) and *Chicago* (Rob Marshall 2002), prison science fiction, *Space Rage* (Conrad E. Palmisano and Peter McCarthy [reshoot] 1985), *Wedlock* (Lewis Teague 1991) and *Fortress* (Stuart Gordon 1993), the sport/ prison film featuring American football in *The Mean Machine* (Robert Aldrich 1974), boxing in the *Penitentiary* series (all Jamaa Fanaka 1980, 1982, 1987), and football in *Escape to Victory* (John Huston 1981). The latter could also be classed as prisoner-of-war film, of which there have been many, including *Stalag 17* (Billy Wilder 1957), *Prisoner of War* (Andrew Marton 1954), *The Great Escape* (John Sturges 1963), *King Rat* (Bryan Forbes 1965) and *The Dirty Dozen* (Robert Aldrich 1965). In addition we could add the exploitation prison movie, a large number of which were made in the 1970s, such as *The Big Dolls House* (Jack Hill 1971), *Women in Cages* (Gerardo De Leon 1971) and *The Big Bird Cage* (Jack Hill 1972). As well as these subgenres, there are prison films in which the *mise-en-scène* of punishment does not dominate, such as the Bogart comedy vehicle *We're Not Angels* (Michael Curtiz 1955), Charles Bronson's jail break, *Breakout* (Tom Gries 1975) and Oliver Stone's postmodern media critique, *Natural Born Killers* (Oliver Stone 1994).

I am a fugitive from theory

Despite the growth in contemporary research on prison cinema, much of this work has, on the whole, been theoretically lightweight. With the exception of excellent work by Jarvis (2004, Chapter 10, this volume), Nellis (2003, Chapter 13, this volume) and Schauer (2004), much of the literature is reductive, offering little more than narrative description with no attempt critically to engage with broader epistemologies. I have already proposed that genre theory allows for a full exploration of the corpus of prison film and its consequent cultural and sociopolitical significance. However, I want to extend this to consider whether Hollywood's construction of incarceration can be considered in Foucauldian terms as a discursive practice, which contributes to the fixing of the meaning of imprisonment within a particular discourse at a particular time.

Foucault has argued that discourse constructs versions of social reality, such that although things may exist outside a given discourse, it is only through discourse that knowledge and meaning are produced (Foucault 1972). Thus, as Hall has suggested, discourse 'governs the way that a topic can be meaningfully talked about and reasoned about' (1997a: 15). Consequently, meaning is always fixed and refixed (Shapiro 1989) by discursive and representational practices at particular moments, what Foucault termed the 'episteme' (Foucault 1972). Drawing on Nietzsche's argument that central values and ideas are culturally and historically constructed (Dean 1994), and reinforcing Derrrida (1973), Foucault contends that there are simply histories of the present – 'genealogies' (Foucault 1972) – which reinterpret the past within socially, culturally and politically situated discourses: a slippage between historical moments that emphasize the discontinuity of historic events. Thus, for Foucault, terms such as 'homosexuality' (Foucault 1973), 'madness' (Foucault 1978) and 'criminality' (Foucault 1979) are historically and culturally specific.

If we adopt Foucault's approach here, three questions arise. First, to what extent can we say that Hollywood's prison film output is a discursive practice, a dominant *regime of representation* with the power to re/present prison in a particular way? Secondly, what does this representation look like and consist of? Thirdly, if meaning floats, only to be temporarily anchored in specific historic moments, has Hollywood contributed to ruptures and discontinuities in the discourse of prison between one period and another, and if so what have these meanings been? Finally, have there been what Hall calls different 'transcoding strategies' (1997b) of reappropriating the meaning of imprisonment within Hollywood's output; or counter-discourses which exploit the ambivalences and complexities within Hollywood's dominant discourse of prison? These are clearly considerable questions that require more space than is available here; consequently, I aim to offer some preliminary thoughts on the first two questions through a genealogy of the Hollywood prison film and an exploration of discourse it has constructed about prison over the last 90 years.

Towards a regime of representation

For Foucault, discourses are 'a series of discontinuous segments whose tactical function is neither uniform nor stable' (1990: 100). Thus, to view Hollywood's prison films as *the* discursive practice, constructing what can be said and known about prison would be problematic. Not least because, as others have illustrated in this book, a number of other discourses exist which construct knowledge of prison, such as the entertainment and news media, government rhetoric, parliamentary debate, pressure group campaigns and public opinion (King and Maruna, Ryan, Jewkes, Solomon, Allen, Chibnall, Nellis – all this volume). However, what is particular about prison compared to other arms of the criminal justice system – the police and the courtroom, for example – is their inaccessibility, their shrouding in secrecy which negates informed public knowledge about them. Further, despite Foucault's genealogical account of the disappearance of the *ancient regime*'s spectacle of punishment, of gallows and guillotine replaced by the birth of the prison, visual spectacle persists in cinematic representations.[2] Jarvis is right when he suggests that one can read the prison film as 'a dark panopticon that regulates the public gaze on law and order' (2004: 173).

The Hollywood prison film then contributes significantly to the discursive practice around prison. Further, as a regime of *re/presenting* penalty, Hollywood dominates. In what Maltby (2003) calls the 'commercial aesthetic', Hollywood has driven the commodification of entertainment in postwar Western cinema, ensuring that like all corporate strategy, its films are seen by the most number of people in the most number of cinemas the most number of times. Hollywood produces, and contributes to, a discourse of imprisonment through its power to represent prison in particular ways; more specifically, it is 'the exercise of *symbolic power* through representational practices' (Hall 1997b: 259, emphasis in original). In Foucault's terms, Hollywood's prison films are an example of power *producing*, through a regime of representation, discourse on imprisonment. Thus power is not primarily repressive and restrictive but constructs new objects, in this case 'imprisonment'. Further, power does not simply flow from a centralized source, it circulates, and is 'exercised through a net-like organization' (Foucault 1980: 98), so rather than the top-down coercion and force suggested by Marx (1867/1976) power can solicit consent at micro-levels of society. To investigate this power/knowledge through the discourse of prison as constructed by Hollywood, we need to trace, historically, its prison film output.

Mapping the Hollywood prison film landscape

I am sceptical of the historical taxonomies of the prison film that have been undertaken thus far (Crowther 1989; Cheatwood 1996; Rafter 2000; Wilson and O'Sullivan 2004). In constructing such time periods and attributing terms to them, those writers who offer historical schemas of the prison film succeed in producing mere internal generic chronologies with little recourse to Hollywood's industrial or historic context. Cheatwood (1996), for example, traces the prison film through 'the depression era' of the 1930s, the 'rehabilitation' era from 1943 to 1962, 'confinement' from 1963 to 1980 and, finally, contemporary prison films which he terms the 'administration era'. However, Cheatwood's taxonomy is forced, claiming, for example, that *Cool Hand Luke* is part of the 'confinement era' where 'toughness and the image of the Bad Dude have replaced loyalty and the Square John as primary values' (1996: 223) is surely to miss the point that *Cool Hand Luke* is about the horrors of a chain gang in Southern America, owing much, in spirit at least, to *I am a Fugitive from a Chain Gang* (Mervyn LeRoy 1932), made 30 years previously and in what Cheatwood terms the 'depression era'. A similar approach is also adopted by Wilson and O'Sullivan (2004), who argue that periodizing the genre in this way aids rather than reduces prison film analysis but fail to elucidate this claim, or justify imposing such a periodization.

These oversimplified taxonomies become tautologous, where historical periods narrowly defined (either using a small number of films, in a cultural and industrial vacuum, or built solely on UK and/ or US criminal justice policy developments) serve simply as artificial frames wedged round an ill-fitting pile of prison films which may or may not be justifiably grouped together based on their release date. This practice becomes a one-eyed decontextualizing of the prison film, the purpose of which seems to be seeking out films which *prove* the category works, rather than exploring what discourse(s) Hollywood constructs through its representation of prison at particular historic moments. Under the former regime, the prison film is confined to a small cell and subject to unreasonable conditions. I want to liberate the prison film from this restrictive analysis, instead tracing its developments and re/presentation since the beginning of the twentieth century.

My research suggests Hollywood has produced around 350 prison films since the Barnsdale production company made the silent melodrama *Prison Bars* in 1901. Many accounts of the prison film begin in the 1930s. However, there were at least 30 made before that, including the silent comedies *Pimple's Prison* (1914), *No Place Like Jail* (Frank Terry 1918), *Big Town Ideas* (Carl Harbaugh 1921) and *See You in Jail* (Joseph Henabery 1927), the latter featuring Stan Laurel who also appeared with Oliver Hardy in the prison comedies *The Second Hundred Years* (Fred Guiol 1927), *The Hoose Gow* (James Parrot 1929) and later in their best known prison comedy and first full-length talkie, *Pardon Us* (James Parrot 1931). Whilst it is true that few remarkable prison pictures came out of Hollywood during this period, a number of directors, who went on to make more significant contributions to the genre, made their first prison films before 1930.[3]

As I have previously noted (Mason 2003), the 1930s remains the most prolific decade for the production of prison films in Hollywood, with over 80 being made. As well as *I am a Fugitive from a Chain Gang*, the decade's prison films included the Oscar-nominated *The Criminal Code* (Howard Hawks 1931) and *The Big House* (George W. Hill 1930). The latter was described by *Variety* as 'Not a two-dollar talkie but a virile, realistic melodrama' (Walker 1997: 71). Nellis notes: 'the failure of prison to rehabilitate, together with scenes of admission to prison and solitary confinement have become integral to the narrative and iconography of subsequent prison films, and have helped to give *The Big House* its status as a minor classic' (1982: 15). Some of the subsequent legends of Hollywood starred in prison films during the 1930s, including James Cagney (*The Mayor of Hell* (Archie Mayo 1933), *Angels with Dirty Faces* (Michael Curtiz 1938) and *Each Dawn I Die* (William Keighley 1939)); Edward G. Robinson (*Two Seconds* (Mervyn LeRoy 1932), *The Last Gangster* (Edward Ludwig 1937)); and George Raft (*Each Dawn I Die* and *Invisible Stripes* (Lloyd Bacon 1940)).

The self-regulation of Hollywood's Production Code in 1930, devised to counter external regulation and censorship,[4] in essence 'amounted to a consensus about what constituted appropriate entertainment for an undifferentiated mass audience in America and, by default, the rest of the world' (Maltby 2003: 61). This led to a 'negotiated struggle and eventual convergence' (Parker 1986: 146) between the film industry and the institutional regulators, producing recurring cinematic narratives in which crime never paid. Hollywood's most famous gangster actors metamorphosed into dynamic cops: Edward G. Robinson (*Outside the Law* (Tod Browning 1930), *Little Caesar* (Mervyn Leroy 1931), *Smart Money* (Alfred E. Green 1931)) became cop Johnny Blake in *Bullets or Ballots* (William Keighley 1936) and James Cagney (*The Public Enemy* (William A. Wellman 1931), *Blonde Crazy* (Roy Del Ruth 1931), *The Mayor of Hell* (Archie Mayo, 1933) turned heroic G-Man Brick Davis out to avenge the murder of his best friend in *G-Men* (William Keighley 1935).

Both Roffman and Purdy (1981) and Parker (1986) argue that the prison film during this time was 'the ultimate metaphor of social entrapment, where the individual disappears among the masses in an impersonal institution' (Roffman and Purdy 1981: 26). Thus prison cinema in the 1930s regularly constructed the protagonist as an innocent man wrongly convicted, such as James Allen (Paul Muni) caught up in a hold-up in *I am a Fugitive from a Chain Gang*; Chick Wheeler (Edgar Edwards) wrongly convicted of murder in *Convicted* (Leon Barsha 1938); or James Larrabee (Donald Woods) framed on grand larceny charges by corrupt politician Shields (Joseph Crehan) in *Road Gang* (Louis King 1936). If our hero was guilty of a crime, then it often came with mitigating circumstances such as Robert Graham (Philips Holmes) protecting his sweetheart in *The Criminal Code* (Howard Hawks 1930) or young orphan Jimmy Mason (Junior Durkin) persuaded to work for a boot-legger in *Hell's House* (Paul Gangelin 1932). A third variation on this narrative was predicated upon the reforming con who, having reformed or redeemed himself in some way, suffered an unjust death whilst still incarcerated. Tom Connors (Spencer Tracy) goes willingly to the chair, for an unjust execution in *20,000 Years in Sing Sing* (Michael Curtiz 1933) for example, and 'Killer' John Mears (Preston S. Foster) ends a prison riot by his suicidal walk towards the guards' machine-guns, enabling a death row reprieve for new inmate Walters in *The Last Mile* (Samuel Bischoff 1932).

As Roffman and Purdy argue, such films reflected the dejection of the recession in 1930s America: 'the films' evocation of innocence living in subjugation and terror clearly reflects the despair of the nation faced with incomprehensible social and economic upheaval...the cells and bars and chains eloquently re-create the sense of frustration and restriction in a land of lost opportunity' (1981: 28). During the 1940s, in the climate of postwar readjustment in America, Hollywood's production of prison films declined both in number and in quality. Rafter (2000) argues that the influence of the European directors and the consequent, but contested,[5] corpus of 'film noir' reconstructed the crime film adding complex narratives and a confusing moral order. This is perhaps best illustrated by *Brute Force*, Jules Dassin's bleak representation of prison life. Dark in tone and fractured in its narrative, with flashback sequences of four inmate's stories, Parish (1991) argues its lip-service to prison reform allowed Dassin more licence for gratuitous horror.

Along with several notably prisoner-of-war films, such as *Stalag 17* and *Prisoner of War* (Andrew Marton 1954) and prison comedies, *We're Not Angels* and *My Six Convicts* (Hugo Fregonese 1952), the juvenile delinquent and social problem films such as *The Wild One* (László Benedek 1953), *The Blackboard Jungle* (Richard Brookes 1955) and *Rebel without a Cause* (Nicholas Ray 1955) were evidence of Hollywood's realignment to incorporate the growing teenage market during the 1950s. *Girls in Prison* (Edward L. Cahn), and the Elvis prison film vehicle *Jailhouse Rock*, further echoed this trend. The former also illustrated the development of women protagonists in prison narratives (Chapter 11, this volume) in films such as *Caged* (John Cromwell 1950), *Yield to the Night* (J. Lee Thompson 1956) and *I Want to Live!* (Robert Wise 1958). The producer of the latter, Walter Wanger, was also involved in the Don Siegel picture, *Riot in Cell Block 11*, filmed at Folsom Prison and featuring some of its inmates amongst the cast. Having spent three months in prison in 1951 for attempting to shoot his wife's agent, Siegel was moved to make the film following the riots in American jails between 1951 and 1953, and offered a serious treatise on prison reform (Nellis and Hale 1982). Kiminsky comments that the film 'broke two cardinal Hollywood rules: the good guys lost and there were no women in the picture' (1974: 83).

The Kennedy years in the 1960s witnessed 'a new domestic agenda... reflected and to some extent reinforced by American film' (Neve 1992: 212) and this was perhaps echoed in the final release of *The Birdman of Alcatraz* (John Frankenheimer 1962) based upon the true story of Robert F. Stroud, who had spent 42 years in solitary confinement. The film's release coinciding with Stroud's transfer from Alcatraz to Springfield Prison following extensive campaigning by, amongst others, journalist Thomas Gaddis. Hollywood's liberal agenda was also evident in *The Defiant Ones* (Stanley Kramer 1958), a tale of two escaped convicts, one black and one white, chained together at the ankle, exemplifying Hollywood's exploration of racism in American society. Although prison film production continued to decline in the 1960s, with Hollywood producing less than 30 prison films, alongside *The Birdman of Alcatraz* was *Cool Hand Luke* in which Paul Newman played Lucas Jackson, sentenced to hard labour on a Southern correctional camp for knocking the heads off parking meters. In many ways the film echoed the horrors of the chain gang previously explored in films such as *I am a Fugitive from a Chain Gang*, *Hells Highway* (Roland Brown 1932) and *Blackmail* (H.C. Potter 1939). Worthy of mention is *In Cold Blood* (Richard Brooks 1967) based on Truman Capote's case study of two killers on death row following the Clutter family murders in Kansas City in 1959. There were also several prison-of-war films, including *The Great Escape*, *King Rat* (Bryan Forbes 1965) and *The Dirty Dozen* (Robert Aldrich 1965) in which the eponymous convicted murderers were assigned to destroy a Nazi-occupied fortress.

The 1970s, too, produced few prison films of note, although my research suggests Hollywood produced around 35. These included the run of women-in-prison exploitation films, such as the women's penitentiary series, *The Big Doll's House* (Jack Hill 1971), *Women in Cages* (Gerardo De Leon 1971) and *The Big Bird Cage* (Jack Hill 1972) and comedies such as the Burt Reynolds' vehicle *The Mean Machine*, recently remade under its US title *The Longest Yard* (Peter Segal 2005) and still featuring Burt Reynolds. Nellis and Hale, however, note an interesting development prompted by the MGM release of *Fortune and Men's Eyes* (Harvey Hart 1971) which dealt frankly[6] with homosexuality in prison. They suggest that a 'series of press exposés, the rise of gay liberation and the greater frankness of cinema generally combined to ensure that the new prison movies gave considerable space to it, in both its violent and affectionate forms' (Nellis and Hale 1982: 35). True stories provided Hollywood with the narratives for several prison films during this period, notably *The Sugarland Express* (Steven Spielberg 1973) and *Straight Time* (Ulu Grosbard 1978), as well as *Midnight Express* (Alan Parker 1978), based on Billy Hayes' account of life in, and escape from, a Turkish prison. Both *Midnight Express* and the earlier *Papillon* (Franklin J. Schaffner 1973) highlighted conditions in prisons outside America, in the case of *Papillon*, Devil's Island in French Guiana.

Whilst interesting and challenging prison films were being made outside Hollywood, such as *The Kiss of the Spider Woman* (Hector Babenco 1985) and Jim Jarmusch's monochromed prison/road movie romp, *Down by Law* (1986), Hollywood continued to offer familiar prison narratives throughout the 1980s which focused on violence (*Lock Up* (John Flynn 1989), *Penitentiary II*) (Jamaa Fanaka 1982), escape in *Escape from Alcatraz* (Don Siegel 1980) and corruption and miscarriage of justice in *Fast Walking* (James B. Harris 1982). There were occasional highs, in particular, *Brubaker* (Stuart Rosenberg 1980) in which Robert Redford played the eponymous warden, attempting prison reform against a backdrop of corruption at local and government level. The film was based upon the revelations of Thomas O. Murton who was appointed superintendent at two prison farms in Arkansas in the late 1960s (Murton and Hyams 1970).

In the 1980s, prison films began to look forward as well as back, in science fiction prison films such as *The Chair* (Waldemar Korzeniowsky 1988), and future dystopian punishment narratives in *Escape from New York* and *The Running Man* (Paul Michael Glaser 1987) (Chapter 13, this volume). This continued into the 1990s with *Fortress* (Stuart Gordon 1993) and *No Escape* (Martin Campbell 1994). Cheatwood notes how these futuristic prisons were run by faceless, mechanistic wardens: in *No Escape*, the warden is a hologram, whilst in *Fortress* he is part robot. In the mid-1990s the catalyst for the increased popularity and production of the prison film was *The Shawshank Redemption* (Frank Darabont 1995). In the immediate years that followed the release of *The Shawshank Redemption*, Hollywood studios also released *Murder in the First* (Marc Rocco 1995), *Just Cause* (Arne Glimcher 1995), *Dead Man Walking* (Tim Robbins 1996), *Last Dance* (Bruce Beresford 1996), *Con Air* (Simon West 1997), *Return to Paradise* (Joseph Ruben 1998), *Brokedown Palace* (Jonathan Kaplan 1999), *The Green Mile* (Frank Darabont 1999), *American History X* (Tony Kaye 1999), *The Hurricane* (Norman Jewison 1999) and *Life* (Ted Demme 1999).

Guaranteed first on the list when anyone mentions prison movies, *The Shawshank Redemption* is the best known and most popular example of the genre of all time, a regular in many 'greatest films ever made' lists.[7] Director Frank Darabont has said of it 'I've gotten mail from people who say "Gosh, your movie got me through a really bad marriage...or it got me through a really bad patch in my life or a really bad illness; or it helped me hang on when a loved one died"' (Kermode 2003: n.p.). Darabont later directed *The Green Mile* (1999) which also proved a commercial success, although Tom Hank's feel-good Mom's apple-pie portrayal of guard Paul Edgecomb proved rather too sweet for some tastes. Peter Bradshaw in the *Guardian* wrote if 'you can stand the three-hour-plus stretch of saccharine gibberish and patronizing racial politics then you've got a stronger stomach than me' (25 February 2000).

Since 2000, Hollywood has produced few prison films. Apart from another remake of *The Mean Machine* (Barry Skolnick 2001) in a British prison with football replacing American football, and Alan Parker's first foray back into prisons since *Midnight Express* in the death row film *The Life and Death of David Gale* (2003), Steven Spielberg's DreamWorks SKG produced *The Last Castle* (Rod Lurie 2001) in which Robert Redford takes over a military prison from the brutal Colonel Winter (James Gadolfini); and echoing the earlier boxing in prison films in the *Penitentiary* series was *Undisputed* (Walter Hill 2002). There have been some interesting films which fall outside Hollywood and the prison genre as discussed thus far, but none the less worthy of note. These include Spike Lee's film about a man's final 24 hours before his seven-year prison sentence begins – *25th Hour* (2002) – and two hard-edged treatments of American penal culture by independent cinema, *Animal Factory* (Steve Buscemi 2000) and *Down Time* (Sean Wilson 2001).

Hollywood grammar: the discourse of imprisonment

So what does Hollywood's discourse of imprisonment look like within the prison film genre? In offering some thoughts on this question, my aim is somewhat modest. Indeed, I propose *not* to do three things. First, to explore all facets of the prison discourse, nor as I have discussed above, to investigate the fixing and refixing of the meaning of imprisonment across the genealogy of prison cinema outlined above. Thirdly, I do not explore here Hollywood's counter-discourses which challenge the dominant regime of representing prison. In the space available, I will outline one aspect of Hollywood's prison discourse which has remained ubiquitous in the prison film genre. Jarvis rightly points out that 'the prison film is a repeat offender on the counts of character, plot and mise en scène' (2004: 167). He also notes the centrality of the penal built environment to Hollywood's treatment of prison, and it is this iconography and its mechanistic resonance that I wish discuss.

Hollywood's mechanistic discourse of incarceration

The discourse of machine pervades the prison film like the slamming of doors and the turning of keys. For Hollywood, the prison is a system with impenetrable swathes of regulations which grind on relentlessly. This mechanical representation of punishment emphasizes the inmate's struggle to survive and the process of dehumanization and othering, inherent in incarceration within the penal system. The monotony and regulation of prison life are most often depicted by the highly structured movement of prisoners. In the opening scene of *Numbered Men* (Mervyn LeRoy 1930), for example, the inmates trudge round the prison landings with the number of years of their sentence superimposed above their heads. From *The Criminal Code* (Howard Hawks 1931) to *The Mean Machine* frequent shots of prisoners making their way along steel landings, up and down stairwells to and from their cells, have been used to convey the system within prison, echoing Roffman and Purdy's description of a scene from *The Big House*:

> Rows of cell doors open simultaneously and hundreds of prisoners tramp in unison to the yard. In the cavernous mess hall, they sit down to eat the mass-produced fodder their keepers call food. The camera tracks along a row of prisoners to reveal faces mainly individuated by the manner in which they express their revulsion at the meal (1981: 26).

Prison films frequently depict inmates undertaking repetitive tasks, which acts both as a narrative device to move from one scene to another and as a constant reminder to the audience of the mundane regime of prison. As Abu Jamaal suggests, the 'most profound horror of prisons lives in the day-to-day banal occurrences that turn into months, and months into years, and years into decades' (cited in Jarvis 2004: 166). The banality is constructed in the limited movement of the exercise yard, in inmates collecting food; and in the half-whispered conversations taking place on stairwells or in and outside cells. The constraint in and uniformity of movement serves both to underscore the highly structured system and routine of prison life, and to extend the machine allegory further. The visible movement of inmates against the backdrop of cold steel and grey concrete which contains them mirrors the workings of a machine – prisoners are the cogs that turn, driving the huge mechanism of punishment relentlessly onward. Long tracking shots in many films reveal the prison interior, dwelling on landings, stairwells, bars and cell doors, stressing the quasi-industrial nature of the prison. In *Wedlock*, for example, the audience follow new inmate Magenta (Rutger Hauer) around the high-tech maximum security prison to which he has been sent. The camera sweeps around the dripping silver pipes, huge fans and metal columns accompanied by an insistent humming noise.

Hollywood's representation of Alcatraz in films such as *The Birdman of Alcatraz, Escape from Alcatraz* and *Murder in the First* all dwell on their grim surroundings.

As if to emphasize its dominance still further, the prison film habitually demonstrates the inflexibility of rules of the prison machine, as Robert Stroud (Burt Lancaster) notes in *The Birdman of Alcatraz*: 'I know 'em. They're the same in all Pens. They tell you when to eat, when to sleep, when to go to the privy.' Although used primarily to exemplify injustice, the harsh penal regulations serve to accentuate the unyielding processing of inmates through the prison system. This is expressed through seemingly trivial regulations such as James Stewart's chain gang routine in *Carbine Williams* (Richard Thorpe 1952), paralleled in (amongst many others) *Chain Gang* (Lew Landers 1950) and *Hell's Highway* (Rowland Brown 1932). Breach of these regulations is often punished by long periods of solitary confinement, a penalty often represented as harsh given the original offence, for example *Papillon* and *Cool Hand Luke*. Mechanistic discourse has been fundamental in Hollywood's prison cinema, producing other narratives in the genre: escape from the machine, riot against the machine, the role of the machine in processing and rehabilitating inmates, and entering the machine from the free world as a new inmate.

A second pervasive aspect of Hollywood's prison discourse, and one linked to the mechanistic process and systematic nature of imprisonment, is the emphasis on a dehumanizing process: the death of the men and women from the outside world, and the birth of the prisoner as a number and statistics of the inside prison world. This process is initiated at prison reception, and is often shot from the inmate perspective, underscoring for the audience the routine and regime that will stay with the inmate for the length of their sentence. Frequently this process involves the relinquishing of worldly possessions to an intransigent prison guard, stripped naked, scrubbed or hosed, and clothed in prison issue uniform and shoved unceremoniously into a cell. Versions of this routine are present in many films, initiating, particularly visibly, the dehumanizing process, what we might call the othering of the prisoner from his or her outside world self in Hollywood discourse. I have noted elsewhere (Mason 2003) how this mastering of the body of the condemned is perhaps most symbolic in the cutting of hair, which historically has represented an attack on liberty and personal autonomy and is the most visible difference between inmate and free citizen. The speed and mechanical interpretation of this process, implemented almost immediately the inmate arrives at the prison is the first, and perhaps therefore the most striking, example of the regulated institutional nature of prison the viewer sees.

This process has another important function other than highlighting the process of turning men into prisoners. The entrance of the protagonist into a prison resonates with audiences, whose limited knowledge of prison ensures they empathize with the ignorance and fear felt by the new inmate. The audience are subjected to the harsh regime of prison life, the stern officers and claustrophobic cells. Hollywood uses audience ignorance to elicit sympathy for the new inmate: the naivety of Carmen (Ena Hartman) in falling for an inmate prank in *Terminal Island* (Stephanie Rothman 1977) and freshly convicted Billy Hayes being administered a horrendous beating after trusting another inmate in *Midnight Express*. Hayes' beating exemplifies Hollywood's pattern of new inmates often meeting with a violent introduction from guards. Chain gang films like *Road Gang*, *Hell's Highway*, *I am a Fugitive from a Chain Gang*, *Cool Hand Luke* and *Chain Gang Women* (Lee Frost 1971) depict guards whipping inmates new to the rigours of hard labour. Whilst in *The Mean Machine* Paul Crew (Burt Reynolds) is beaten by Head Guard Captain Kennauer, in *Murder in the First* Henry Young (Kevin Bacon) had his foot sliced with a razor by Chief Warden Glenn (Gary Oldman). The introduction of violence serves to establish what Jarvis terms 'the exitlessness from the theatre of cruelty' (2004: 167).

Conclusion

My brief discussion of one aspect of the discourse of imprisonment constructed by Hollywood serves merely to begin fleshing out the skeletal frame of my argument. Other important aspects of Hollywood's prison discourse concern, for example, constructions of masculinity and the body, and of prison reform. There are also key questions around the dis/continuity of these discourses at particular historical moments and counter-discourses within the Hollywood prison genre. Further, a wider analysis might include discourses in punishment narratives outside the prison film genre, in other crime cinema and thrillers for example; and, of course, in films made outside Hollywood. I am aware that I have asked more questions than I have answered here. My aim has been to offer a framework for analysing the Hollywood prison film through combining genre theory and Foucauldian discourse analysis and ideas of representation. A full and comprehensive analysis which adopts this position is like the escape route of many a prison film inmate: a lengthy dig, but one which promises light at the end of the tunnel.

Notes

1   A version of this chapter appears in H. Albrecht *et al.* (forthcoming) *Images of Crime III*. Freiburg: Max-Planck-Institut.
2   I have discussed elsewhere Foucault's genealogy of modern penalty and its application to the prison film (Mason 2000, 2003) and do not propose to repeat that work here.
3   For example, Raoul Walsh, director of *The Honor System* (1917) and *Me, Gangster* (1928) who later directed James Cagney in *White Heat* (1949); and Lloyd Bacon, best known for his direction of musicals such as *42nd Street* (1932) who also directed the Bogart films *San Quentin* (1937) and *Invisible Stripes* (1940) but previously worked on the silent prison film *Brass Knuckles* (1929) and with Al Jolson in the improbable mawkish prison yarn, *Say it with Songs*. The 1920s also saw prison films directed by Joseph Von Sternberg (the noir-ish *Thunderbolt* 1929) and Cecil B. DeMille (*Manslaiughter* 1922), the latter Parish notes as '[b]esides being a self-serving moral essay, DeMille craftily interwove flashbacks into the proceedings, allegedly for historical comparisons. However it was just an excuse to introduce lavish Biblical settings, risqué costuming and debauched behavior' (1991: 271).
4   Maltby (2003) notes that the Supreme Court ruling that films were 'mere representations' and thus not entitled to the First Amendment right to freedom of speech remained in force until 1952.
5   See, for example, Cook (1990), Neale (2003), Silverman and Ursini (2004).
6   In fact, MGM insisted that the original, much more provocative, stage play originally shown off Broadway in 1967 and again in 1969 was toned down for the screenplay.
7   For example it was ranked third in Channel Four's *100 Greatest Films of All Time* (www.filmsite.org/filmfour.html), second in the Internet Movie Database *Top Rated 250 Films of All Time* (www.imdb.com/chart/top) and third in 'The ultimate movie poll', *Empire Magazine* (November 2001).

References

Baudrillard, J. (1983) *Simulations*. New York, NY: Semiotext.
Buscombe, E. (1970) 'The idea of genre in the American cinema', *Screen*, 11: 43.

Cheatwood, D. (1996) 'Prison movies: films about adult, male, civilian prisons: 1929–1995', in F. Bailey and D. Hale (eds) *Popular Culture, Crime and Justice*. Belmont, CA: Wadsworth.

Clowers, M. (2001) 'Dykes, gangs and danger: debunking popular myths about maximum security life', *Journal of Criminal Justice and Popular Culture*, 9: 22–30.

Cook, D. (1990) *A History of Narrative Film*. London: W.W. Norton.

Crowther, B. (1989) *Captured On Film – The Prison Movie*. London: Batsford.

Dean, M. (1994) *Critical and Effective Histories: Foucault's Methods and Historical Sociology*. London: Routledge.

Derrida, J. (1973) *Speech and Phenomena*. Evanston, IL: Northwestern University Press.

Foucault, M. (1972) *The Archaeology of Knowledge*. London: Tavistock Press.

Foucault, M. (1973) *The Birth of the Clinic*. London: Tavistock Press.

Foucault, M. (1978) *The History of Sexuality*. Harmondsworth: Penguin Books.

Foucault, M. (1979) *Discipline and Punish*. Harmondsworth: Penguin Books.

Foucault, M. (1980) *Power/Knowledge: Selected Interviews and Other Writings, 1972–1977*. Brighton: Harvester Books.

Foucault, M. (1990) *The History of Sexuality. Volume One: An introduction*. London: Penguin Books.

Hall, S. (1997a) 'The work of representation', in S. Hall (ed.) *Representation: Cultural Representation and Signifying Practices*. London: Sage.

Hall, S. (1997b) 'The spectacle of the other', in S. Hall (ed.) *Representation: Cultural Representation and Signifying Practices*. London: Sage.

Hutchings, P. (1995) 'Genre theory and criticism', in J. Hollows and M. Jancovich (eds) *Approaches to Popular Film*. Manchester: Manchester University Press.

Jarvis, B. (2004) *Cruel and Unusual: Punishment and US Culture*. London: Pluto Press.

Kermode, M. (2003) *BFI Modern Classics: The Shawshank Redemption*. London: BFI.

Kiminsky, S. (1974) *Don Siegel: Director*. New York, NY: Curtis Books.

Levenson, J. (2001) 'Inside information: prisons and the media', *Criminal Justice Matters*, 43: 14–15.

Maltby, R. (2003) *Hollywood Cinema* (2nd edn). Oxford: Blackwell.

Marx, K. (1867/1976) *Capital: A Critique of Political Economy. Vol. 1*. London: Penguin Books.

Mason, P. (1998) 'Systems and process', *Images* (available at <www.imagesjournal.com//issue06/features/prison.htm).

Mason, P. (2000) 'Watching the invisible: televisual portrayal of the British prison 1980–1991', *International Journal of the Sociology of Law*, 28: 33–44.

Mason, P. (2003) 'The screen machine: cinematic representations of prisons', in P. Mason (ed.) *Criminal Visions: Media Representations of Crime and Justice*. Cullompton: Willan Publishing.

Mason, P. (forthcoming) *From Fugitive to Redemption: Exploring the Prison Film*. London: Wallflower Press.

Mathiesen, T. (2000) *Prison on Trial* (2nd edn). Winchester: Waterside Press.

Muncie, J. and McLaughlin, E. (2002) *Criminological Perspectives: Essential Readings*. Milton Keynes: Open University Press.

Murton, T.O. and Hyams, J. (1970) *Accomplices to the Crime: Arkansas Prison Scandal*. New York, NY: Grove Press.

Neale, S. (2003) *Genre and Hollywood*. London: BFI.

Nellis, M. (2003) 'News media, popular culture and the electronic monitoring of offenders in England and Wales', *Howard Journal of Criminal Justice*, 42: 1–31.

Nellis, M. and Hale, C. (1982) *The Prison Film*. London: Radical Alternatives to Prison.

Neve, B. (1992) *Film and Politics in America: A Social Tradition*. London: Routledge.

O'Sullivan, S. (2001) 'Representations of prison in nineties Hollywood cinema: from *Con Air* to *The Shawshank Redemption*', *Howard Journal of Criminal Justice*, 40: 317–34.

O'Sullivan, S. (2003) 'Representing "the killing state": the death penalty in nineties Hollywood cinema', *Howard Journal of Criminal Justice*, 42: 485–503.

Parish, A. (1991) *Prison Pictures from Hollywood: Plots, Critiques, Casts and Credits for 293 Theatrical and Made-for-television Releases*. Jeferson, NC: McFarlane.

Parker, J. (1986) 'The organizational environment of the motion picture sector', in S. Ball-Rokeach and M. Cantor (eds) *Media, Audience and Social Structure*. Beverly Hills, CA: Sage.

Querry, R. (1973) 'Prison movies: an annotated filmography 1921–present', *Journal of Popular Film*, 2: 181–97.

Querry, R. (1975) 'The American prison as portrayed in the popular motion pictures of the 1930s.' Unpublished PhD thesis, University of New Mexico.

Rafter, N. (2000) *Shots in the Mirror*. Oxford: Oxford University Press..

Roffman, P. and Purdy, J. (1981) *The Hollywood Social Problem Film: Madness, Despair and Politics from the Depression to the Fifties*. Bloomington, IN: Indiana University Press.

Root, J. (1981) 'Inside', *The Abolitionist*, 10: 12–13.

Ryall, T. (1998) 'Genre and Hollywood', in J. Hill and G.P. Church (eds) *The Oxford Guide to Film Studies*. Oxford: Oxford University Press.

Schatz, T. (1981) *Hollywood Genres: Formulas, Filmmaking, and the Studio System*. New York, NY: Random House.

Schauer, T. (2004) 'Masculinity incarcerated: insurrectionary speech and masculinity in prison fiction', *Journal for Crime, Conflict and Media Culture*, 1: 28–42.

Shapiro, M. (1989) 'Textualising global politics', in J. Der Derian and M. Shapiro (eds) *International/Intertextual Relations*. Lexington, MA: Lexington Books.

Silverman, A. and Ursini, J. (2004) *Film Noir Reader: The Crucial Films and Themes. Bk. 4*. Pompton Plains: NJ.

Sparks, R. (1992) *Television and the Drama of Crime: Moral Tales and the Place of Crime in Public Life*. Milton Keynes: Open University Press.

Tudor, A. (1989) *Monsters and Mad Scientists: Cultural History of the Horror Movie*. Oxford: Blackwell.

Walker, J. (ed.) (1997) *Halliwell's Film Guide*. London: HarperCollins.

Wilson, D. (1993) 'Inside observations', *Screen*, 34: 76–9.

Wilson, D. and O'Sullivan, S. (2004) *Images of Incarceration*. Winchester: Waterside Press.

Chapter 13

Future punishment in American science fiction films

Mike Nellis

Introduction

> There are some prison administrators who stress the need to create small maximum security facilities for the most troublesome offenders – 'maxi-maxi' institutions. Their plans read like the design of the inner circles of hell (Morris 1974: 88).

This chapter tentatively explores the cultural significance of the dystopian penal imagery that is to be found in a number of American movies over the last 30 years, an era in which, it is widely agreed, penal practice has become markedly more punitive than hitherto (Garland 2001). Crudely put, it is concerned with the image of punishment contained within a number of – often well-known, widely watched and highly popular – science fiction 'action' films. Whilst I will take for granted that such movies – like science fiction generally – are often an oblique, and sometimes satirical, commentary on the social context which spawned them, I will also suggest that they can legitimately be taken at face value, as projections of possible, if not necessarily probable or plausible, futures. They may have no standing whatsoever as serious predictions of things that might happen, but precisely because they are signified to audiences as 'set in the future' (usually the *near* future, somewhere around the mid-twenty-first century), and made to look technologically distinctive, they do inform, stimulate and constrain our mental image of what could happen. They may get the particulars – in terms of events, actions and institutions – wrong, but still get the 'mood and temper' of an emerging future right – or vice versa, getting a particular technology right, but misjudging the political context in which it will be used. Either way, science fiction movies are one cultural resource amongst several which impinge on our collective endeavour to imagine and anticipate the future. We are never in complete thrall to them, but to deny them any cultural significance at all closes down an important source of understanding our contemporary hopes and fears. I suggest that the movies considered here are so consistently and remorselessly dystopian that, in the absence of any cultural counterweights of comparable popular appeal and visual vividness, they cannot but add to a sense of pessimism and despair about future penal practices.

The movies in question are not always prison-movies-of-the-future *per se*. Some are indeed set almost wholly in futuristic penal institutions, but others only contain sequences set in such places. Even within those, however, the tropes, conventions and set pieces familiar to students of the prison movie genre (Nellis 1982; Mason 2003; Wilson and O'Sullivan 2004) are often to be found. Several could, however, be read as commentaries on something quite other than penality – urbanism, masculinity or cyborgization, for example. They are 'action movies' as much as 'science fiction movies'. Some of them are hybrids of 'cop movies' and 'science fiction movies' – nowadays a rather extensive category, which, like cop movies set in the present day (and traditional 'detective fiction'), usually stop short of the point at which apprehended offenders receive legally sanctioned punishment. But, just as in the real world, 'policing' and 'punishment' are blurring – the police impose minor penalties on minor offences of disorder and supervise offenders released from prison – so film has reflected this, most graphically in *Judge Dredd*, who combines in one person the function of constable, judge, jury and executioner. He embodies an enduring cop movie tradition of simply killing villains who are deemed undeserving of legally sanctioned punishment (by dint of being 'too bad'), or who have already proved impossible to hold in prison, or who are not willing to be taken alive. Such incorrigibles have often died spectacularly *obliterative* deaths – defiant escaped con Cody Jarrett (James Cagney) atop an exploding gas tank in *White Heat* (Raoul Walsh 1948) comes to mind from an earlier era – but the visually sophisticated special effects of which science fiction films are now capable have made possible some novel forms of obliteration.

Science fiction *films* are not easily or sensibly separated from the literature (novels and short stories), comics, artwork, TV series and, nowadays, computer games that constitute the cultural field of science fiction. The literature alone has been notoriously self-referential, an accumulating stock of themes, tropes, motifs, stereotypes and conventions which different writers continually adapt and add to; this intertextuality actually encompasses a range of different media. That said, science fiction has never been insular. Literature exploring the possible social impact of real and imagined technology originated in the nineteenth century and was named 'science fiction' in the 1920s but, once established, the genre drew on, and integrated into itself, the far older forms of *utopian literature* (Plato's Republic, Thomas More's *Utopia* itself) and *fabulist literature* (ancient mythology, Dante's *Inferno, Gulliver's Travels*). Both these were literatures which originally had deep social (or perhaps spiritual) purposes, pointing men towards the good society or depicting the fates which awaited them beyond death. 'Punishment', writes John Carey (1999: xiv), 'is a subject that inevitably concerns the creators of utopias, since the eradication of wrongdoing is one of their prime targets', whilst justice – the absolute righting of wrongs in this world or the next – has featured repeatedly in fabulist literature. Given these emphases it is unsurprising, though under-acknowledged by criminology, that science fiction itself has paid regular and insightful attention to questions of crime and punishment (see Clute and Nicholls 1999: 274–7). The science fiction films considered here thus draw, probably unconsciously, on a rich ideational and iconographic heritage, in which, I will eventually argue, the spirit of Dante's *Inferno* lives on. The recently envisaged penal future is Hell. It was not always so.

Utopia and penality

The single most celebrated contribution to nineteenth-century North American utopian literature anticipated that well before the year 2000 imprisonment would have been abolished. In Edward Bellamy's (1888) *Looking Backward 2000–1887*, Julian West, a resident of late nineteenth-century Boston, is accidentally induced into a deep hypnotic trance and awakes over a century later to find that his home city has been transformed from an exploitive capitalist city into an attractive, peaceable, egalitarian – essentially socialist – metropolis. From conversations with a contemporary historian, Dr Leete, West learns how the transition from capitalism to socialism occurred in the USA in the mid-twentieth century, and how life in Boston has now changed. Amongst other things, Leete explains 'the total disappearance of the old state prison ... All cases of atavism are treated in the hospitals ... The idea of dealing punitively with those unfortunates was given up at least fifty years ago, and I think more' (Bellamy 1888: 150–1). He describes how 'property crime' had dwindled with the ending of inequality and the coming of socialism, obviating the need for an extensive legal and penal apparatus. The few violent offenders remaining, 'unconnected with any idea of gain', were committed by 'the ignorant and bestial, ... explained as the outcropping of ancestral traits' and responded to with an 'attitude of compassion and firm restraint' (1888: 150–1).

Capitalism, of course, triumphed. Socialism as Bellamy understood it was stifled by the 1930s. Regarding crime, the Lombrosian (and ultimately Darwinian)-derived notion of 'atavism' had been discredited in the early years of the twentieth century, although isolated eugenic experiments continued well after that. The rehabilitative ideal did indeed grow stronger, and more influential, at least until the 1970s, but was never fully realized in practice, and was never exclusively – or even mainly – a *medical* project. Its most humane and progressive expressions were arguably derived from social and psychological theories of criminal behaviour rather than biological ones, although even they were not without their repressive variants. Boston, and the state of Massachusetts generally, were the locus of constructive penal innovations throughout the twentieth century – notably probation and the later deinstitutionalization of young offenders – but as a new century dawned it, 'like most of the rest of America, [had] all but abandoned the notion of prisons as places to rehabilitate criminals into upstanding citizens' (Flynn 2000: 19) and simply sent them there, *en masse*, as – and perhaps also *for* – punishment. The USA in 2000 was aptly characterized as 'lockdown America' (Parenti 2000), a 'prison nation' (Hallinan 2001), a host to a 'perpetual punishment machine' (Dyer 2000).

The treatment ideal, influential as it had become by the mid-twentieth century, always had precarious foundations. Although Bellamy drew on the available scientific criminology of his day to argue that the treatment of criminals was a *realistic and desirable* possibility, he also borrowed from Samuel Butler's (1872) earlier, influential utopia, *Erewhon* (an anagram of 'nowhere'). This likened the punishment of criminals (deemed not responsible for their actions) to the punishment of the sick and infirm, although the intent here was anti-Christian satire, not science. Either way, the humanistic rehabilitative ideal was always tainted by simplistic utopian hopes, and did not survive the broad collapse of confidence in social progress that began in the 1970s (Allen 1979; Jacoby 1999). Fearing that the waning of rehabilitative aspirations might presage a return to crude, vindictive punishments, or to the development of ethically dubious, technology-based forms of social and psychological manipulation – the proposed super-max prisons embodied both – some liberals, notably Norval Morris (1974), began promoting a new, constructive, but less treatment-dependent vision of imprisonment. Interestingly, Morris heeded the warnings of Aldous Huxley, George Orwell and Anthony Burgess about 'the dangers to liberty in techniques of behaviour modification' (1974: 22), sensing the dark potential of what were later to be called 'technocorrections'. He wrote appreciatively of Burgess's (1962) novel *A Clockwork Orange* – although oddly made no mention of Stanley Kubrick's (1971) film version – in order to explore the limits of 'coercive curing'. It was arguably Kubrick's England-set, but internationally influential film (and the boost it gave to the novel itself), which triggered Hollywood's subsequent interest in future punishments. These tapped into, and extrapolated from, 'the new punitiveness' (Pratt *et al.* 2005) in tones that were as often celebratory as they were critical.

Early 'future punishment' movies

American independent cinema, at least, was ahead of liberal penal reformers in recognizing that the dominant forms of state control in America were becoming less and less benign. The very first movie to be concerned with future punishments was not, strictly speaking, a prison movie or even a science fiction movie, nor was it intended, as many subsequent such movies were, as mainstream entertainment. Writer-director Peter Watkins' (1970) *Punishment Park* extrapolated from government crackdowns on the anti-Vietnam War protesters, student revolutionaries and political dissidents of the late 1960s. Over several days, a small group of such convicted dissidents, loosely based on the Chicago Seven, are forced to run the gauntlet through the Arizona desert, having been told that if they reach a spot where an American flag has been planted they will be given amnesty for their crimes. At the same time they have to avoid government patrols who are permitted to kill them. A TV crew films the group cinema verite-style. Upon reaching the flag, the dissidents are gunned down anyway. The film clearly drew on the already extant use of wilderness training for offenders and raised the question of whether modern media could be used to turn punishment into a public spectacle, as executions had been in the early nineteenth century. The precise penal strategies envisaged by *Punishment Park* did not come to pass although, in the present century, the issue of televising punishment has both endured as a theme in future punishment movies, and found muted expression in several 'reality TV' shows.

George Lucas's (1971) low-budget feature film *THX 1138* would have been inconceivable without the prior dystopian narratives of Zamyatin, Huxley and Orwell, although Herbert Marcuse's (1964) then influential text, *One Dimensional Man*, also contributed to its conception. Like *Punishment Park*, but on a larger scale and in a more distant (albeit unspecified) future, it expressed prevailing leftist anxieties about the growing repressiveness and regimentation of American society. Only a fraction of its future society is depicted – we see only the workers, and the supervisers and police robots (humanoid in appearance, chrome-faced, helmeted, clad in black leather, armed with electric shock sticks) who monitor and control them. The action unfolds in a vast underground city, throughout which any individual's movements can be tracked using a 'city probe scanner'. Similarly, the whereabouts and viability of each of the city's 35,707 police robots are continually monitored; if one ceases to function it registers instantly on a digital counter in a central control room. Citizen/subjects are known by numbers rather than names, live in small monochromatic cubicles with bare walls and do their shifts at workstations called 'cells'. Surveillance cameras are ubiquitous but unobtrusive.

The eponymous main character, THX 1138 (Robert Duvall), is one of thousands of low-level workers educated from childhood (biochemically) to know only what they need to perform set technical tasks. These workers are more real to their supervisers as images and data than as persons. Whilst wired to their workstations, employee's heart and respiration rates can be monitored for advance signs of anxiety, underconcentration and inefficiency. At worst, supervisers can immobilize workers from a distance, using 'mindlock', switching a person off and on again as if he or she were merely a machine. Pervasive auto-voices encourage them to be good consumers and good workers – 'be efficient, be happy' – and to go on serving 'the masses' from which they are barely individuated. Most crucially in terms of control, the workers are variously sedated or energized with self-adminstered drugs, whose intake is monitored via the computerized medicine cabinets – a fusion of Huxley's soma and Orwell's telescreen – in each bathroom. It is illegal *not* to take these docility/efficiency-inducing drugs but, as an unanticipated, instinctive, all too human, mutual attraction develops been THX 1138 and his female room-mate LUH 3417, they cease doing so and make unlawful love.

THX 1138 is charged with 'criminal drug evasion'. At his peremptory trial THX is deemed 'incurable' (his failure to take his drugs has created a permanent chemical imbalance) but spared immediate destruction. He is sentenced to 'detention' in a 'rehabilitation centre', and to 'reconditioning', a neurological intervention which fails, suggesting that even in this repressive society, total control has not yet been perfected or operationalized – although it is clearly being worked on. The place of detention in which this occurs is a vast, white, horizonless space, utterly disorienting, unnamed in the film, but aptly called 'the white limbo' in Clarke's (2002) commentary. There is a hint in the film – better developed in the novelization (Bova 1978) – that law-breakers are simply kept in this limbo until such time as their bodily organs are needed to keep another, more compliant and valuable member of the masses, alive. THX does in fact escape from 'the white limbo' and indeed from the underground city – in the closing moments of the film he emerges from a deep air vent into natural sunlight, into an unknown landscape in which he may or may not survive. We never learn.

John Carpenter's (1981) *Escape from New York* postulated that by 1997 the whole of Manhattan would have become a walled-off, lawless, self-governing penal colony – into which a dubiously motivated former war hero is sent by the authorities to retrieve a missing VIP. A small explosive device, defusable only by the authorities, is implanted in his neck to ensure he returns within 24 hours. A similar tracking device, though less central to the overall plot, figures in the Arnold Schwartznegger vehicle *The Running Man* (Paul Michael Glaser 1987). It is set in an economically impoverished, politically repressive USA in 2019, where a docile public are entertained by cruel, participatory television programmes, whose wretched contestants risk life and limb for money, and on whose survival audiences bet. The top-rated live show, run jointly by a media corporation and the 'Justice Department–Entertainment Division', is called 'The Running Man'. In it, convicted criminals are pitted against a number of flamboyant 'stalkers', the series regulars, whose job it is to despatch the criminals with chainsaws, flame-throwers or bolts of electricity. Audiences are assured that those 'lucky' criminals who survive get to live abroad in luxury, but the game is rigged – contestants are always killed, onscreen or off. Arnold Schwartznegger plays a framed police officer – blamed for the massacre of food rioters whose death at the hands of his colleagues he had sought to prevent. Having initially been confined in the Wilshire Detention Zone, a huge industrial prison in Los Angeles whose inmates, whilst working 'outside', are kept in check by electronic collars which explode if a perimeter line is crossed, Schwartznegger is selected as a contestant on 'The Running Man'. He outwits and kills all the stalkers, and eventually the odious game show host himself, as well as helping the underground resistance launch a first skirmish against the authorities.

The Running Man was based on a Stephen King (writing as Richard Bachman) novel written in 1972, which ends quite differently from the film – far from surviving, the hero crashes a hijacked airliner into the skyscraper from which the TV show is run, an uncannily prescient piece of image-making which, post-9/11, has lost all innocence. The ending apart, King's novel is disturbingly similar to Robert Sheckley's (1958) much earlier short story 'The prize of peril', and to the French/Yugoslavian film *Le Prix du Danger* (Yves Boisset 1983) that had recently been made of it. Sheckley's central character is not a criminal, just an ordinary man who volunteers to evade trained killers for a week 'live' on TV, just to raise cash for his family. Sheckley's 1958 story seems indubitably to have originated the idea of ratings-driven 'punishment TV' and some of his subsequent satirical science fiction has explored further the idea of punishment as a spectator sport. It was, however, the Schwartznegger movie which popularized the idea for a mass audience, although it might none the less be said that, like Kubrick's film of a *A Clockwork Orange*, but unlike King's originating novel, *The Running Man*, partakes of the very voyeurism it purports to criticize.

'Future punishment' in the 1990s

In the 1990s science fictional prisons became really prominent in American cinema. *Face/Off* (John Woo 1997) was set in the present rather than the future. It contains a brief sequence in a special prison, aptly called Erewhon, used only for exceptionally violent prisoners and terrorists. The guard announces to a newly arrived prisoner, standing naked and alone in a darkened room, that its existence is unknown to the public, even to Amnesty International, and that the Geneva Convention does not apply. Initially, all audiences see are the insides of the prison. The walls and floors are metal rather than stone, and the authorities maintain order by requiring inmates to wear magnetic boots which make them sluggish, identify their location on a control room screen and, at the click of a switch, clamp them to the floor if they need to be immobilized. This device apart – plus the electrified cattle prods occasionally used on prisoners – Erewhon is depicted in conventional prison movie terms – prisoners dress in grey overalls, tramp in a circle round the cavernous hall which stands in for a yard and get thrown in solitary. They fight, and the guards watch a while before they quell it. A mass escape begins from what passes for a hospital unit. The lead character alone makes it to the outside, whereupon Erewhon is revealed to be an offshore oil-drilling platform – whether built in disguise or converted from a working rig we never know – just within swimming distance of the coast of (presumably) California.

Wedlock (Lewis Teague 1990) is a rather conventional prison-and-escape move, set 'sometime in the [very near] future'. Jewel thief Frank Warren (Rutger Hauer) (an ex-military electronic security specialist) arrives at a new private prison, somewhere in rural California. Drolly named after its founder and warden, George Holliday, Camp Holliday is described on the gate as maximum security, yet there are no high walls or fences, and few guards. The warden addresses the newcomers in the yard, telling them they are 'participants in a new penal experiment'. All prisoners are fitted with electronic collars and each prisoner is twinned with one other – 'wedlocked' – though only the authorities know the pairings. If the twinned collars ever get more than 100 yards from each other (i.e. if one partner goes beyond the blue perimeter lines), or if either partner seeks to loosen or remove the collar, both explode. Prisoners thus have good reason to keep a wary eye on each other. The warden demonstrates the technology using collared crash dummies; as they are driven across the perimeter in the back of a truck their heads explode. 'Who needs fences?' sneers the governor. 'Who needs guards? We got the best ball and chain in the world. Your ass'. He later tells Warren that if he makes a success of his penal experiment he will be be able to 'franchise Camp Hollidays across the country like they were taco stalls'.

The early part of Brett Leonard's (1995) *Virtuosity* updates the 'prison reception' sequence found in so many traditional prison movies. Parker Barnes (Denzel Washington), a former policeman imprisoned for murdering the terrorists who killed his family, works day release at the Law Enforcement Technological Advancement Centre (LETAC) using a 'virtual reality' program to train rookies to catch killers, in particular, a murderous adversary called Sid 6 (Russell Crowe). Barnes returns to prison each evening, stands naked in a reception cubicle, gets scanned for contraband and instructed in institutional routines by a feminine auto-voice. He steps from the cubicle into a long, narrow prison wing, only instead of cons jeering from behind barred cells (as in older prison movies), one sees their silhouettes behind toughened, translucent glass and hears only their muted catcalls. As the film opens, Barnes has 17 years left to serve, but is offered his freedom if he volunteers to recapture the now real-life Sid 6 (freed from the 'prison' of cyberspace by an irresponsible LETAC employee, who uses bio- and nano-technology, Frankenstein-like, to 'embody' him). Fearing that an embittered Barnes may simply abscond, the authorities (like those in *Escape from New York*) demand as a condition of his release that a micro-locator implant be inserted in his head, enabling satellite tracking of his movements. Initially unbeknown to Barnes, the device can also be triggered to release lethal toxins if he attempts to escape. Barnes accomplishes his task, spectacularly obliterating Sid 6 in a climactic fight, sinew by sinew, chip by chip – though not before venting his anger on those who would 'tag me like some kind of an animal'.

Both *Fortress* (Stuart Gordon 1992) and *No Escape* (Martin Campbell 1994) are set in the early twenty-first century, the latter specifically in 2022. They concern disillusioned military officers imprisoned in private sector, high-tech maximum security penitentiaries in remote desert settings. Both begin (in traditional prison movie fashion) with a cohort of new prisoners arriving, the former by truck, the latter by monorail, and then being given the introductory talk by the warden, one via CCTV, the other via a large holographic projection of the warden's head. The Fortress is run by the Mentel Corporation. Leviticus (in *No Escape*) (which looks on the outside like an infernal industrial installation) is described more vaguely as serving the 'international prison system'; the warden describes himself as running 'a multinational business...reprocessing garbage'. Little is actually shown of the prison interiors, but prisoners fear that small sensors which detect electrical activity in the brain have been embedded in the walls of their cells, relaying their private moods to the prison authorities. The sentence in Leviticus is natural life, with no contact whatsoever with the outside world: 'to all intents and purposes', new arrivals are told, 'you are already dead'.

The Fortress is the world's largest underground prison, a pit 33 storeys deep, housing both men and women. Inmates descend as though through circles of Hell, and are employed digging ever deeper levels. All prisoners have 'intestinators' inserted into them during the reception process, small metal devices which can be triggered, individually or *en masse*, to inflict excruciating pain, or even to explode if prisoners ignore instructions or stray outside designated zones. Mobile surveillance cameras glide along ceiling tracks and feed multiple images of the prison interior to a screenbank in the warden's office. An artificial intelligence, linked to Mentel's headquarters, co-ordinates the prison's complex management systems, instructing prisoners and advising the warden in an authoritative, feminized monotone. Cells are sealed by searing laser beams rather than bars. Various additional controls and punishments are available: a dream scanner which probes the minds of sleeping prisoners, sensing escape plans and punishing 'unauthorized thought processes', and a 'mind-wipe' technique that can stupefy recalcitrant inmates, erasing memories and sapping volition. The general inhumanity of the warden is underscored by the late-in-the-day revelation that he is a cyborg, reared and 'physically enhanced' by Mentel to perform this job. It is finally by damaging the artificial intelligence – by a combination of technical ingenuity and brute force – that an escape is affected.

Ultimately, *No Escape* dwells on the primitive rather than the high-tech aspects of future punishment. For 15 years, the wealthy, businessman-warden has been sending hundreds of recalcitrant prisoners to Absalom, a remote tropical island whose use for this purpose is not publicly known. These prisoners have split into warring tribes: a mere handful (rather like the more law-abiding Australian convicts of old) have created a small, peaceful village at one end of the island, but live in fear of tribal raids. The island is patrolled at a distance by gunships, scanned by sophisticated satellites, and visited every fortnight by heavily armed, supply-dropping helicopters. The warden treats the internecine warfare as sport, and relishes the cruelties that prisoners inflict on each other, whilst worrying that other satellites may observe and expose what happens on Absalom – implying (without the idea ever being developed) that there is a democratic government out there, to whom he might conceivably be held accountable. At various times, *No Escape* alludes to penal measures in former times – ordeal by combat, penal colonies, lashing, and execution by burning, impaling and guillotining – the suggestion being that however automated control becomes in the future, cruelty and brute force will never be wholly excised from penal practice.

Though set in a high-tech world, *Demolition Man* (Marco Brambillo 1993) also celebrates raw physical strength, as might be expected from a Sylvester Stallone vehicle. By 1996 convicted felons can be frozen in 'cryoprisons', during which time they are neurologically reprogrammed to become law-abiding citizens. Simon Phoenix (Wesley Snipes), a super-gangster, and John Spartan (Stallone), the policemen who captured him, are both sentenced to the cryoprison, the latter to 70 years for having wrongly been found responsible for the death of hostages held by Phoenix. Over the next 40 years, partly because of this and other technology, California becomes a feminized, crime-free, scientifically managed 'utopia', ruled by law and order ideologue (and inventor and owner of the cryoprison), Ramon Cocteau. All middle-class citizens in 'San Angeles' – the conurbation into which San Francisco and Los Angeles has melded – are fitted with electronic implants which enable their whereabouts to be known at all times, and are also subject to high levels of visual and verbal surveillance. A mass of excluded poor people, living beneath the city, organize against this regimentation. To terrorize them back into submission, Cocteau reprograms Simon Phoenix to be *more* violent, and unfreezes him. Lacking expertise with old-style violent gangsters, the Police Department then unfreeze John Spartan to deal with Phoenix. He finally kills him in the cryoprison itself, where the gangster is attempting to unfreeze other inmates. During the mayhem Spartan creates – hence his 'demolition' nickname – Phoenix steps in some leaking liquid nitrogen and instantly crystallizes from the feet up. Spartan gratuitously kicks off his adversary's frozen head, which bursts into smithereens when it hits the floor – an image of obliteration even more spectacular than that of Sid 6. The police and the underground rebels warily befriend each other and San Angeles is freed-up to become a more 'normal' city.

Stallone reprised these themes in *Judge Dredd* (Danny Boyle 1995), the media apotheosis of a comic-strip character created in 1977 to amplify and satirize the emerging 'law and order culture' in Britain. The Judges are a caste of armour-clad warriors raised from infancy to maintain order – 'the Law' – in Mega City One (the old eastern seaboard) in a post-apocalyptic – anti-democratic, militarized – twenty-second-century America. Most citizens are destitute. Many are organized into predatory gangs. The rich live in protected enclaves – all are insecure and fearful. Minor violations of the Law invite draconian penalties, and the Judges routinely kill to maintain order. Judge Dredd, the most ruthless Judge of all, typifies their role as both oppressor and protector of the poor; the satirical point of the comics being to suggest that his indubitably fascist *modus operandi* would become inevitable given the breakdown of social conditions which began in the 1970s, and the logic of the crackdown with which the government responded to it. One does not have to accept Newsinger's (1998: 9) eulogy to the often moronic nihilism of most Judge Dredd stories to agree that they are 'a cultural phenomenon of some importance', disturbingly popular with a late teen/young adult audience for over a quarter century.

The American-made film humanized Dredd (to suit Stallone's 'good guy' persona), portraying him as an 'emotionless automaton' (Newsinger 1998: 35) at the outset but eventually as a champion of (relative) liberty, breaking ranks with the *really* fascist Judges who have enlisted a ruthless super-criminal to help them intensify repression in Mega City One. The criminal has first to be sprung from Aspen Prison, from a special-force field cell within a prison-within-a-prison. The interiors of this remote, razor-wired, granite edifice (to which a framed Dredd is himself eventually sentenced) are only sketchily visualized, but the novel of the film makes plainer the combination of old and new technology – stone dungeons reached by a maze of stairs, entered using palm-and-voice print locks and guarded by wall-mounted autoguns – that ensure security in its hidden chambers. The tone – from first mention of the 'skeletal fingers' of its guard towers to its depiction as a 'tomb of the living … a place of darkness' – is remorselessly Gothic. Dosed with special drugs, over 200 of its prisoners were:

> *men who had committed such unspeakable crimes they were sentenced to live instead of die.* The Judges had decreed that every effort would be made to keep these men alive, that they did not deserve the merciful release of execution … [Their food] contained a drug that that would prevent a man from killing himself, or escaping into any degree of madness that would let him forget about his punishment or his crime. The drugs didn't make a man feel any better, they just made sure he did his forever-after time (Bartlett 1995: 60, emphasis added).

'Forever after-time' has a vaguely theological ring to it, and it is here, perhaps, that the aesthetic influence of Dante's *Inferno* on images of future punishment becomes most obvious. Descriptions of imprisonment, whether in the past, present or future, and especially fictional descriptions, have always lent themselves to infernal metaphors – Hell, after all, has been claimed for centuries as the ultimate punishment in Western Christendom. Prisons have notoriously been 'hell holes' or 'hells on Earth', places of damnation even when intended, forlornly, as places of redemption. Dante's particular rendering was both a part of a larger utopian project and a sociopolitical critique of corruption in fourteenth-century Italy, particularly Florence. His Hell depicted traits which had no place in an ideal society, his Purgatory showed how to remedy them and his Paradise showed the ideal itself (Ferrante 1995). His images of Hell as a dark underworld, subdivided into 24 circles according to the severity and character of the decreed retribution, a place of endless mutual torment and personalized agony (constant awareness of one's *particular* sin and its painful consequences), were long ago severed from their original intellectual moorings, and have permeated Western culture as freestanding motifs of punishment in their own right. Culturally, Dante's *Inferno* might be seen as an ur-dystopia with which all subsequent dystopias have resonated: 'It has profoundly affected not only the religious imagination but all subsequent allegorical creation of imaginary worlds in literature' (Clute and Nicholls 1999: 299). Its themes and iconography have been absorbed into science fiction in both subtle (Smith 1961) and caricatured (Niven and Pournelle 1977) ways, becoming part of the common stock of knowledge for any science fiction (screen)writer who wants to comment on processes of justice and punishment, whether trivially or profoundly. More generally, Dantean themes have permeated world cinema from its inception (Welle 1995), and there is thus nothing intrinsically surprising about the discovery of Dante's latent presence in recent American future punishment movies, even if has not hitherto been remarked upon.

The movies reviewed in this chapter tell us without exception that the American prisons of the future will be hellish places, and that there will surely be villains bad enough to justify their existence. They are envisaged as places of deliberately created misery, occupied by the damned – and perhaps this is an extrapolation of what many already are. The underground prison in *Fortress* may be the most obvious Dantean environment but all the movies which introduce progressively more painful punishments (new 'circles') for ever more recalcitrant inmates are drawing obliquely on the *Inferno*. The mutual torment – guard on inmate, inmate in inmate – whilst being both real life and a staple of the prison movie genre – also has clear Dantean echoes. But it is perhaps the way that 'personalized agony' is depicted in the movies that is most intriguing, because this is not something that imprisonment in the past has actually been able to engineer at will. The personalized agony of Dante's characters comes from an awareness of sin and guilt induced by knowledge of God; in reality prisoners have found a myriad of ways of neutralizing the mental pressure, where it exists, to dwell on the horror of their crime. What the future punishment movies – and indeed some literary science fiction – suggest is that technology may one day be devised to sustain this protracted sense of guilt in offenders' minds, not necessarily to foster remorse or redemption, but simply to torment the offenders concerned.

The idea occurs in Steven Spielberg's (2002) *Minority Report*, a cops-of-the-future movie (with a memorable prison sequence) intended by its director and star (Tom Cruise) to provoke serious debate about contemporary crime control trends (Jarvis 2004). Set in Washington, DC, in 2054, the film deals with a team of precognitive telepaths and the pre-crime police rapid-response squad who act on their 'precognitions', pre-empting otherwise inevitable homicides. The telepath's flickering, mental images of the imminent murders are caught on screen and stored on a holographic disc. Perpetrators of 'pre-crime' are then placed – semi-comatose, in pods – in the Department of Containment, a dimly lit, cavernous chamber with a central control tower (manned by a single wheelchair-bound guard/caretaker), surrounded by several hundred transparent columns in which the individual pods are stacked. On the faceplates before their eyes – which they cannot avert – 'containees suffer non-stop replays of their intended crimes', looped holographic images taken from the police screens. 'Look at how peaceful they are', the guard says sardonically, 'but on the inside…busy, busy, busy!' Although the lead character, a framed policeman, is at one point subject to containment himself, the film says nothing of the personalized punishment's origins. It did not occur in Phillip K. Dick's (1956) originating story, although it did figure in a much later story by Harlan Ellison (1998). The horror of such a technological prospect – the utter antithesis of humanistic rehabilitation – is not entirely assuaged by the upbeat ending of *Minority Report* – the discrediting of infallible precognitions and the (offscreen) release of the containees.

Conclusion

> To designate a hell is not, of course, to tell us anything about how to extract people from that hell, how to moderate hell's flames. Still, it seems a good in itself to acknowledge, to have enlarged, one's sense of how much suffering caused by human wickedness there is in the world we share with others (Sontag 2003: 102).

What, in sum, do the future punishment movies tell us? America will become a quasi-fascist country – but the rule of the strong may well have come about as a result of fears about a dangerous underclass and/or cunning terrorists, so it may be the lesser of two evils, perhaps even fun. These repressive societies of the future will not be so repressive as to preclude the exposing and remedying of atrocities. There will still be political contestation (*The Running Man*, *Wedlock*, *Minority Report*). Those who do the contesting, however, will of necessity be exceptional, superfit men, variants of the rugged-individual-against-great-odds who repeatedly figures in American action movies, and prison movies in particular. What science fiction accentuates is the pitting of the superfit, but still 'natural', masculine body – sometimes augmented by special effects – against technologically enhanced forms of domination. Man still wins over the machine – but only if he has embraced some of the characteristics of the machine itself.

There will be private prisons run by global corporations and these will be bad. The wardens in the private prisons in *Fortress*, *No Escape* and *Wedlock* are all, in varying degrees, sadistic and corrupt. There is often, however, an implied connection between privatization and penal innovation, for within these institutions new control technologies will be devised, aimed either at knowing the minds of the criminals or at responsibilizing their behaviour (exploding tags, implants and collars). The ubiquity of devices which track an offender's location and movement, in or out of prison, has surely gained plausibility because of the widespread adoption of electronic monitoring technologies in the USA (Meyer 2004), although their capacity to inflict pain or death has yet to be emulated in the real world. Regulatory and punitive processes may, these films also suggest, become more automated. Standardized, formulaic procedures (e.g. prison reception) could be reduced to algorithms, and managed by computers. More speculatively, the invariably dehumanized prison guard may quite logically be replaced by the non-human – robot or cyborg – as in *Fortress*.

There may be secret prisons (Erewhon in *Face/Off*, Absalom in *No Escape*) whose whereabouts, perhaps even whose existence, are not known to the populace at large, only to (some of) the authorities. In reality these have traditionally been associated with past totalitarian or quasi-totalitarian societies. They were not associated with America until after the 'war on terror' began post-9/11. Even if they are not, strictly speaking, unlocatable, such prisons might still be 'secret' in the sense of being difficult to get information from, for example Camp X-Ray (a name straight out of science fiction!) at Guantanamo Bay in Cuba. Such prisons may be improvised and transient, and even crudely low-tech – as in Abu Graib. Conversely, there may be also demand for punishment to be *less secret* in the future, to be publicized – not to expose atrocity, but as entertainment – and for it to be sanctioned by people in authority who believe that this may serve deterrent purposes.

If the formulaic conventions of cop and prison movies are mentally subtracted from the appraisal of Hollywood's view of future punishments, the visual and ideational residues can be seen to resonate – all too easily – with trends and tendencies in real-world punishment. Cruelty has made a comeback. Technocorrections are developing. Real-world police patrols and courtrooms already provide TV entertainment. It is not inconceivable that real prisons will too, and some documentaries have already come close to it. Game shows and reality TV in which contestants have to endure hardships and humiliation are commonplace. American popular culture seems to have coarsened to the point where enough of the public would accept – might even demand – the sight of real offenders undergoing their punishment. A JailCam experiment has already been tried (Lynch 2004). Whether this is offset by vicarious, fictional depictions of punishment is a moot point, but it is not inconceivable that the more violent and exploitative prison movies themselves, whether future oriented or not, are already fulfilling this dismal function.

Sophisticated intellectual elites may well interpret future policing and punishment movies as academic film critic J.P. Telotte (2001: 176) reads *Robocop* as 'a darkly satiric fantasy, much in the tradition of the work of Jonathan Swift, and as intent as Swift's work in prodding us into change'. However, quite apart from the dubiousness of Hollywood's *intention* in this respect, the broad cultural effect of such movies is not to warn us against dystopian penalities, but to get us used to bad news and worse times, to stifle our capacity to imagine and communicate something more convivial, and to embrace 'fun fascism' with varying degrees of eagerness. It is not just, as Zedner (2002) has recently argued, that penal dystopias can engender defeatism amongst liberals; Hollywood-style dystopias can actually be made to seem aesthetically appealing. Susan Sontag is right that we can in principle use images of Hell in the present to stir reformist sentiments and create better futures, but when a hellish future has itself been depicted as a half-desirable destination, there is no easy or clear way to forestall it.

References

Allen, F. (1979) *The Decline of the Rehabilitative Ideal*. New Haven, CT: Yale University Press.

Bartlett, N. (1995) *Judge Dredd*. London: Boxtree.

Bellamy, E. (1888/1986) *Looking Backward, 2000–1887*. Harmondsworth: Penguin Books.

Bova, B. (1978) *THX 1138*. London: Granada Publishing.

Butler, S. (1872) *Erewhon* (reprinted London: Penguin Books).

Burgess, A. (1962) *A Clockwork Orange*. Harmondsworth: Penguin Books.

Carey, J. (1999) *The Faber Book of Utopias*. London: Faber & Faber.

Clarke, J. (2002) *George Lucas*. Harpenden: Pocket Essentials.

Clute, J. and Nicholls, P. (eds) (1999) *The Encyclopaedia of Science Fiction*. London: Little, Brown.

Dick, P.K. (1956) 'Minority report', in *Minority Report and Other Stories (2002)*. London: Gollancz.

Dyer, J. (2000) *The Perpetual Punishment Machine: How America Profits from Crime*. Boulder, CO: Westview Press.

Ellison, H. (1998) 'Pulling hard time', in *Slippage*. Boston, MA: Houghton Miflin.

Ferrante, J.M. (1995) 'Hell as the mirror image of paradise', in M. Musa (ed.) *Dante's Inferno: The Indiana Critical Edition*. Indianapolis, IN: Indiana University Press.

Flynn, S. (2000) *Boston Law: The True Story of a War on Crime*. London: HarperCollins.

Garland, D. (2001) *The Culture of Control*. Oxford: Oxford University Press.

Hallinan, J.T. (2001) *Going up the River: Travels in a Prison Nation*. New York, NY: Random House.

Jacoby, R. (1999) *The End of Utopia: Politics and Culture in an Age of Apathy*. New York, NY: Basic Books.

Jarvis, B. (2004) *Cruel and Unusual: Punishment and US Culture*. London: Pluto Press.

King, S. (1982) *The Running Man*. London: Hodder & Stoughton.

Lynch, M. (2004) 'Punishing images: JailCam and the changing penal enterprise', *Punishment and Society*, 6: 255–70.

Marcuse, H. (1964) *One Dimensional Man*. London: Routledge & Kegan Paul.

Mason, P. (2003) 'The screen machine: cinematic representations of prison', in P. Mason (ed.) *Criminal Visions: Media Representations of Crime and Justice*. Cullompton: Willan Publishing.

Meyer, J.F. (2004) 'Home confinement with electronic monitoring', in G.A. Caputo (ed.) *Intermediate Sanctions in Corrections*. Denton, TX: University of North Texas Press.

Morris, N. (1974) *The Future of Imprisonment*. Chicago, IL: University of Chicago Press.

Niven, L. and Pournelle, J. (1977) *Inferno*. London: W.H. Allen & Co.

Nellis, M. (1982) 'Notes on the American prison film', in M. Nellis and C. Hale (eds) *The Prison Film*. London: Radical Alternatives to Prison.

Newsinger, J. (1999) *The Dredd Phenomenon: Comics and Contemporary Society*. London: Libertarian Education.

Parenti, C. (2000) *Lockdown America: Police and Prisons in the Age of* Crisis. London: Verso.

Pratt, J., Brown, D., Brown, M., Hallsworth, S. and Morrison, W. (eds) (2005) *The New Punitiveness: Trends, Theories Perspectives*. Cullompton: Willan Publishing.

Sheckley, R. (1958) 'The prize of peril', in R. Sheckley (ed.) (1973) *The Robert Sheckley Omnibus*. Harmondsworth: Penguin Books.

Smith, C. (1961) 'A planet named Sheol', in J. Merril (ed.) *The Best of Sci-Fi 2*. London: Mayflower Dell.

Sontag, S. (2003) *Regarding the Pain of Others*. London: Hamish Hamilton.

Telotte, J.P. (2001) *Science Fiction Film*. Cambridge: Cambridge University Press.

Welle, J. (1995) 'Dante in the cinematic mode: a historical survey of Dante movies', in M. Musa (ed.) *Dante's Inferno: The Indiana Critical Edition*. Indianapolis, IN: Indiana University Press.

Wilson, D. and O'Sullivan, S. (2004) *Images of Incarceration: Representations of Prison in Film and Television Drama*. Winchester: Waterside Press.

Zedner, L. (2002) 'Dangers of dystopia in penal theory', *Oxford Journal of Legal Studies*, 22: 341–66.

Index